POWER TOOLS

for
Reason 6

Master Propellerhead's Virtual Studio Software

INCLUDES DVD-ROM!

Andrew Eisele

HAL LEONARD BOOKS
An Imprint of Hal Leonard Corporation

Published in 2012 by Hal Leonard Books
An Imprint of Hal Leonard Corporation
7777 West Bluemound Road
Milwaukee, WI 53213

Trade Book Division Editorial Offices
33 Plymouth St., Montclair, NJ 07042

Book design by Kristina Rolander

Library of Congress Cataloging-in-Publication Data

Eisele, Andrew.
 Power tools for Reason 6 / Andrew Eisele.
    p. cm.
1. Reason (Computer file) 2. Software synthesizers. 3. Software samplers.
4. Software sequencers. I. Title.
 ML74.4.R43E373 2012
 781.3'4536--dc23
                                        2012002112

ISBN 9781458402271

www.halleonardbooks.com

Contents

CHAPTER 7
SAMPLING   105

REASON DRUM AND
PERCUSSION INSTRUMENTS

REASON EFFECTS

CHAPTER 10
UTILITY DEVICES   187

PART FOUR   **209**

CHAPTER 11
ADVANCED ROUTING   211

Part One

Setting Up Your
Studio for Reason 6

Before we dive into the tutorials that will instruct you on the basics, let's first have a look at the system requirements for running Reason 6. I've also compiled some information with regard to the kind of equipment you may wish to consider purchasing, to enable you to get the most out of your computer-based studio. These recommendations are based on my own personal experience as an audio engineer, and so, by all means, do your own research and, if possible, check out each product before purchasing. Most major music retailers will have this type of gear readily available and often have showrooms at which you can test out products. Also make sure the store from which you are purchasing has a decent return policy, in the event you are unsatisfied with your purchasing decision.

PREREQUISITES FOR RUNNING REASON

To effectively run Reason 6 you will need a computer that meets the following minimum requirements.

Computer

MAC OS X

- Intel Mac (multiple cores highly recommended)
- 1 GB RAM or more
- Mac OS X 10.5.8 or later
- 3 GB free hard disk space (program may use up to 20 GB scratch disk space)
- Monitor with 1024x768 resolution or larger
- A MIDI interface and a MIDI keyboard recommended
- Internet connection for registration

- Free USB port for ignition key
- CoreAudio-compliant audio interface or built-in audio hardware

WINDOWS
- Intel Pentium 4/AMD Opteron or better (multiple cores highly recommended)
- 1GB RAM
- Windows XP SP3, Vista, or Windows 7 (Vista or Windows 7 required for 64-bit)
- 3 GB free hard disk space
- Monitor with 1024x768 resolution or larger
- A 16-bit Windows-compatible audio card, preferably with an ASIO driver
- Internet connection for registration
- Free USB port for ignition key
- A MIDI interface and a MIDI keyboard recommended

Audio Interface

It is possible to run Reason with the built-in soundcard that comes preequipped with your computer; however, it is recommended that you invest in a proper audio interface, as this will allow your computer to perform better when recording and playing back audio. It will also alleviate much of the headaches associated with working with subpar equipment. You are looking for an audio interface that meets the demands of digital audio. Audio interfaces that are designed for gaming are not always adequate, so you may need to supplement your interface. Luckily, there are a number of low-cost options on the market, so with little effort you should be able to easily find something suitably sufficient for music production.

FIREWIRE
FireWire is a technology that allows for fast data throughput and greater performance. My favorite low-cost interface is the Apogee Duet. It features two microphone inputs, two line inputs, two line outputs, and MIDI I/O (input and output). It also features two high-quality microphone preamps. This unit usually sells for just under $500 brand new. It's the best bang for the buck, as there's really nothing else of this quality in this price rage. Apogee has just released the Duet 2, so you could also look for sales on the original version.

Other manufacturers of FireWire interfaces are MOTU, M-Audio, PreSonus, RME Hammerfall, Focusrite, and TC Electronics.

USB
USB stands for "universal serial bus" and is the most popular connection means for computers today. There are a number of USB audio interfaces on the market, but I highly recommend using an interface with USB 2.0 or higher, as the data put-through is much faster (on par with or faster than FireWire 400).

Propellerhead has just released an interface called Balance that's designed to work with Reason 6 (and any other software). It integrates seamlessly and affords many fantastic features, such as the built-in ignition key and Clip Safe technology.

I'd also recommend the Apogee Duet 2, as the sound quality is superior to anything in its price range.

Other manufacturers of USB interfaces are MOTU, M-Audio, PreSonus, RME Hammerfall, Focusrite, TC Electronics, Native Instruments, Avid/Digidesign, Mackie, and Alesis.

MIDI Interface

A MIDI interface is usually a USB device with one or more inputs and outputs, which allows for the connection of MIDI equipment, such as keyboards and synthesizers. Fortunately, most audio interfaces have built in MIDI interfaces. There are also MIDI controllers that have built-in MIDI interfaces and connect directly to your computer via USB.

MOTU, Cakewalk, Roland, Midisport, and M-Audio are popular manufacturers of MIDI interfaces.

Monitors (Speakers)

A studio monitor is designed to give you an accurate representation of your music and is often calibrated to have a flat frequency response. It is possible to use regular hi-fi audio speakers or bookshelf speakers from your home stereo, but more often than not, the consumer speakers are designed to make the music sound "better" with the use of digital processing. This is fine if you are simply listening to music. For example, commercially released CDs should sound great on these systems. However, if you are actively mixing a song, this playback system is not ideal as, due to the calibration, it will fool you and your mixing won't translate well to other playback systems. Your music might sound fine on your home stereo, but listening to it in your car or on a club system, you'll discover that your mixes often won't sound the same.

There are two types of studio monitors: passive and active.

PASSIVE

Passive monitors are usually a little cheaper, but they require the use of an audio amplifier, which is an additional expense and will require extra room in your studio.

ACTIVE

Active monitors have the amplifier built into the speaker. This is a space saver and has the added benefit of the manufacturer's building the amplifiers to match the speakers perfectly, resulting in both better performance and sound quality.

SUBWOOFER

Depending on the type of music you are producing and the size of your studio monitors, you may wish to invest in a subwoofer, which is a low-frequency speaker capable of producing powerful bass output. Designed to pick up where your studio monitors leave off, subwoofers will help immensely when producing bass-heavy music such as hip-hop, drum and bass, dubstep, cumbia, glitch, electro house, techno, and other forms of electronic music.

There are a number of manufacturers of studio monitors. Some even package subwoofers as part of a set. Check out KRK, Event, Genelec, Tannoy, M-Audio, Blue Sky, Yamaha, and Dynaudio for suitable options.

Headphones

Headphones are a good investment, as they will allow you to work without bothering loved ones and neighbors. They can also give you a different take on your mix, with the added intimacy. However, they are not an adequate replacement for a good pair of studio monitors. Look for good quality, comfort, and ideally headphones that don't overemphasize bass frequencies. My personal favorites are the Sony MDR 7506. They usually cost about $99 and sound great without overhyping the bass. Also, Focusrite has released the VRM Box, which uses DSP (digital signal processing) to emulate different studio monitors from within your headphones. The wonders of modern technology!

Other manufacturers of headphones include Sennheiser, AKG, Audio-Technica, Sure, and Beyerdynamic.

Controllers

MIDI controllers come in all sorts of shapes and sizes, from MIDI guitars, keyboards, and drum pads to full-size harps and pianos. If you own a keyboard or synthesizer that has a MIDI output, you can use this in conjunction with a MIDI interface. Most audio interfaces also have a MIDI input, which would be a replacement for a dedicated MIDI interface. A simpler solution is to use a USB controller.

KEYBOARD

USB MIDI keyboard controllers aren't an absolute must if you wish to produce music in Reason 6, but I highly recommend utilizing one, as it speeds up the process of recording MIDI. keyboard controllers come in various sizes, some with more features than others. I recommend finding a controller that has at least a two-octave range with velocity sensitivity and dedicated pitch bend and modulation control.

Some recommended manufacturers include M-Audio, Novation, Akai, Yamaha, Korg, Roland, and Alesis.

CONTROL SURFACE (MIXING)
Another USB controller used to control mix parameters is the control surface. It is a dedicated controller that often looks like a mixing board, but no audio passes through it, as it's used to control software parameters. These range in price from $50 (Korg nanoKONTROL) to over $20K (SSL Matrix). It's nice to have the hands-on control for mixing, but I find that it's not a necessity. Check out Novation Zero SL for a good-quality control surface.

Microphone

If you are planning on recording your own samples in Reason 6, you'll need a good-quality microphone. Fortunately, a number of low-cost microphones are available on the market. Several types are available, but the most popular are the dynamic and the condenser.

DYNAMIC
A dynamic microphone is a great, all-purpose microphone. These are often used in both live sound and studio recording. They are hardy and very rarely break unless seriously abused., Audix, AKG, Audio-Technica, Sennheiser, and Sure make great dynamics microphones.

CONDENSER
Condenser microphones are most often used in recording studios. They are extremely sensitive and perfect for home recording; however, they do require a microphone preamplifier with 48-volt power—often referred to as phantom power. Fortunately, most audio interfaces have microphone preamps with phantom power built into them. Because of their sensitivity, they need to be handled with care. They can break if dropped, but if properly cared for, can last a lifetime. Røde, Studio Projects, Cascade, MXL, Blue, Audio-Technica, and Sure are just a few manufacturers of inexpensive high-quality condenser microphones.

Microphone Accessories

MICROPHONE STAND
Be sure to invest in a mic stand. Budget ones are fine, but can break over time. I prefer a tripod stand with a boom extension, as this allows for greater flexibility when recording.

MICROPHONE CABLE
Cables come in a variety of lengths and quality. I've been making my own cables for years, but if you're not handy with a soldering iron, invest in the lowest tier of a quality manufacturer such as Monster or Mogami.

POP FILTER
If you were planning on recording vocals, it would be wise to invest in a pop filter. This device will help prevent plosives (excessive *p*'s and *t*'s) from ruining a recording. There are

some name brands, but I've always been happy with the inexpensive no-name brand usually costing about $20.

Other Accessories

POWER CONDITIONER

Although not a necessity, a power conditioner with surge protection is a great investment. These typically are either the channel strip type or studio rack mounts and will offer multiple A/C plugs (usually eight plugs). Depending on the specs, they can condition the power to cut down on electronic noise created by appliances in your home or studio. Some offer protection from power spikes and lightning (however, I still unplug my gear during electrical storms). Some manufacturers offer insurance, so if something does go wrong, they can help with replacing the damaged equipment. Some power conditioners even have battery backup, so if you lose power, you've got a few minutes to save and turn off your computer properly.

Furman, ETA, Monster, and APC are a few manufacturers of power conditioners.

CABLES

One often overlooked aspect of your studio is cables. When purchasing your software and hardware, make sure that you don't forget to buy the right cables. There are a number of manufacturers of cables. As I said in the microphone section, I prefer to make my own, but if you're not handy with a soldering iron, invest in the lowest tier of a quality manufacturer such as Monster or Mogami.

With that said, keep your cable runs as short as possible. Don't buy a twenty-five-foot cable if you really only need ten feet. Longer cables may also add interference. Also, when in doubt, use balanced cables (XLR or TRS). This will help cut down on excessive noise and interference, especially when working over long distances.

SETTING UP YOUR STUDIO

Selecting Your Room

When selecting a space to install your studio, look for a room without parallel walls or ceiling, if possible. Odd-shaped rooms with slanted ceilings (such as an attic) are great for a mixing environment. The last thing you want is a perfectly square room where the walls, ceiling, and floor are equidistant. If this is not possible, buying some room treatment to help with reflections will help improve your mixing environment.

Room Treatment

There are a number of manufacturers of room treatment materials available for purchase. Prime Acoustics, Real Traps, Auralex, and Clearsonic are a few manufacturers to consider.

Another low-cost alternative is using compressed fiberglass (the same material used in air ducts). This can be purchased from a home store such as Home Depot. I recommend framing with wood, covering with material, and hanging on your walls and on the ceiling above the mix position.

Room Correction

Another option for getting the best mixing environment is the advent of room correction hardware/software. These typically come with a special calibration microphone that works with software to analyze your room's acoustics and correct any issues found. This is not a necessity for you to use Reason 6, but will help insure your mixes sound their best.

IK Multimedia, KRK, and JBL offer room correction packages.

Setting Up Your Mix Position

Once you've got your equipment ready, I recommend setting your studio monitors equidistant from your head in what is known as the mix position. The ideal mix position is to have the high-frequency drivers (tweeters) at ear level and measured in equal distances between your left and right monitors. You're trying to create an equilateral triangle between your monitor and your ears. For instance, if your monitors are spaced four feet apart, then the optimum mix position is four feet from the monitors. Use of a tape measure is recommended, as the precision of the distance is important.

Hooking Up Your Monitors

Connect your audio cables to your audio interface. The Left output (Output 1) connects to the Left monitor as it faces you. The Right output (Output 2) connects to the Right monitor as it faces you.

INSTALLING DRIVERS

If your audio interface is class compliant, then your computer should recognize it automatically. But, if your interface requires drivers, I recommend going to the manufacturer's website and checking for the latest version of the drivers. If the website has newer software available, skip the CD that ships with the product and install the newer software directly from the website.

The same process applies your MIDI interface or MIDI controller. Always check the manufacturer's website for updates to the software before installing from a CD.

Check to see if your device is available on your computer.

On a PC, this will usually be displayed at the bottom right corner of the screen or you can check the Control Panel for the devices.

On a Mac, open the AMS (audio MIDI setup) found in the Utilities folder within the Applications folder. Once open, your devices should be present in their respective windows (Audio Devices and MIDI Studio).

INSTALLING REASON

The installation process is fairly simple. Simply insert the DVD-ROM into your computer and either double-click on the installer application or simply drag the Reason 6 folder to your Applications folder.

Reason 6 uses copy protection based a USB device called the Propellerhead ignition key. When you first launch Reason 6, you'll be asked to input the ignition key into a USB port on your computer, followed by entering a code found in your Reason 6 materials. The Authorizer application will automatically connect you with the Propellerhead website and you can finish registering your ignition key and software.

There has been a lot of criticism regarding using a USB dongle for copy protection. What would happen if you lost your ignition key? Not to worry, as Propellerhead has come up with a very reasonable solution. There are, in fact, three modes available with which to launch and use the software.

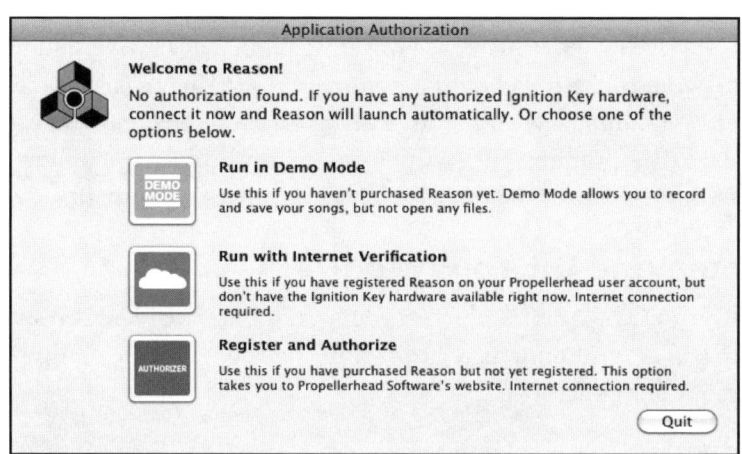

Fig: 1-1

Ignition Key

This is by far the easiest to use. With the ignition key inserted into a USB port, you launch the program and get right to work.

Internet Verification

If you forgot or lost your ignition key and you have access to an Internet connection, the Authorizer application will launch and you simply input your user name and password. This is followed by a brief connection to the Internet and the software launches.

Demo Mode

If you don't have your ignition key or access to the Internet, you can still use the program in demo mode. Demo mode allows you to fully use Reason 6; however, you cannot open any preexisting sessions or export your song.

If you lose your ignition key, you'll have to pay a nominal fee to get a replacement.

SETTING UP PREFERENCES

Before you can begin to use Reason 6, you must first set up the preferences, which will allow Reason 6 to communicate with your peripherals.

The setup wizard asks you questions about your audio interface and MIDI keyboard controller and will facilitate setting things up for you.

If by chance you didn't have your hardware set up or you'd like to make some changes to your set up afterward, you'll want to be familiar with the Preferences selection process. On rare occasions, Reason 6 may lose communication with your MIDI controller and/or audio interface and you will need to reselect the options in Preferences.

As a result, it's a good idea to become familiar with the process of selecting your preferences.

Let's begin by launching Reason 6. Once the software is open, select Preferences from the Reason drop-down menu.

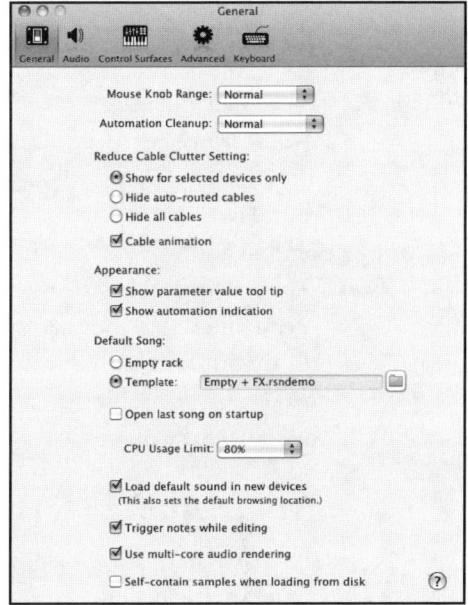

Fig: 1-2

GENERAL PREFERENCES

Under this first tab, you can set a lot of Reason's behavior and the visual look of the program. It also gives you options on how the program should open. This page can be left in its default state.

Empty Rack

Opens Reason with a blank rack.

Template

This setting allows for creating a song start or template file, which is useful for a quick session start. When you first launch reason, the template Empty + FX.rnsdemo will automatically load. You'll learn how to create and select other templates in a later chapter.

Open Last Song on Startup

This setting opens the last project you were working on in the previous session.

Next, select the drop-down menu at the top of the page, which currently says General. Select the next option, Audio.

AUDIO PREFERENCES

If you had your audio interface connected when the Reason started its setup wizard, it should automatically display your sound card. If you didn't have it connected, it may say "Built in" or "No Sound."

To change this setting, press the drop-down menu and select your audio device.

If you don't see your audio interface listed, make sure you've downloaded the latest drivers or contact the manufacturer.

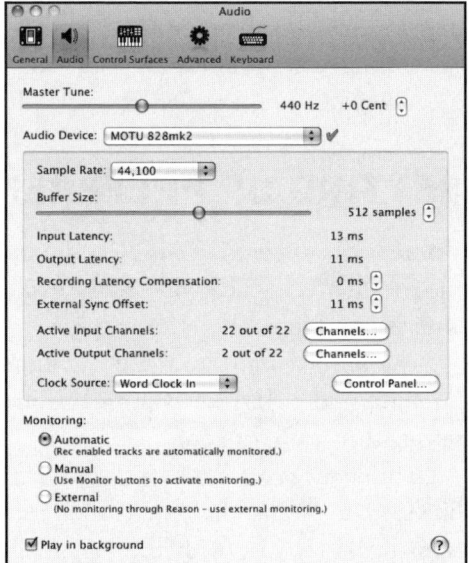

Fig: 1-3

Other Audio Options to Consider

Sample Rate—Reason supports sample rates from 44,100 up to 96,000. You're going to maintain the default setting of a 44,100 sample rate.

Buffer Size—This slider increases or decreases your buffer size. Let's leave this at the default setting of 512 samples.

LATENCY AND BUFFER SIZE

Latency is a delay that is caused by the processing of data. In regard to your audio system, it takes a certain amount of time for your computers to capture, process, and send audio information. The time this process takes is directly related to the buffer size. A higher buffer setting may result in an audible delay, which can manifest in a delay when recording with a microphone or pressing a note on your MIDI controller, which makes playing and recording difficult.

Imagine setting up a microphone and strumming a guitar, only you hear the guitar one second after you've played it. Setting a lower buffer setting enables you to reduce the delay to an acceptable amount and allows yourself to play along in real time.

As you build your song, you'll inevitably use several tracks with effects, and with the addition of virtual instruments, it won't be long before your computer's processor is overtaxed. The result is a slow, sluggish response with crackles, pops, and audio dropouts.

To compensate for this you must increase the buffer, thereby increasing latency. Most audio interfaces today produce very good results. The idea is to find a good balance with buffer settings to allow acceptable performance with lower latencies. I tend to use a lower buffer setting when recording and then increase the buffer setting when mixing.

Let's move back to the Preference drop-down menu and select Keyboards and Control Surfaces.

KEYBOARDS AND CONTROL SURFACES

Select Auto-detect Surfaces.

Reason will first scan your computer for any available MIDI interfaces and keyboard controllers. If your controller does not show up under Auto-detect, select the Add button and manually choose the manufacturer and model of controller.

If your multiple controllers are found and you only wish to use one in particular, then deselect Use with Reason for any controller you don't wish to use with Reason.

Keep the Standard option setting for the Master Keyboard Input. You'll explore using multiple controllers in the live performance chapter.

ADVANCED MIDI

This preference is used to set Reason up for use with external sequencers. It offers four banks of sixteen channels, thereby affording a total of sixty-four MIDI channels to work with. This function, however, is beyond the scope of this series.

COMPUTER KEYBOARD

Reason features a piano keyboard that is controlled by the QWERTY keyboard (computer keyboard). This utility gives you a virtual MIDI keyboard controller. It's a fantastic way to record MIDI or audition sounds when a proper MIDI keyboard controller is not available. The preferences allow for the customization of the setup of the QWERTY keyboard. For your purposes, the default setting is fine. The computer keyboard can be accessed

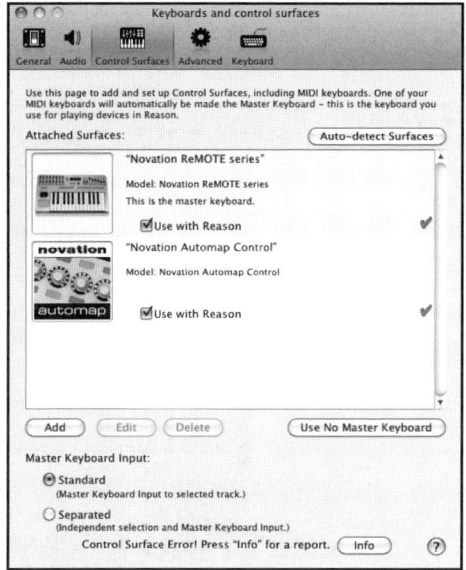

Fig: 1-4

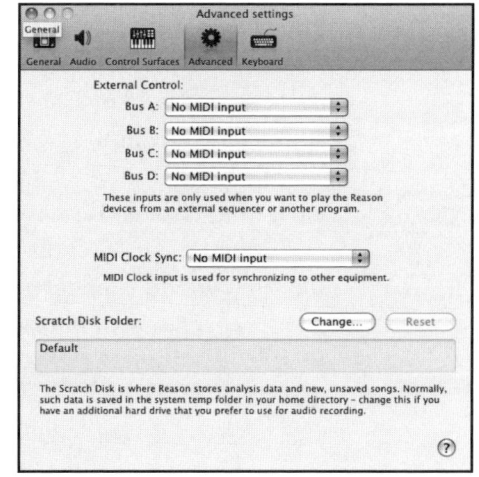

Fig: 1-5

by selecting F4 on your QWERTY keyboard or "Show On-Screen Piano Keys" from the Windows drop-down window on the Reason menu.

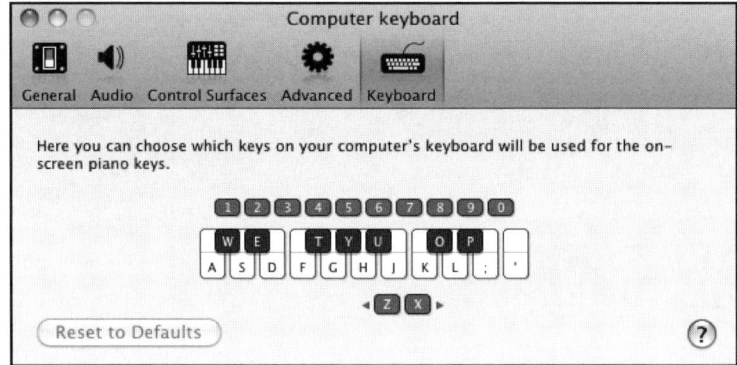

Fig: 1-5

SETTING F-KEYS FOR LAPTOP USERS

By default, your laptop's function keys are set to control hardware functions such as brightness and volume. It is possible to access the Function keys for software, by selecting FN while pressing the F-key, but this seemingly simple step will slow your work process down. I highly recommend changing the settings so you have direct software control using the F-keys. You can still access the hardware functions by using the FN key with the appropriate function.

The F4 to F8 keys are instrumental for navigating through Reason 6 quickly.

If you did not select this option during the setup wizard configuration and would like to change this option, select System Preferences from the Mac or Windows menu.

Under Keyboard, you'll find a check box with the settings for "Use all F1, F2, [etc.] keys as standard function keys."

When changing this option on a laptop, you'll now have to use the FN key with the F-key hardware functions to adjust the brightness.

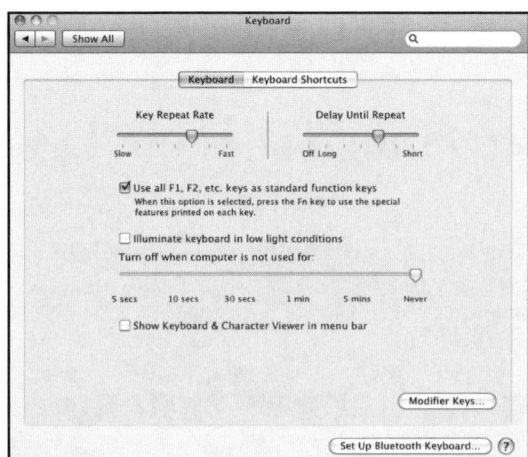

Fig: 1-6

Reason Overview

Finding the right software application for proper musical production can be quite a challenge, especially when you need one that is as powerful as it is easy to use, yet operates smoothly on even the most basic computer setups and includes all the virtual tools required for making music in just about every possible style. Congratulations for making Reason 6 your software of choice. Without question, Reason 6 is one of the most powerful yet easy-to-use music-making software applications available today. For example, consider how just the massive collection of instruments and effects available in Reason alone has revolutionized individual music production. Prior to its introduction in 2000, obtaining all of these instruments and effects required the purchase of separate hardware, literally costing several thousand dollars, in addition to costly hardware sequencers or expensive sequencing software to even utilize these tools. However, the introduction of Reason by Propellerhead changed all this by enabling individual production of music easily and effectively with simply a personal computer, a MIDI controller, quality audio interface, and adequate monitoring. The tools and instruments included in Reason enable anyone to achieve professional music production results easily and effectively without such additional costs or hardware. Now in its sixth incarnation, this powerful studio tool, upgraded with a vast array of samplers, drum machines, synths, and so much more, gives you all the tools you need to produce professional-quality music.

Furthermore, with this Power Tools book, which has been specifically designed to get you up and running quickly and efficiently, you will be producing music easily in no time, without having to overlearn every detail or spend inordinate time learning the basics. In short, this book is not a mere rehash of the instruction manual; rather, it is a focused guide created to rapidly bring you up to speed so that you can transition seamlessly into mastering advanced production techniques, enabling you can take full advantage of all the benefits this amazing music production software has to offer.

WHAT IS REASON?

Reason is the software equivalent of a full-blown audio and MIDI production suite—a virtual studio, if you will. Replete with a plethora of synthesizers, drum machines, samplers, and effects, this software is broken into three easy-to-understand windows: the mixer, modeled after an SSL9000K recording console; the rack, a virtual equipment cabinet designed to look like a nineteen-inch rack case, which houses an infinite number of instruments and effects; and the sequencer, which is used to record and play back MIDI and audio data.

UNDERSTANDING THE LAYOUT

To understand the basic operation of Reason 6, you'll begin by focusing on each section of a demo song. Your goal here is to become familiar with the different sections of the software so as to create a common dialogue. As we move through the different tutorials, I will explain and elaborate on each section in greater detail. Let's start off by opening a demo song and examining each of the three sections.

OPENING A DEMO SONG

Begin by opening up the demo song "Everything" by Little Jinder.

Select Open from the Reason file menu. The Song Browser window will open and you'll see a column on the left titled Locations and Favorites.

Fig. 2-1

Select the Reason folder, followed by the Demo Song folder in the center section of the browser.

Once inside the demo folder, select "Little Jinder—Everything.rnsdemo."

Fig. 2-2

When the song opens, you'll see the screen split into three segments. Let's put those F-keys to work and have a closer look at Reason 6's interface.

EXPLORING THE MIXER

Press F5 to change the view to Reason's mixer, which is modeled after the world-class recording console by Solid State Logic—the SSL9000K.

Fig. 2-3

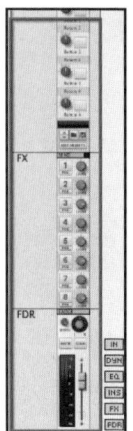

Fig. 2-4

At first glance, this may seem a bit overwhelming, but don't panic! We'll break down the Channel Strip and Master sections in a later chapter, but for now, explore the interface by scrolling up and down with the channel strip navigator located on the right side of the mixer.

Notice the blue outline that designates the viewing area. By clicking and dragging the blue outline, you can scroll up to the top of the mixer. In order from the top, you'll see the following:

- Inputs
- Signal Path
- Dynamics
- Equalizers
- Inserts
- FX Send
- Fader

Another useful feature for managing the look of the mixer is the Show/Hide button located on the bottom right of the mixer. Selecting any of the available options will collapse that section of the mixer to allow for a more focused view. This is a great way to keep the mixer manageable and you'll be putting this technique to good use in the upcoming chapters.

EXPLORING THE RACK

The rack houses all the instruments and effects within the program and offers a fantastically visual way of working with each device.

Fig. 2-5

Press F6, and the window will now display all of the instruments and effects used in the demo song. The rack itself is modeled to look like a high-end piece of studio furniture, down to the wooden panels and nineteen-inch rack rails. By default, the rack is shown with two columns, but you can create as many columns as you deem necessary, which allows for flexible organization as you can group devices together in separate racks.

On the upper right corner of the rack is the rack navigator, which functions exactly like the mixer navigator.

Click and drag the blue highlighted box to move throughout the rack.

Starting from the very top of the rack, you'll find the Hardware Interface, then the Master Section, followed by several effects, instruments, and audio devices.

All of the devices will be explained in greater detail in a later chapter, but for the time being, check out the rear of the rack by pressing Tab on your computer keyboard.

I personally find this is one of the most amazing things about Reason 6. As you can see, the back of the rack is designed to allow you to visually understand the physical wiring of an actual production rack. It is possible to trace the cables that are routed from your instruments and effects to see how they actually attach to the mixer.

It may seem complicated, but most of the physical wiring is done for you by Reason. You'll explore advanced routing techniques in a later chapter.

Fig. 2-6

You may be asking yourself, "How exactly does everything connected to the mixer?" The easy answer is that it is done with virtual connections, which will be covered in more detail in the Signal Flow section of the next chapter.

EXPLORING THE SEQUENCER

The sequencer section allows you to record, edit, and play back MIDI and audio data.

Press F7 to toggle the window to the sequencer. The sequencer is broken up into three main sections: the track list, Arrangement/Edit pane, and track navigator.

Fig. 2-7

Track List

The track list is the vertical column that runs down the
right side of the sequencer page.

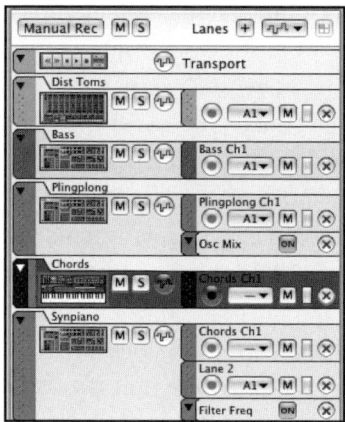

Focus your attention on the Chords track for a moment.
When you select a track, the instrument icon appears
with a red border around it. Two other buttons become
illuminated as well. The first button, which resembles
a circle with squiggly lines inside, is the Record Enable
Parameter Automation button, and is used to record
parameter automation (more about this later). The second,
appearing as a circle with a solid black dot in the center,
is the Record Enable button, which tells Reason that it
should record MIDI to this track.

Fig. 2-8

By default, you have your Master Keyboard Input set
to Standard, which automatically enables the master keyboard
input to the selected track. It is possible to have independent or
separated control over a track's record enable when using multiple
MIDI controllers.

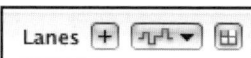

Fig. 2-9

There are three types of lanes used to record data on any given track: note, parameter
automation, and pattern automation.

For instance, if you focus your attention on the track Synpiano (below the Chords
track), you'll see this track contains two note lanes and a parameter automation lane.

To create new lanes, select one of the three buttons on the upper right corner of the track
list section. You'll explore these parameters in greater detail in a later chapter.

Arrangement/Edit Pane

The main section of the Sequencer window is called the Arrangement/Edit pane. This is
where your record, edit, and play back MIDI audio and automation data.

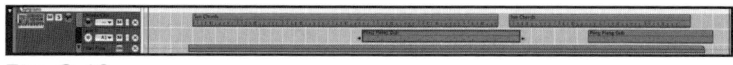

Fig. 2-10

All data on the Arrangement/Edit pane are referred to as clips. You'll be working with
four types of clips: audio, note, parameter automation, and pattern.

In Fig. 2.10, you can see the arrangement view of the Synpiano track.

Double-click on the clip Pling Plong dub track to enter into a MIDI editor. You are now
inside the clip, which allows for direct access to MIDI notes, velocity data, and parameter
automation for filter frequency. We'll be delving into deeper detail regarding usage of the
Edit windows over the next few chapters.

To exit Edit mode, click the Edit button located in the upper left corner of the sequencer window. Another and perhaps faster way of exiting Edit mode is to simply hit the ESC key on your computer keyboard.

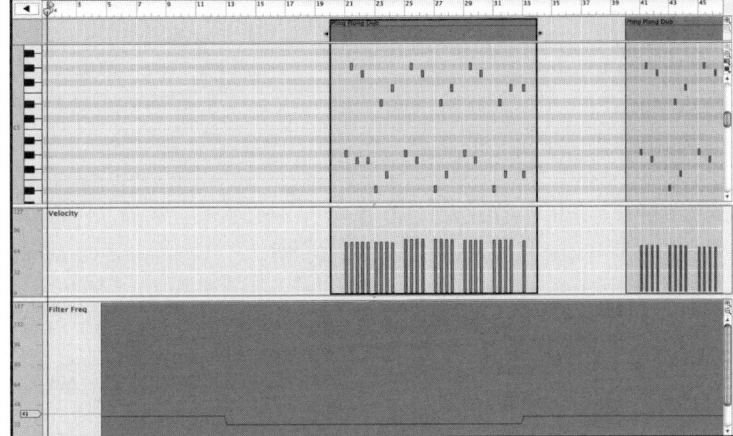

Reason 6 now has the ability to record, edit, and play back audio data. In Fig. 2.12, you see the arrangement view of the audio clip Lead Vox.

Fig. 2-11

Fig. 2-12

Double-click on the Lead Vox clip, to enter into the Audio editor, which gives you the ability to perform edits to the audio waveform, create a composite of several audio tracks, and work with the parameter automation.

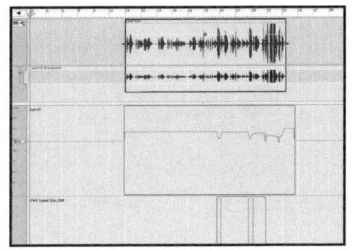

Track Navigator

The third section of the sequencer is the track navigator.

Fig. 2-13

Just like the mixer and rack navigator, the track navigator provides an overview of all the tracks used in the sequencer window, using device icons.

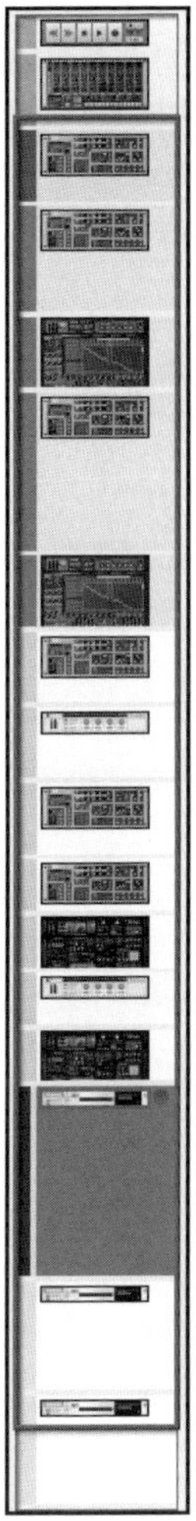

Fig. 2-14

The Ruler

Running along the top of the Arrangement/Edit pane is a ruler.

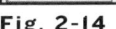

The ruler provides the timeline for your song. Functions of the ruler include the Left Locator (L), the SPP or Song Position Pointer, the Right Locator (R), and the Song End Marker (E). Depending on your zoom settings, the ruler may display bar, beat, and/or division increments.

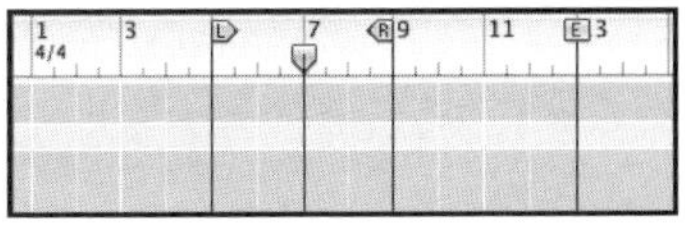

Fig. 2-15

Snap

The Snap function forces any data to lock into to a specific increment of time. In this case, Snap is set to Bar, which would cause any clip or note to be moved in one-measure increments.

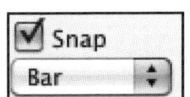

The options at which you can set this time frame to range from one bar to 1/64 of a measure.

Fig. 2-16

Inspector

The inspector feature is much like a window into any selected data on the Arrangement/Edit pane.

Position	Length
5. 1. 1. 0	3. 0. 0. 0

Fig. 2-17

In this particular instance, the clip starts at measure 5 and is a total of seven measures long. The inspector is incredibly useful for making sure all of the data are set in the desired position, as well as duration. It will change, depending on what type of clip or event is selected.

For instance, here's how the inspector would read if you had an individual MIDI note selected. Notice that in addition to the position and length, you also see that the

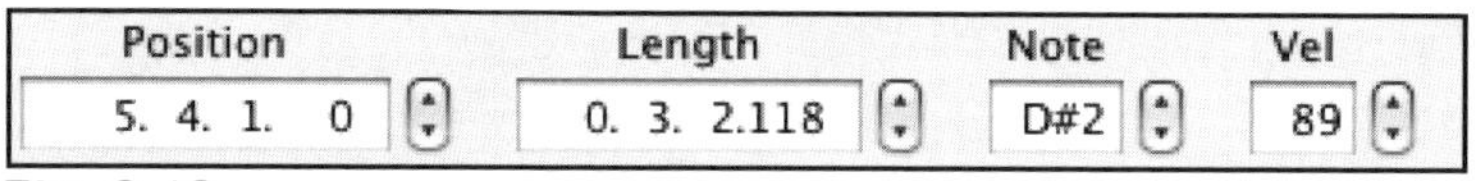

Position	Length	Note	Vel
5. 4. 1. 0	0. 3. 2.118	D#2	89

Fig. 2-18

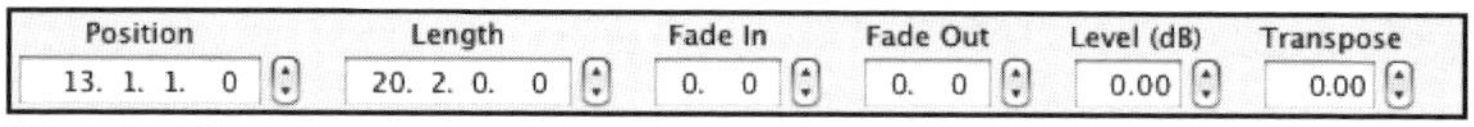

Position	Length	Fade In	Fade Out	Level (dB)	Transpose
13. 1. 1. 0	20. 2. 0. 0	0. 0	0. 0	0.00	0.00

Fig. 2-19

note and velocity information is also displayed as well.

Selecting an audio clip yields even more control parameters, including position, length, fade in, fade out, level, and transposition.

Tool Palette

In the upper left corner of the sequencer window, you will find the Tool Palette.

The Tool Palette allows you to create, edit, delete, and modify both MIDI and audio data.

Fig. 2-20

SELECTOR TOOL
Selects one or more events for editing

PENCIL TOOL
Adds MIDI events or draws automation

ERASER TOOL
Erases MIDI events and automation

RAZOR TOOL
Splits MIDI events, clips, and automation

MUTE TOOL
Mutes individual notes, clips, and automation

MAGNIFY TOOL
Zooms in or out (To zoom out, press down the Option key.)

HAND TOOL
A navigation tool

Another great feature of the Tool Palette is the assignation of quick key commands, which can be used to quickly select each tool as needed. Press Q, W, E, R, T, Y, and U to respectively select each tool. This can be a great time saver once you get accustomed to each command!

SONG NAVIGATOR

The song navigator always available, regardless of what window is being used. It is located just above the Transport pane at the bottom of the screen. This function affords a bird's-eye view of the entire song and allows you to navigate to any section of the song very quickly.

You can change your zoom setting by using the magnifying glass (+ or –) on the left side of the song navigator or by moving the song

Fig. 2-21

navigator handles on the left or right side of the navigator pane. Hold Shift while moving a navigation handle to cause both handles to move proportionately together, providing a focused zoom over a specific area.

TRANSPORT

The Transport is a global device that is always available for use whether you're looking at the mixer, rack, or sequencer. It is an extremely useful

Fig. 2-22

feature, not just for playback and recording. It further offers a whole host of necessary and useful functions described as follows.

IN
Audio Input meter

OUT
Audio Output meter

DSP
DSP stands for "digital signal processing." This shows how much of your computer's processor is being used for the current function.

CALC
CALC stands for "calculation." This displays activity when Reason is processing and/or loading samples.

BLOCKS

This is an advanced Arrangement tool that will be addressed in Chapter 12 – Building an Arrangement. To disable, deselect the Blocks button.

METRONOME

Provides a click track with preroll

TAP TEMPO

Repeatedly tapping this button sets the song tempo.

TEMPO

Calculated in beats per minute (bpm)

TIME SIGNATURE

The default setting for this is 4/4.

SONG POSITION

Displayed in two formats:

    1. Musical (Bar . Beat . 16th Note . Tick) and
    2. Time (hours:minutes:seconds:frames)

TRANSPORT CONTROLS

Rewind / Fast Forward / Stop / Play / Record

DUB

New take

ALT

Alternate take

Q REC

Quantize during Record

LEFT AND RIGHT LOCATORS

These are used in conjunction with the ruler on the Arrangement/Edit pane and afford the ability to set up a loop for recording and editing.

IN CONCLUSION

By now you should now have a pretty good idea of the overall layout and basic functions of Reason. In the next chapter, you will take a closer look at the signal flow of MIDI in Reason 6.

Getting Started

This chapter will guide you through Reason's MIDI signal flow and explore how to create instruments and browse patches. But before you begin your journey into this process, let's start with an overview of the concept of MIDI.

WHAT IS MIDI?

MIDI (musical instrument digital interface) is a universal programming protocol, that was adopted as the music industry standard by every major manufacturer of electronic instruments since the early '80s to standardize parameters dealing with musical production. Prior to MIDI, every manufacturer had already developed its own unique means of communication regarding its own respective products; however, this, in turn, created much difficulty on the user end by requiring multiple methods for varying instruments or devices to be used simultaneously. The MIDI protocol created standardized settings for information, such as note volume, pitch, velocity, aftertouch, and so on, thereby enabling compatibility across all products.

One of the most important concepts to consider with regard to MIDI is that it contains no audio data. When you record MIDI data, the variables performance, not actual audio waveforms, are the primary focus. Once recorded, the MIDI data parameters can then be edited into the desired performance effect with a variety of enhancement tools. For example, if you wish to edit a particular variable such as the pitch or key of the instrument you have just recorded, with audio waveforms you would need to rerecord the entire instrumentation sample to change or enhance certain variables. However, with MIDI, you simply adjust just the patch of the instrument or even change the instrument itself, without having to rerecord. This makes editing an incredibly easy, flexible, and even fun process, thereby making even the most minute adjustment to any variable simple.

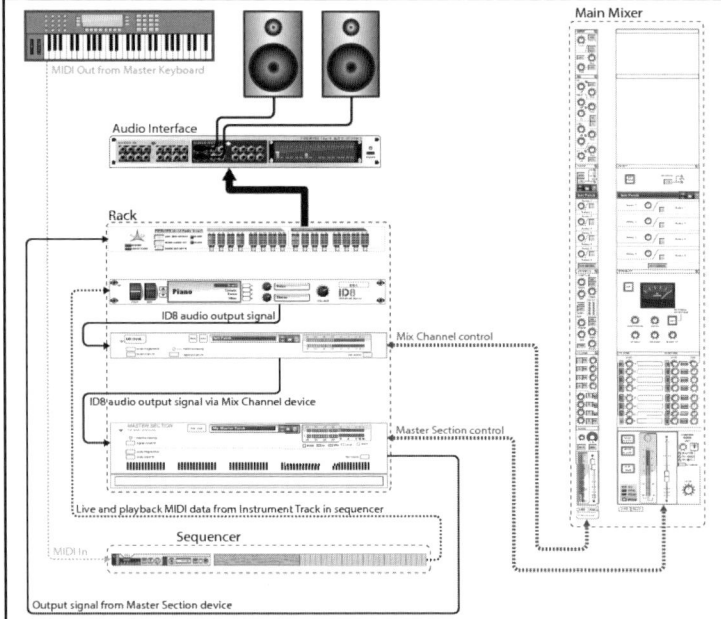

Fig. 3-1

MIDI SIGNAL FLOW

Begin by opening the Chapter 3.reason song file found on the enclosed DVD or available for download from the Hal Leonard website. Once it is open, you'll find it is a blank session.

You'll first look at how audio flows from Reason to your monitors.

In Fig. 3.1, you'll find a signal flow diagram taken from the Reason 6 manual.

Let's break down the signal flow diagram, while looking at Reason song file. Please make sure that your audio and MIDI controller settings are working correctly.

Audio Interface

The audio interface is the physical device used to transmit audio into and out of your computer. For more information with regards to audio interfaces, see chapter 1.

In the diagram, you'll see an interface containing sixteen input and outputs. Please note that the only actual physical connection present is to the studio monitors.

Hardware Interface

The Hardware Interface is the software representation of your physical audio interface.

A number of useful functions are available on the front of the Hardware Interface device. The active Audio Driver window is displaying MOTU 828mk2, which lets you know that Reason has accurately identified

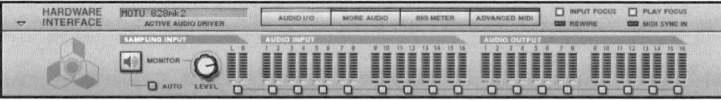

Fig. 3-2

the interface you are using. To the right of this window are four buttons: Audio I/O, More Audio, Big Meter, and Advanced MIDI.

AUDIO I/O

By default, the Audio I/O (Input/Output) is selected. Just below, you see three sections: Sampling Input, Audio Input, and Audio Output. Sampling Input will be covered in greater detail in the chapter on sampling.

The Audio Input section shows sixteen inputs, while the Audio Output section shows sixteen outputs. Each pair of inputs and outputs has LEDs to indicate status. The gold color indicates the active inputs and outputs for the audio interface; in this case you can see eight inputs and eight outputs are active. Green LEDs indicate channels that are in use, and in this case you can see that Outputs 1 and 2 are in use.

Now, press Tab and take a look at the rear of the rack for a moment.

On the rear of the rack, you'll find the Master Out is connected to Slots 1 and 2 of the To Audio Output section of the Audio I/O. Devices connected to Reason's mixer are combined and sent from the Master Out to the Audio Output section, which is connected directly to the studio monitors.

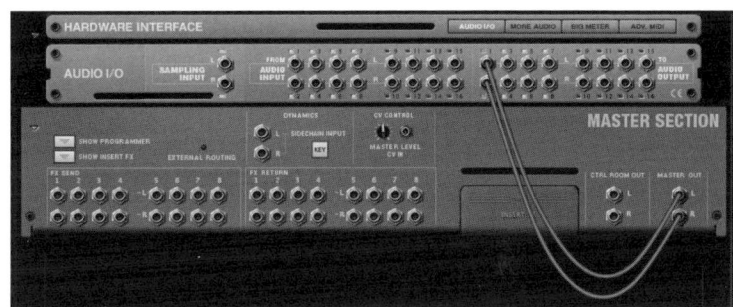

Fig. 3-3

MORE AUDIO

If you select the More Audio tab, an additional panel initiates to reveal a total of sixty-four inputs and outputs. Most audio interfaces do not have this many inputs and outputs, but this feature comes in quite handy when implementing ReWire, a method of connecting Reason 6 to another DAW such as Logic or Ableton.

BIG METER

Press Tab to toggle your view back to the front of the rack. The Big Meter provides an accurate depiction of levels. In this case, the red button under Outputs 1 and 2 indicate that the meter is focused on the Master level. This function is also useful when setting levels for recording or sampling.

ADVANCED MIDI

The Advanced MIDI tab allows for the set up of Reason devices to be used with an external sequencer.

Create an Instrument

Create an ID8 by selecting Create > Instruments > ID8 Instrument Device.

An ID8 instrument is created, along with a Mix Channel device.

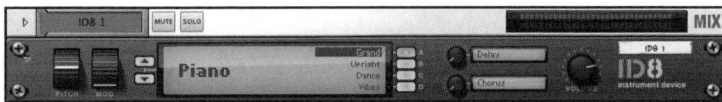

Fig. 3-4

On the Mix Channel device, select the right-facing triangle in the upper left corner. The triangle will shift downward and the device will unfold to reveal its control parameters.

Tab to the rear of the rack and note that the ID8 instrument has been cabled to the inputs of the Mix Channel device.

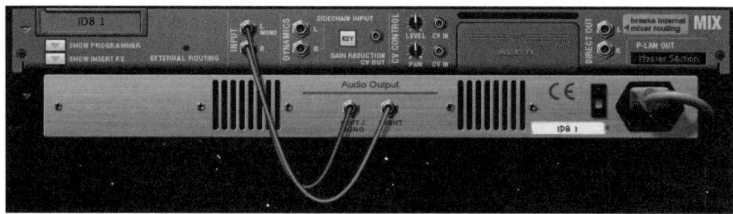

Fig. 3-5

The Mix Channel device has an invisible connection to the channel strip on the mixer.

In addition to the ID8 and Mix Channel device, a track is also created in the sequencer

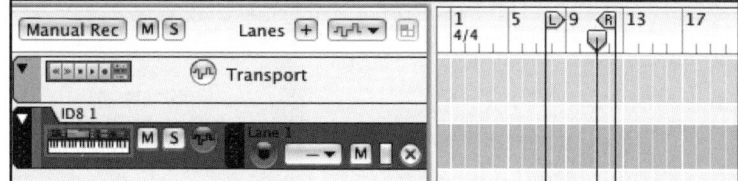

Fig. 3-6

window. If you play a few keys on your MIDI controller keyboard, you will hear a piano sound from the ID8.

Following MIDI Signal Flow

Referring back to Fig. 3.1, let's trace the signal flow from MIDI out of the master keyboard.

- Pressing a key generates a MIDI Note-On message.
- The signal travels to the ID8 sequencer track.
- The sequencer track passes the signal to the ID8 instrument and sound is generated.
- The generated sound of the ID8 flows into the Mix Channel device.
- The Mix Channel device sends the signal to the Mix Channel control or channel strip, where it is processed and sent back to the Mix Channel device.
- The Mix Channel device sends the processed signal to the Master Section device.
- The Master Section device then sends the signal to the Master Section control or Master channel strip for processing.
- The signal is sent back to the Master Section device and on to the Hardware Interface.
- The Hardware Interface sends the signal to your audio interface.
- The audio interface connects to your studio monitors.

When recording, the MIDI information is printed to the sequencer track. This allows you to record, edit, and play back the MIDI data. With every new instrument created, a Mix Channel device track and sequencer track are created. Now that you have a basic understanding of how the signal flow works, let's explore methods for browsing patches.

EXPLORING SOUNDS

Begin by first creating a Subtractor Synthesizer.

From the Create menu, select Instruments > Subtractor Analog Synthesizer.

The Subtractor will appear located underneath the ID8 instrument in the rack. Also, notice the new track appearing in the sequencer and mixer, titled Subtractor 1.

Make sure the Subtractor is selected. By default, this should have happened when you created the

Fig. 3-7

Subtractor. If you are unclear of track selection, please review the Track List section of Chapter 2.

Play a few notes on your MIDI keyboard controller. The sound you will hear is the default Bass Guitar patch.

Browse Subtractor Patches

Let's explore how to create and select patches on a few different instruments in Reason 6.

Fig. 3-8

Select the Browse Patch button on the Subtractor, which is the center button with an icon shaped to resemble a file folder.

The Patch Browser window will open to reveal all categories of the patches available for use in the Subtractor Synthesizer.

Select the Bass folder and explore some of the different bass sounds the Subtractor provides. First, click on a patch name and then play a few notes on your MIDI keyboard to audition the sounds. A Select Next/Previous button, located on the bottom right, allows you to select the next patch

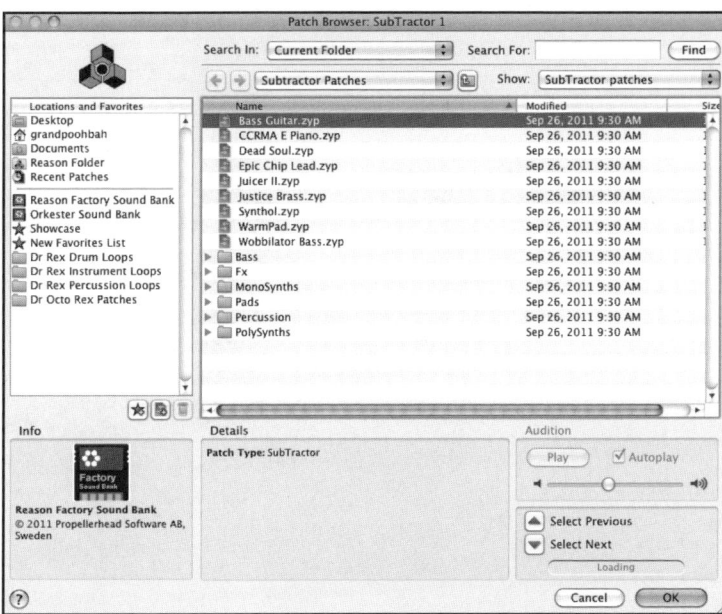

Fig. 3-9

Fig. 3-10

while browsing. For even more convenience, you can use the Up and Down arrows on your computer keyboard to select patches.

An alternate method for quickly selecting patches is to use the Next/Previous Patch button located to the left of the Browse Patch button. This allows you to browse patches in a given folder without having to open the patch browser. By selecting the top or bottom triangle, you will move either forward or backward within the Bass Patch folder of the Subtractor.

Once you are finished exploring some of the bass sounds of the Subtractor, select the ReasonBass patch, which we'll use in the next chapter about recording.

Browse ReDrum Patches

Next, create a ReDrum drum machine.

From the Create menu, select Instruments > ReDrum Drum Computer.

The ReDrum is a powerful yet easy-to-use drum machine modeled after the vintage Roland TR series drum machines. It features ten sounds, each with its own sound-shaping capabilities. You'll explore every facet of the instrument in a later chapter, but for now, let's use it as a drum module.

To play the ReDrum as a module, you must use the C1 octave on your MIDI keyboard controller. If you are using a small two-octave controller, you may have to use the octave shift to lower the controller's range. The note range is C1 to A1. C1 will typically trigger a kick drum sound.

By default, the Disco Kit 1 patch is selected. Feel free to explore the other available kits via the patch browser. The browse patch functions exactly like the Subtractor.

After you're done exploring a few of the different kits, please select the House Kit 08, which you'll use in the next chapter.

Now that you have a basic understanding of Reason's MIDI signal flow, and how to create instruments and select patches, you'll next take a look at how to record and edit MIDI.

Fig. 3-11

Part Two

Recording and Editing MIDI

This chapter will guide you through the ins and outs or recording and editing MIDI data. If you already have the chapter 3 song file open and you've been following along, you may begin right away. If you're starting chapter 4 anew, first please open the Reason song file titled Chapter 4.reason, found on the enclosed DVD.

SELECTING A TRACK

The very first step you should always take when starting a recording session is to confirm that you have the correct track selected. This refers back to the concept of signal flow and knowing where to route the incoming MIDI data that's being triggered by your MIDI controller.

On the sequencer rack, select the ReDrum track.

Notice how the background color of the selected track changes to a darker shade. Furthermore, note there is now a red border highlighting the Instrument icon, which resembles a miniature version of the ReDrum. This is an indication that the Master Keyboard selection is set up correctly within the keyboard controller preferences. Also observe of how both the Parameter Automation and Record Enable buttons are

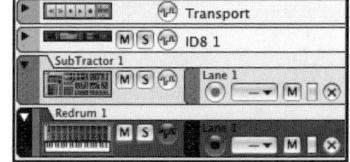

Fig. 4-1

now red. Your focus will be the red button containing a solid black circle: the Record Enable button.

Play a few notes in the C1 to A1 range of your MIDI keyboard, and you will hear the ReDrum playing the House Kit 08 patch you selected in the previous chapter.

Next, you'll want to set up a metronome, for time referencing during production.

THE METRONOME

Setting up a metronome is a great way to work when producing music, because it provides a timing reference that is very useful in the editing and arranging processes. If you record a MIDI section without a timing reference, it is highly likely that the ruler will not match the recording, which makes the editing and arranging process much more difficult.

For example, pretend you are recording a one-measure MIDI clip with a tempo of 160 bpm. If the Reason sequencer tempo is set to 120 bpm, the result would manifest as a MIDI section that doesn't match the tempo of your ruler. This mismatch in timing would then render the Snap function useless in editing.

Fig. 4-2

Next, let's take a closer look at the metronome and its settings.

On the Transport window located at the bottom of the screen, use the Click button to engage the metronome.

Press the space bar to initiate playback.

Notice how there is a higher-pitched sound on the first beat of every measure, followed by three sound beats at a slightly lower pitch. Also, note the Time Signature section on the Transport window, which is set by default to 4/4 time. The first number shown is equivalent to the first beat (or the higher-pitched sound) followed by the three beats at the lower pitch. This can be adjusted, for example, by changing the time signature to 3/4 time so that the metronome only cycles through three beats instead of four, with the first beat as the higher-pitched sound, followed by only two beats at the lower pitch. For the purposes of this tutorial you will be working in 4/4 time, so be sure to return the setting to this default.

Press the space bar again to stop the transport.

Next, engage the Pre button located under the Click button in the Metronome section.

Fig. 4-3

The Pre button engages the Precount function, which is essentially a count-off that occurs before recording begins. This is quite helpful because it allows you to hear the tempo at which you will be recording just prior to starting the recording session. By default, this is set to run for one measure; however, you can easily modify the length of the Precount by selecting Options on the main menu and navigating to Number of Precount Bars to select either 1, 2, 3, or 4 as possible settings.

Now, select 2, to set the Precount to occur for two bars (eight beats) before recording begins.

If you determine that the metronome is either too loud or not loud enough, you can easily modify the volume adjusting the Click Level knob.

Now you are ready to record a MIDI section. Your goal is to record four measures of a quarter-note kick pattern.

RECORDING MIDI

From the Transport window, click the square Record button or simply use the quick keyboard command Command + Return if using a Mac, or Control + Return if using Windows.

Fig. 4-4

Now, using your MIDI controller, play C1 with each click of the metronome. When you have finished recording this four-bar section of kick drum, simply tap the space bar to stop recording.

Congratulations! You've just created your very first recording in Reason 6.

You will find there is now a MIDI clip visible inside the Arrangement window.

Fig. 4-5

To return to the beginning of the newly recorded section, click the Stop button in the Transport window or simply use the keyboard command Shift + Return to perform the same function.

Now, when you press Play or tap the space bar, you can listen to your recording.

EDITING MIDI

While listening to your newly recorded kick drum track, you may notice that your timing might have been less than perfect. One or more of the notes may be a little late or early. Let's open up the Drum editor and first work with one of sequencer tools called Quantize, which is designed to quickly and efficiently correct timing anomalies.

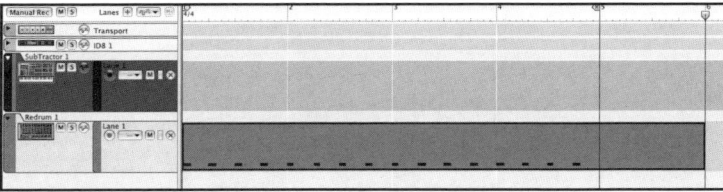

Fig. 4-6

Start by zooming in on the MIDI clip. An easy way to doing this is to use the Magnify tool. Simply click and hold your mouse as you draw a box around the MIDI clip. You may

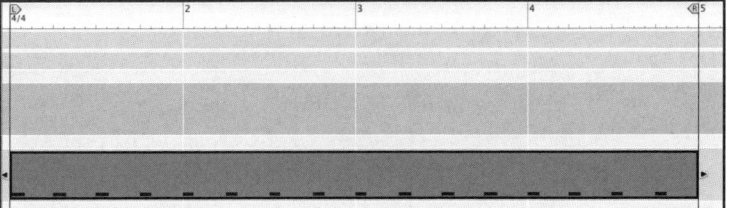

Fig. 4-7

also like to use the Magnify tools on the bottom left and right of the sequencer window, which allow for horizontal and vertical zooming. Additionally, you may also use the keys G and H on your computer keyboard to zoom horizontally.

For example, your recorded clip may not be exactly four measures. Select the clip by clicking on it once with the Selector tool. Two small triangles will appear at either end of the clip. Also notice the inspector at the top displays the length as five measures.

Grab the right triangle and move it to the start of Measure 5.

Next, press P on your computer keyboard, which sets the Left and Right locators to the size of the clip, turns the Loop function on, and begins playback.

Drum Editor

Double-click the clip and the sequencer window changes from the Arrangement view to the Edit view with the Drum editor.

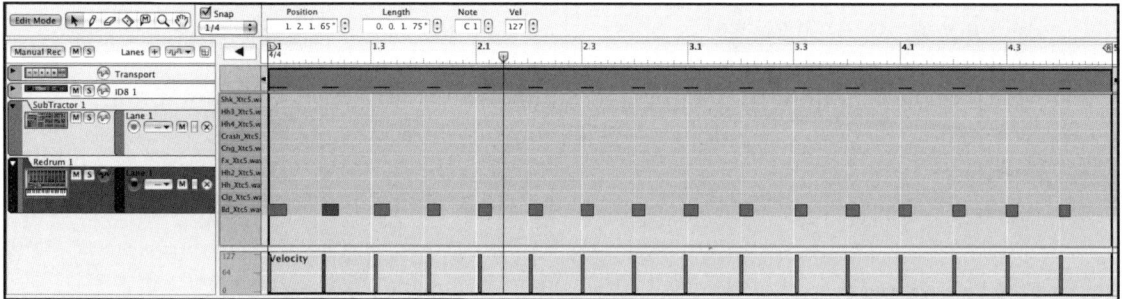

Fig. 4-8

The Drum editor is the default editor used for the ReDrum drum machine. It features a column on the right with samples used, and creates a matrix with the ruler. The notes are on the BD_Xtc5.wav sample row.

The Snap is set to quarter notes, which define the vertical white lines. Notice how each MIDI note more or less lines up with the quarter-note grid, but closer examination reveals that the notes are not perfectly aligned to the grid.

Also note the second MIDI note has been selected and the inspector shows a position of 1.2.1.65* (The Inspector position is broken down into numbers signifying, respectively, Bar . Beat . Division . Tick), the asterisk indicating the position of this note is not on a whole tick, but falls in between two values.

Sequencer Tools

Press F8 or select Show Tools from the Window menu.

Select the Sequencer Tools button at the top, which resembles a wrench and screwdriver. Here you'll find a list of available tools to help with MIDI editing. First, we will be working with the Quantize section.

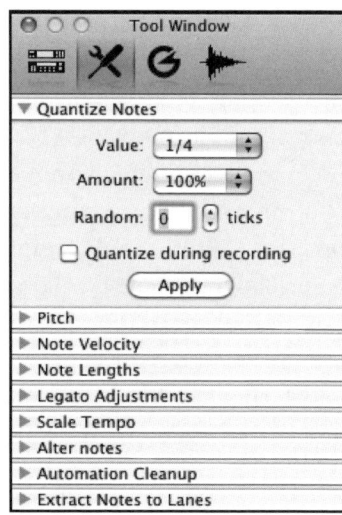

Fig. 4-9

QUANTIZE

Change the Quantize value to quarter notes. You may select individual notes and hit Apply, which is helpful if you don't wish to quantize every note within the clip. In this case, you need to quantize everything. The easiest way to select everything is to simply click on the clip at the top of the screen. Alternatively, you may use the key command Command + A if using a Mac, or Control + A if using Windows, or you can rubber-band select all the notes by clicking and dragging around all the notes within the clip.

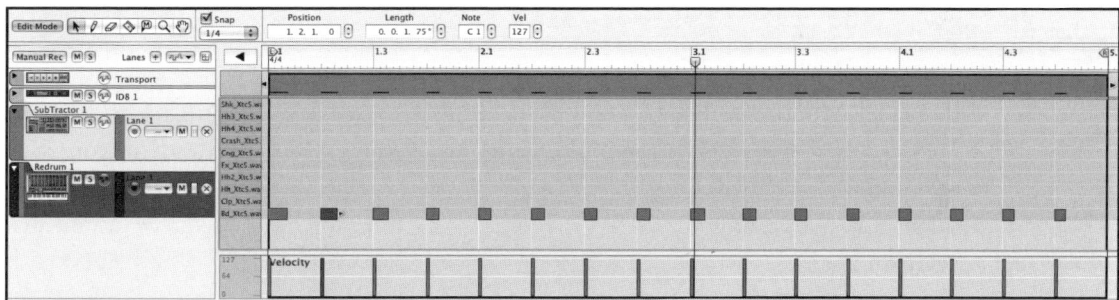

Fig. 4-10

Next, hit Apply on the Quantize window.

You will notice that all the notes have snapped to the nearest quarter-note position.

Now, press Play and listen to the drum track again. Notice how the kick drum is now in perfect synchronization with the metronome. You can now disable the click on the Transport, as you've just created a timing reference. Leave the Pre button engaged, as it's always helpful to have a preroll when recording.

COPYING NOTES

Next, you are going to build up the drum track by adding more notes to the sequence. You could use the Pencil tool to draw in these notes, but by copying, you can quickly build up the sequence in a few short steps.

Begin by changing the Snap value to eighth notes.

Next, select all the notes on the kick drum row. By right-clicking or using Control + Click on a note, the Edit menu appears and you may select the function Select Notes of Same Pitch. Once all the notes have been selected, copy the notes up to the Hh2_Xtc.wav row.

To copy, hold the Option key if using a Mac or the Alt key if using Windows while dragging the notes upward with the mouse. Move the notes over one eighth-note to the right. Remember to release the mouse button before releasing the Option/Alt key to execute the copy.

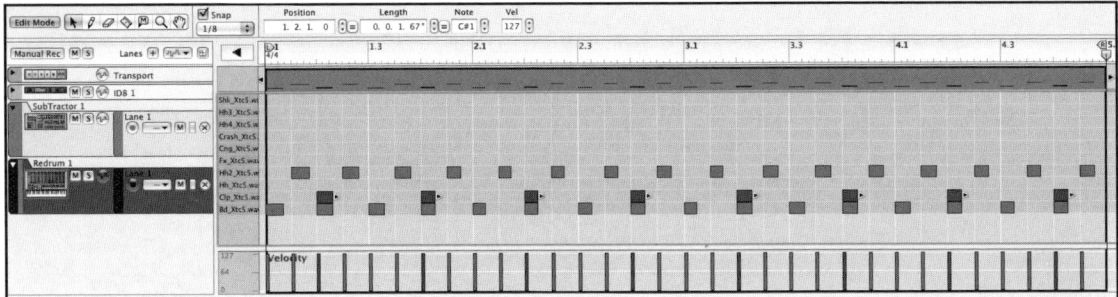

Fig. 4-11

On the kick drum row, click on every even-numbered note and copy the notes up to the Clp_Xtc5.wav row. Use the Option + Click method if using a Mac or Alt + Click method if using Windows, and again, remembering to release the Option/Alt key last.

Hit Play and marvel at your work. Give yourself a pat on the back, as you've just created a house drum track.

QUANTIZE DURING RECORDING

Another useful feature is the Quantize During Recording function. This will automatically correct your timing as you record on the fly. You many not wish to use this all the time, but it will certainly speed up your workflow.

To engage this function, either select it from the Transport via the Q Rec button or from the Quantize window from within the Sequencer Tools window.

Next, create a new lane by selecting the New Note Lane button with a + symbol on it at the top of the track list of the sequencer window. Alternatively, you can create a new note lane by pressing the Dub button located on the Transport.

Either option will yield a new note lane above the newly created drum track.

Next, change the Quantize value to sixteenth notes.

Move the SPL back to the beginning by clicking on the Stop button or using the keyboard command Shift + Return.

Hit Record and play the notes G-sharp 1 and A1 in any rhythm you choose.

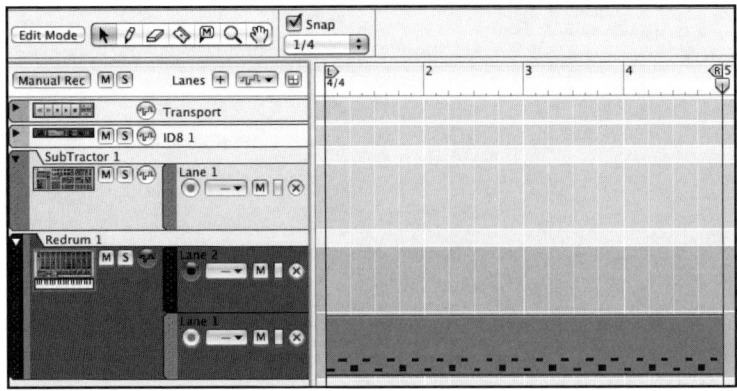

Fig. 4-12

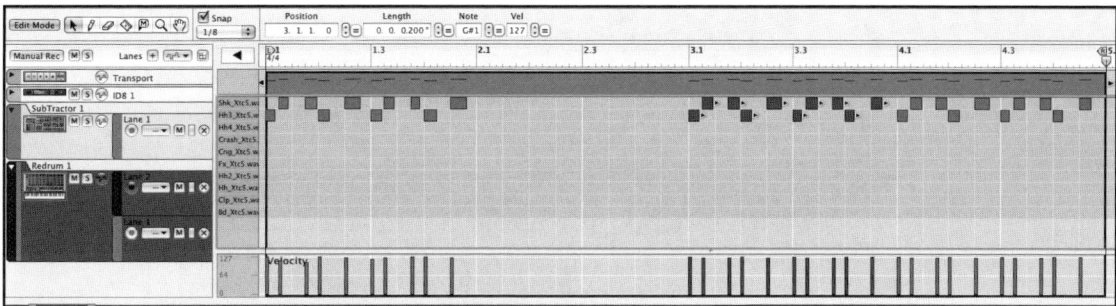

Fig. 4-13

After you've recorded a performance through the four-measure cycle, listen to you work. Even if you didn't play your sequence perfectly, the notes themselves are locked to a sixteenth-note grid. In my case, there were some mistakes in the second measure that I would like to fix, so I selected all the notes in Measure 2 and deleted them. Next, I copied the notes from Measure 3 to Measure 2, using the Option + Drag method to replace them with the correct notes.

RECORDING A BASS LINE

Next, record a bass line using the Subtractor synthesizer.

In Fig. 4.14, I played a two-measure sequence twice. The image shows a simple bass line using notes G1 and A-sharp 1 for the first two measures.

To the best of your abilities, play the bass line as shown. If you find are having trouble playing it, you can also use the Pencil tool to draw in the notes at their respective position and length. Keep in mind that the Snap value is set to eighth notes.

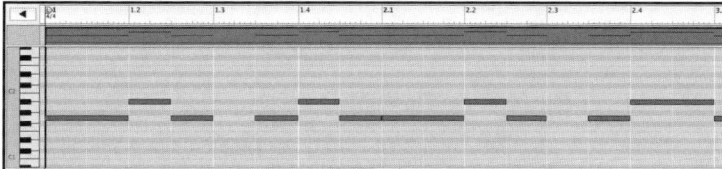

Fig. 4-14

Key Editor

Most instruments will default to the Key editor as shown.

Instead of sample names on the left column, as on the Drum editor, here you will find a piano keyboard. The editing functions here are exactly the same as for the Drum editor, only the view has changed.

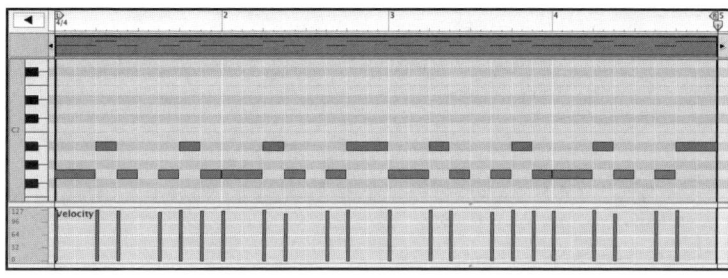

Fig. 4-15

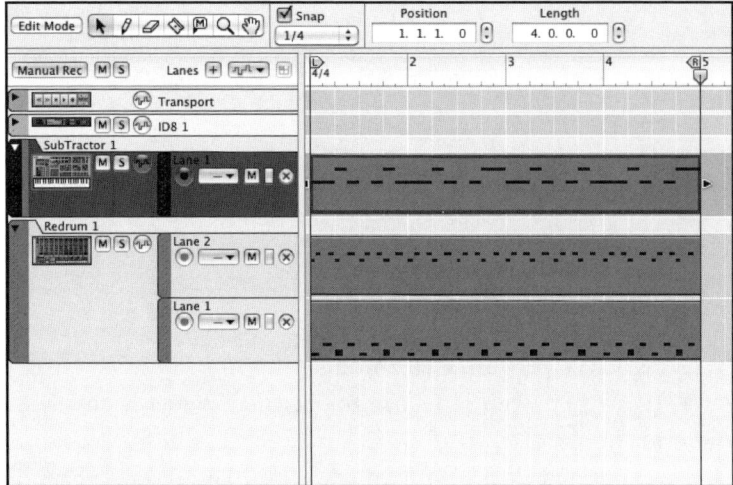

Fig. 4-16

Next, press the Edit button in the upper left corner of the sequencer window to leave the Edit view.

You should now be back in the Arrangement view of the sequencer. Copy the three MIDI clips to Measure 5. You may also use the Copy and Paste function from the Edit menu or the keyboard commands Command + C for copy and Command + V for paste if using a Mac, or Control + C for copy and Control + V for paste if using Windows.

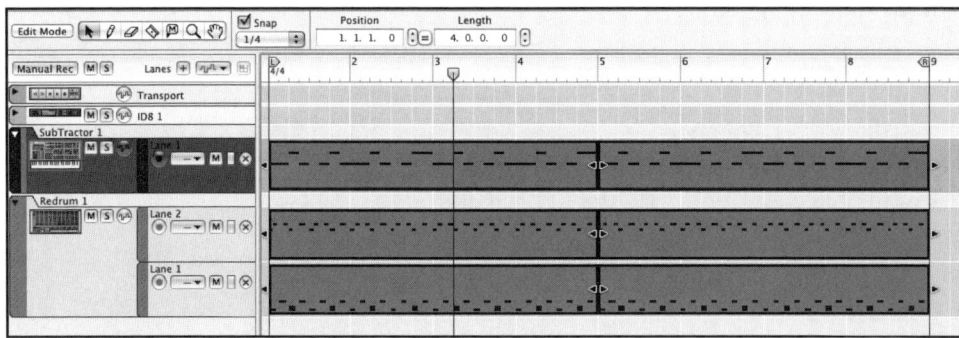

Fig. 4-17

With the sequence doubled, you should now have MIDI clips that plays Measures 1 to 9, an eight-measure sequence.

Using the Razor tool, make a slice on the bass line clip at Measure 7.

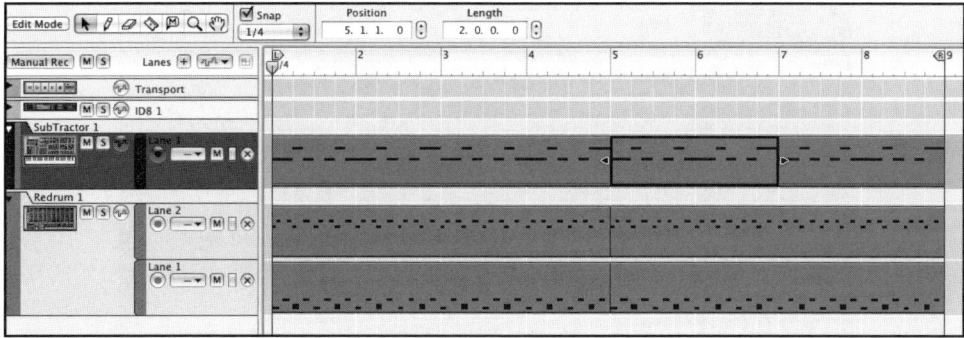

Fig. 4-18

SEQUENCER TOOLS—TRANSPOSE

Select the bass line clip, starting at Measure 5.

   Open the Sequencer Tools window and go to the Pitch section.

   With the Transpose button selected, use the Up arrow to select four semitones.

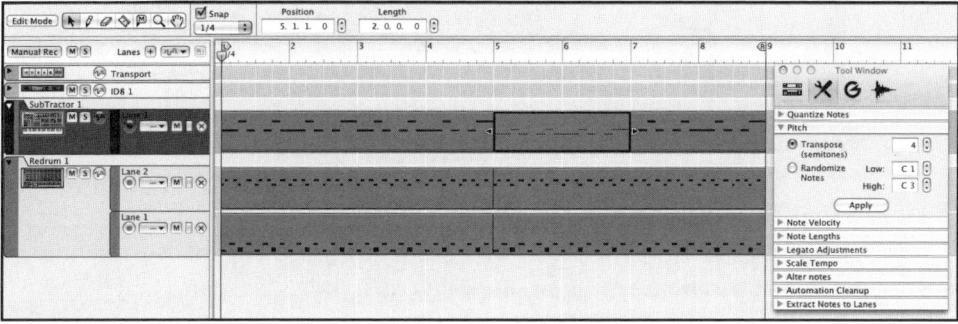

Fig. 4-19

Hit Apply and listen to the sequence. As you can hear, the clip starting at Measure 5 has been transposed up four semitones, or notes. Entering the Key editor, manually selecting the notes, and moving them up four notes on the keyboard can achieve the same result.

CREATING A LAYER

Next, let's add some depth to this bass line by layering a new sound. This is the process of creating a new instrument and copying the MIDI clips on to its sequencer track. Reason allows this to occur easily, by simply selecting the Subtractor track and using the command Duplicate Tracks and Devices from the Edit menu.

   Reason makes a duplicate copy of both the MIDI clips and instrument. On the Subtractor 1 Copy instrument in the rack, select the patch DirtStep from the Bass folder.

Fig. 4-20

Press Play and hear the layered bass sound.

Layers are a great way to build up a track very quickly without having to do a lot of sound design. The sum of both synths far out weigh their individual parts, and because they are playing the exact same notes, it sounds like one sound.

ADDING A PERCUSSION LINE

Next, let's create a percussion line with a Dr. OctoRex.

From the Create menu, select Instruments > Dr. OctoRex Loop Player.

Click the patch browser and navigate to Percussion > Conga/Bongo 125 bpm.

The Dr. OctoRex Loop Player is a unique instrument designed to work with .rex files and allows for some pretty creative functionality. You'll explore all the facets of the Dr. OctoRex in a later chapter, but for now, let's cover the basics.

The main interface features eight loop slots, six of which have been loaded with loops.

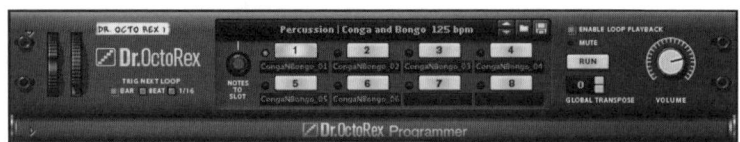

Fig. 4-21

To listen to the loops, click the Run button on the right side of the interface. Take a minute to explore the six loops.

Recording Patterns

One way to work with the Dr. OctoRex is to record the switching of different loops.

To begin, make sure the Run button is off and Slot 1 is selected. Move the SPL to the beginning of the sequence. You might also wish to raise the volume level on the Dr. OctoRex to enable you to hear the loop over the rest of the instruments.

Next, press Record. Just before the SPL reaches measure 3, select Loop Slot 3.

As the SPL reaches Measure 7, select Loop Slot 6.

Stop recording when you've reached Measure 9 and the sequence loops around.

You should now have a new pattern lane with the three selected patterns. Also note the green box around the loop slot selection on the main interface that indicates the section has been automated.

Play back the sequence and watch as the slots change automatically at the designated times.

Fig. 4-22

Copy Loop to Track

Another useful option and my preferred way of working, is the Copy Loop to Track function.

Begin by right-clicking or using Control + Click on any loop slot button on the interface and select Clear Automation. This will remove the automation and delete the pattern lane.

Also, deselect the Enable Loop Playback button found on the upper right side of the Dr. OctoRex interface.

Next, unfold the Dr. OctoRex programmer by selecting the right-facing triangle on the lower left corner of the Instrument interface. The programmer will unfold,

Fig. 4-23

revealing several audio control parameters. You'll be going over all the controls in a later chapter, but for now, focus your attention on the silver rectangular box on the left of the programmer. At the center top of this section, there is a button labeled Copy Loop to Track.

Before you use this function, you must first designate the range of the loop you wish to copy by setting the left and right locators on the sequencer page.

Move the right locator to Measure 3.

Next, select Loop Slot 1.

Finally, select the Copy Loop to Track button.

You should now have a two-bar MIDI clip on the Dr. OctoRex sequencer track.

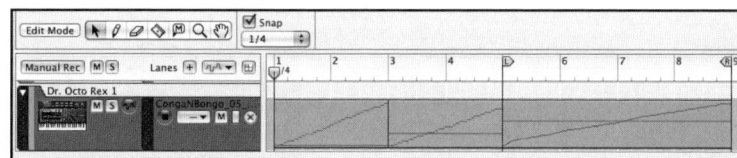

Fig. 4-24

Next, move the right locator to Measure 5 and the left locator to Measure 3.

Select Loop Slot 3, followed by the Copy Loop to Track button.

Finally, move the right locator to Measure 9 and the left locator to Measure 5.

Select Loop Slot 6, followed by the Copy Loop to Track button.

Move the left locator to Measure 1 and press Play. As you can hear, the MIDI data that has

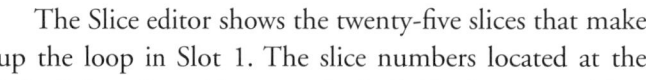
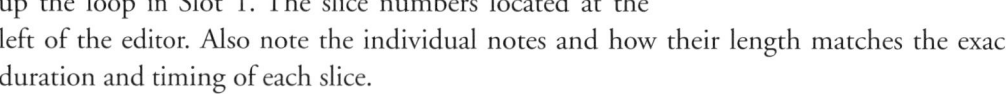

Fig. 4-25

been copied to the track plays back the different loops just like the pattern sequencer, with the additional benefit of your having access to the individual notes that have been assigned to each slice.

Slice Editor

Double-click on the MIDI clip, starting at Measure 1. The view changes from Arrangement to Edit with the Slice editor in view.

The Slice editor shows the twenty-five slices that make up the loop in Slot 1. The slice numbers located at the

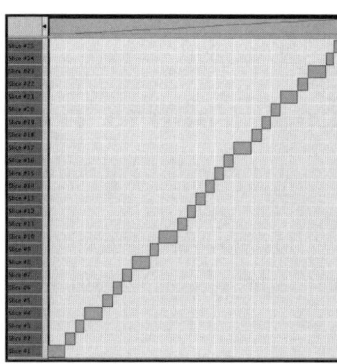

Fig. 4-26

left of the editor. Also note the individual notes and how their length matches the exact duration and timing of each slice.

You can reorder the slices to create a custom sequence.

Alternatively, it is possible to play the slices from your MIDI keyboard controller, starting from the C1 octave.

VELOCITY

Fig. 4-27

Now, let's take a look at the Velocity editor. Velocity is the speed at which something travels. With regard to MIDI, this is how quickly you strike or play a MIDI trigger, such as a key or pad. Most MIDI controllers transmit velocity data and I highly recommend using those that do.

The velocity information is translated into some form of expression, usually controlling volume. Yet, as you move through the book, you will find that at the Velocity window you may control any number of parameters.

The Velocity window is located at the bottom of the Drum, Key, and Slice editors. Each vertical bar is synced to a corresponding note. To edit note velocity, simply use the Pencil tool to adjust these levels. We'll explore more about the Velocity window in greater detail in later chapters.

IN CONCLUSION

You should now have a basic understanding of how to record and edit MIDI data. You'll be delving deeper into these functions and more as we move throughout the book.

If you would like to check your work, I've included a Reason song file named Chapter 4—Finished.reason that's available on the accompanying DVD or via download from the Hal Leonard website.

In the next chapter, you'll examine audio signal flow and how to record and edit audio data.

Recording and Editing Audio

Reason 6 now offers the ability to record, edit, and play back audio data. This chapter will guide you through Reason's audio signal flow and explore Reason's audio recording and editing capabilities. But before you begin your journey into this process, let's start with an overview of sound.

SOUND PRIMER

Sound is defined, on the micro level, as the disruption of air molecules. As the sound pressure level is being disrupted, our eardrums act as transducers, converting the minute variations in sound pressure levels into signals that our brain then recognizes as sound.

Sound moves in waves, which oscillate up and down. A good example is to pluck the string on a guitar and watch it vibrate or oscillate. Depending on the density and length of the string, you'll discover that the string vibrates at a different rate.

Frequency

The frequency, or how frequently the sound oscillates is measured in hertz (Hz), which is defined by how many oscillations occur per second.

A string oscillating thirty times a second would be equivalent to 30 Hz.

Amplitude

The amplitude of a sound wave is defined by how large the waveform is, regardless of its frequency. The larger the waveform, the louder we perceive it to be.

We measure amplitude of a signal in units called decibels (dB), which are a tenth of a bel, a seldom-used logarithmic unit.

Human Perceptions of Sound

Human beings can generally hear sounds from 20 Hz to 20,000 Hz, or 20 kHz. At what amplitude humans hear is based on the frequency of the sound because human hearing is logarithmic, which means we are more sensitive to certain frequencies than to others.

Following is a chart with common sounds and their measured level of decibels:

- Threshold of Hearing: 0 dB
- Soft Whisper: 30 dB
- Quiet Room: 40 dB
- Quiet Street: 50 dB
- Normal Speech: 60 dB
- Vacuum Cleaner: 70 dB
- Heavy Traffic: 80 dB
- Hearing Damage (Long-Term Exposure): 90 dB
- Subway at 200 ft.: 100 dB
- Jackhammer: 110 dB
- Rock Music: 120 dB
- Threshold of Pain: 130 dB
- Jet Engine at 100 Feet.: 140 dB
- Death of Hearing Tissue: 180 dB
- Loudest Sound Possible: 194 dB

DIGITAL AUDIO

Recording audio as a digital waveform, or digitizing, has been around since the late '70s. However, it wasn't until the mid-'90s that the first computer-based digital audio workstation was released.

Flash-forward sixteen years and the possibilities seem endless with unlimited track counts and processing capabilities, hindered only by the power of the computer's processor.

DIGITIZING AUDIO

The process of recording a signal into a computer (or other digital device) is called digitizing. The analog sound must be converted to electrical energy. For instance, the motion of the diaphragm on a microphone is based on changes in sound pressure levels. The moving diaphragm converts the sound into an electrical signal that feeds your audio interface.

Analog to Digital Converters

Within the audio interface, is a device that converts the electrical signal into a digital signal, essentially assigning values of either 1 or 0. Once the signal has been converted to digital, the digital signal processing is used to refine and adjust the sound.

Digital to Analog Converters

The reverse of this process takes place to hear the digital signal in the analog domain. Another device converts the digital signal back to an analog electrical signal that, in turn, is sent to a transducer, such as your headphones or studio monitors. Typically both analog-to-digital converters (ADC) and digital-to-analog converters (DAC) are housed in the same audio interface; however, some high-end interfaces offer devices for a specific function, such as a dedicated ADC or DAC, housed in a separate box.

DIGITAL AUDIO RESOLUTION

Because we hear in terms of frequency and amplitude, most audio interfaces will offer several choices of resolution to adequately capture sound. The digital equivalent of these units of measurement are called sample rate and bit depth.

Sample Rate

Nyquist's theorem states we must have a frequency range of twice the highest frequency of the signal. Any resolution less than this theorem will cause aliasing, which is heard often as distortion or artifacts. Humans can hear up to 20 kHz, so based on Nyquist's theorem, our audio capture sample rate was set to 44.1 kHz. This is the standard sample rate for CDs.

Today, we have audio interfaces that will capture at up to 192 kHz. An increase in sample rate will limit the number to tracks that can be played and recorded simultaneously by the computer's processor. The file sizes for recordings at these sample rates are very large.

Bit Depth

Bit depth refers the amplitude of a recorded frequency and how many levels of amplitude can be recorded digitally. A 16-bit setting will offer 65,536 different levels of amplitude, whereas a 24-bit setting offers much more resolution, at 16,777,216 levels. If possible, use 24-bit resolution when recording, as it offers a greater dynamic range and a greater signal-to-noise ratio. Although a 24-bit recording's file size will be slightly larger than that of a 16-bit, the gain in quality is worth it.

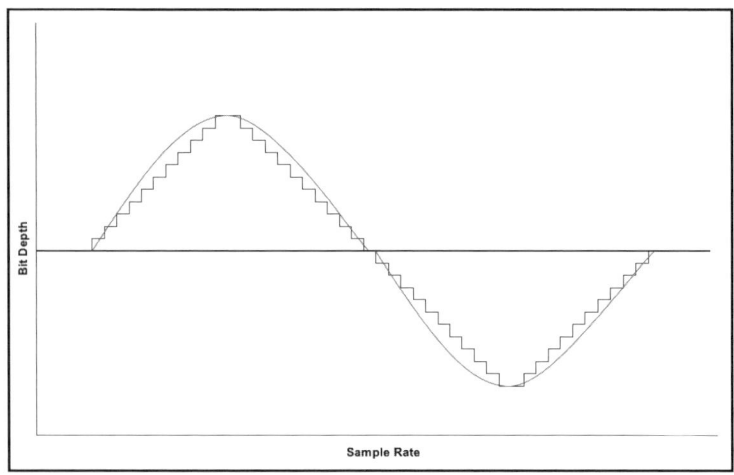

Fig. 5-1

Here is an image of both an analog signal (in red) and what occurs when you digitize audio. Although the image isn't entirely accurate, it illustrates the concept of what happens when you are digitally recording an analog waveform.

AUDIO SIGNAL FLOW

There are two Reason song files associated with this chapter, Recording and Editing.

Begin by opening the Chapter 5—Recording.reason song file found on the enclosed DVD or available for download from the Hal Leonard website. You'll find a session with one audio track created, which you'll use to examine the audio signal flow into and out of Reason 6.

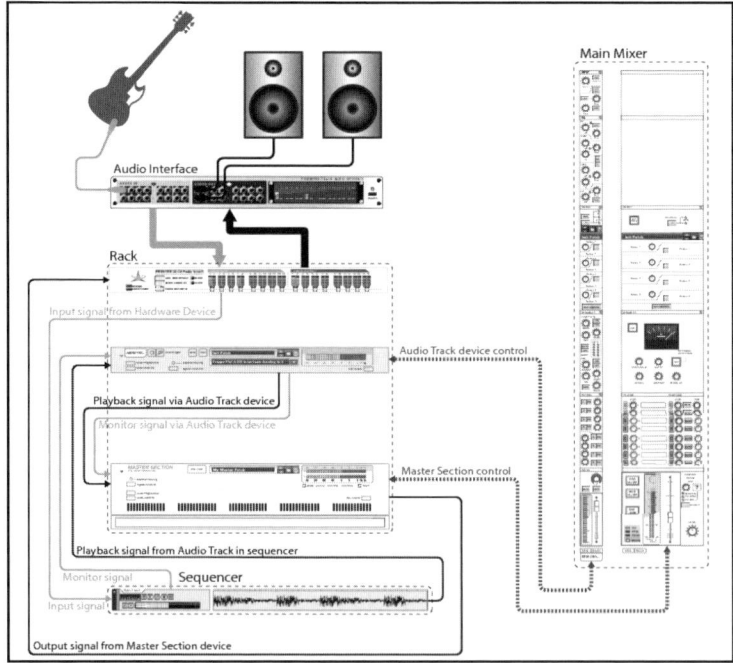

Fig. 5-2

In Fig. 5.2, you'll find a signal flow diagram taken from the Reason 6 manual.

Let's break down the audio signal flow, while referencing the Chapter 5—Recording. reason song file. You'll notice that the diagram looks very similar to the MIDI signal flow, so you should be familiar with the process. If you are unclear about this, please refer to the beginning of chapter 3.

Sound Source

This can be a microphone, instrument, or line level device, essentially anything capable of generating sounds. These devices will connect to your audio interface. Be sure to connect them to the appropriate inputs. Many audio interfaces will have microphone and line level inputs. Many interfaces may have a DI (direct input), which is designed to convert the high impedance signal of a guitar or bass instrument to a low-impedance balanced input. Using the right input ensures the best-quality conversion of an analog signal into the digital realm.

Audio Interface

The audio interface is the physical device used to get audio into and out of your computer. For more information in regard to audio interfaces, refer to chapter 1.

In the diagram you see an interface with sixteen input and outputs. Your sound source connects to one or more inputs of your audio interface, while the output section is routed to a pair of studio monitors.

Hardware Interface

As mentioned in the MIDI Signal Flow section of chapter 3, the Hardware Interface is the software representation of your physical audio interface.

Fig. 5-3

With your sound source connected to the audio interface, the signal makes its way into Reason via the input section of the Hardware Interface. The number of inputs is dependent on your audio interface. By default, you should have at least 1 and 2 of both the inputs and outputs activated.

To activate more inputs and outputs, you will need to configure them from the Audio Preferences.

Select Preferences from the Reason menu and navigate to the Audio tab.

Under Audio Preferences, you will see the familiar Audio Devices selection, which in my case has the MOTU 828mk2 selected. In the section below, you'll see Active Input Channels and Active Output Channels. By selecting the Channels button, the Select Active Channels button opens and you can select any of the available channels. In my case, I've chosen to activate Inputs 1, 2, 3, and 4.

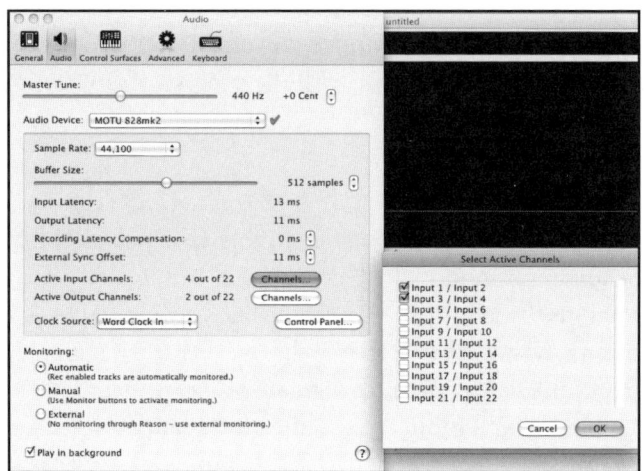

Fig. 5-4

Looking back to the Hardware Interface, you can see that Channels 1, 2, 3, and 4 have illuminated yellow LEDs, indicating these channels are active. If virtual cables were connected, they would be green, denoting that they were in use.

It is not necessary to physically wire virtual cables to audio tracks, as the connections are invisible.

AUDIO TRACK DEVICE

Just like Instrument tracks, when you create an audio track, an Audio Channel device

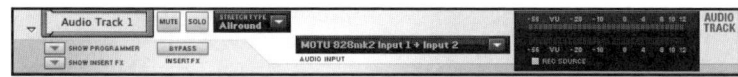

Fig. 5-5

is created in the rack as well. The Audio Channel device serves as the connection to Reason's mixer.

The front panel of the Audio Track device has the same parameters as the Mix Device rack, with some additional features.

Audio Input

Clicking the Audio Input section reveals a drop-down box where you can select to work in mono or stereo, plus any available inputs. In my case, I've chosen stereo input MOTU 828mk2 Input 1 + Input 2.

Stretch Type

When you start recording into Reason, the audio file has been locked into the song tempo. With the Stretch feature, you are able to adjust the song tempo so that the audio file will conform to the new tempo. There may be an instant that you don't wish to use the Stretch algorithm. Select the clip(s) and choose Disable Stretch from the Edit menu to achieve this easily.

ALL AROUND

All Around is an algorithm designed for most polyphonic material, including drum loops or full songs.

MELODY

The Melody algorithm is well suited for monophonic instruments or notes playing one note at a time, such as during solos.

VOCAL

As the name suggests, the Vocal algorithm is best suited for vocal tracks. It focuses on preserving the formants and helps prevent unwanted artifacts when stretching or transposing vocal tracks.

Rec Source

The Rec Source button, located just below the meters, offers the ability to use the Track device as an input source. This is an excellent feature as it enables you to rerecord a track with effects and automation. You'll explore this feature in more detail later in this chapter.

AUDIO SEQUENCER TRACK

The audio sequencer track functions just like an instrument sequencer track, only audio data is recorded instead of MIDI data.

In the track list column you'll find the header for the audio sequencer track displayed. It contains the familiar controls Record Enable and Parameter Automation Enable, as well as a few additional features.

Fig. 5-6

Tuning Fork

Selecting this button opens the tuner, a feature that allows for the tuning of instruments, which is an extremely convenient feature for guitarists.

Select Audio Inputs

This button, located next to the tuning fork, offers the same input selection as the Audio Input section of the Audio Track device.

Meters

The LED meters offer a basic view of a signal's loudness.

Enable Monitor for Track

This is the green button with the speaker icon. Depending on how you have set your preferences, this may be set to Automatic, Manual, or External.

AUTOMATIC
Record enabled tracks are automatically monitored.

MANUAL
Allows for the manual selection of monitoring for record-enabled tracks.

EXTERNAL
No monitoring through Reason. This option is designed for using Reason with an outboard hardware mixer.

By default, the monitor is set to Automatic. Changes can be made at the bottom of the Audio Preference window. Due to the signal flow of Reason, the audio is recorded without effects, but you're able to monitor it with effects. You'll explore how to record with effects later in this chapter.

FOLLOWING AUDIO SIGNAL FLOW

Referring back to Fig. 4.2, let's trace the signal flow from an audio source.

- The audio source generates sound that enters the audio interface and into the Hardware Interface.
- From the Hardware Interface, the signal is directed to a record-enabled track.
- The Audio track records the audio signal to the track and passes the signal to the Audio Track device.
- The Audio Track device sends the signal to the Audio Track device control or channel strip, where it is processed and sent back to the Audio Track device.
- The Audio Track device sends the processed signal to the Master Section device.
- The Master Section device sends the signal to the Master Section control or Master channel strip for processing.
- The signal is sent back to the Master Section device and on to the Hardware Interface.
- The Hardware Interface sends the signal to your audio interface.
- The audio interface connects to your studio monitors.

Once the audio signal is recorded to the sequencer track, it can be edited and processed. With every new audio track created, an Audio Track device is created. Now that you've achieved a basic understanding of signal flow, let's explore how to record and edit audio.

SETTING UP TO RECORD

Recording in Reason is fairly straightforward; however, there are a few things to keep in mind when starting the process.

Your recordings are only as good as the weakest link in your audio chain. For instance, don't expect to get the same results when using a budget $50 microphone as you would when using a $2,500 microphone. That said, don't buy a $2,500 microphone unless you've invested in a high-quality preamp and audio interface.

Another thing to consider is the room you are recording in. Be aware of your surroundings and how sound will bounce off the surfaces of the walls, ceiling, and floor. Any reflective surface will have an effect on your recordings. If you are recording vocals in your home, try to avoid as much ambient sound as possible. Using a walk-in closet filled with clothes will dampen any reflections and often yields great results.

There's a ton of information about the recording process and a little research goes a long way. That said, let's take a look at the recording process from the inputs of your audio interface.

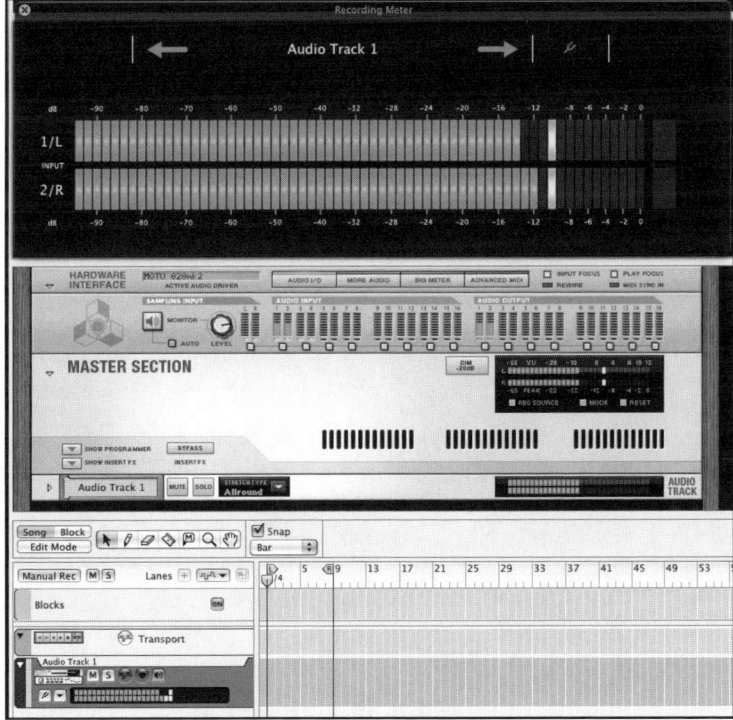

Fig. 5-7

Assuming you have set up your source, inputs selected and ready to record, you'll want to keep an eye on the Level meters to insure that you are not clipping. If you are working at 16 bits, you'll want to have your recording close to 0 dB to mask the noise floor, the low-level noise that's generated by machines and ambient room tone. The problem with working at 16 bits is that you'll be in danger of clipping with such a high-gain setting, and digital clipping is completely unforgiving.

If possible, it's better to record at 24 bits, as you can technically record at –20 dB and you still have more headroom than recording at 16 bits, which it reduces the possibility of digital clipping.

Recording Meter

Pressing F3 brings up the floating recording meter, a high-resolution meter that gives you a detailed view of your input signal.

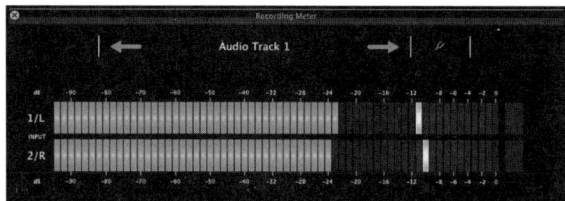

Fig. 5-8

There is no way to control the level of your source from within Reason. Adjust all levels from your source or audio interface to ensure the optimum setting.

I typically aim for about –12 db on the meters while working in 24 bits. This offers a strong signal, but gives 12 dB of headroom in case there are any spikes in the audio signal.

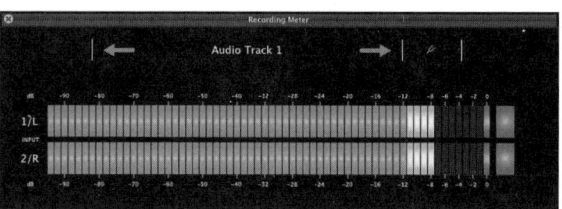

Fig. 5-9

In Fig. 5.9, note that I have intentionally raised the level to show you the clip meters, located on the right side of the recording meter. They appear in the shape of two red rectangles, next to 0 dB. If these are lit, there's a chance you've ruined the take.

If persistent problems with clipping occur, it may be worth investing in a hardware processor, such as a limiter. Such a device is placed before the inputs of your audio interface and can help tame an erratic dynamic range as well as prevent clipping.

It's worth mentioning that it is possible to record multiple tracks simultaneously. You can record as many tracks as you have audio inputs. This feature is a must when multitracking drums or even a whole band. After creating the audio tracks, select the inputs, set Record Enable, and then record away!!

Latency

As explained in Chapter 1 in the Audio Preferences section, the buffer-size slider controls the amount of latency within the program. If you are monitoring through Reason, you'll want to make sure your buffer is set low enough that there is no audible delay while recording.

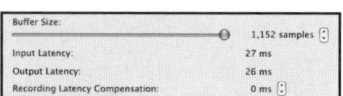

Fig. 5-10

To understand this concept, I highly recommend setting up to record with an instrument or microphone and adjusting the buffer size while monitoring yourself.

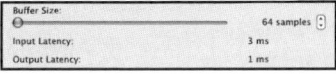

Fig. 5-11

Try moving the buffer slider to the right all the way. You'll notice the input and output latency increases considerably and there is a definite delay between the microphone or instrument and the monitored signal.

Now, move the buffer size to its lowest possible setting.

The latency (input latency + output latency) has decreased to four milliseconds (ms) with no discernable delay.

As a general rule for monitoring, a delay of 9 ms or less is more than adequate for recording. However, most people will get acceptable results with a buffer setting of 256 samples offering a total latency of 12 milliseconds. It is possible to record at higher settings, but doing so becomes increasingly difficult.

Remember to increase your buffer when mixing, as this will give your computer more processing power.

Now, let's explore Reason's audio-editing capabilities.

AUDIO EDITING

Audio editing in Reason is quite similar to editing MIDI data, only you are working with digitized audio files instead of performance data. The digital audio files are represented as waveforms within a clip. With the help of Reason's comprehensive tool set and features, audio editing is fairly straightforward. You'll explore how to make basic edits, as well as how to perform composite edits and work with files at different tempos. You'll also explore how to record with effects.

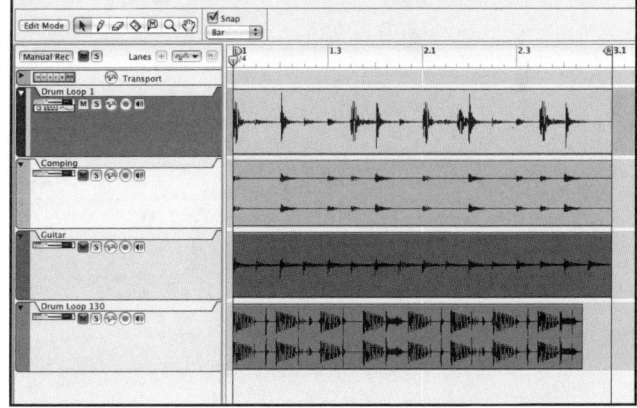

Fig. 5-12

Start by opening the Reason song "Chapter 5—Editing," found on the enclosed DVD or available for download from the Hal Leonard website.

You'll find four tracks each, containing audio files that you'll be using to perform edits. Note all tracks are muted except for one.

BASIC EDITING

On Track 1, you will find a drum loop. Hit Play on the Transport and it will begin playing.

Start by selecting the clip. You will notice the inspector appears and the audio clip has the usual triangular tags on either side of

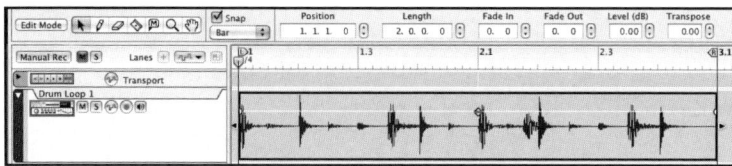

Fig. 5-13

the clip for resizing. This function is exactly the same for resizing MIDI clips and should be familiar.

Level Control

A white line runs horizontally across the clip, with two vertical triangles facing up and down.

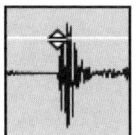

By grabbing the triangles and moving up or down, you can control the level of the clip. Also note the inspector's level control will move with it. Clicking on either the white line or in the level box will have the same effect. Adjusting the level of the audio clip also will change the amplitude of the audio waveform.

Fig. 5-14

Creating Fades

On either side of the audio clip, where the white line meets the ends of the clip, you will find a node, which is used to create fades on the file. Grab the left node and move it to 1.3 on the ruler.

Notice that with each cycle of the loop, the first half of bar one fades up. The same effect may be had with the fadeout function at the end of the loop.

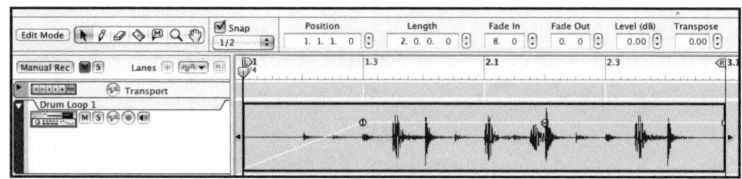

Fig. 5-15

You can also use the inspector's Fadeout box to adjust the fade length.

Remove the fades and return the level back to 0 dB.

Cut, Copy, Paste

Next, change the Snap value to 16 and select the Razor tool from the Tool Palette.

Using the Razor tool, make two cuts as shown in Fig. 5.16.

Now, using the Option + drag method, copy the cut audio to positions 2.2.3.0, 2.2.4.0, 2.3.1.0, and 2.3.2.0. You will now hear a short drum roll.

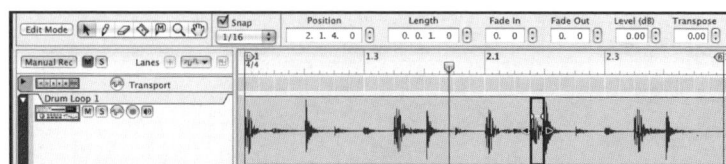

Fig. 5-16

Transpose

For each of the new clips copied, adjust the transpose. Starting with the first, raise each new drum hit up by odd-numbered increments.

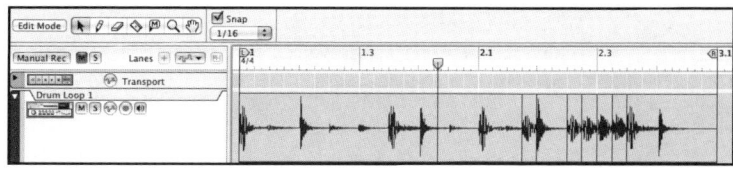

Fig. 5-17

- Drum copy 1: up one semitone
- Drum copy 2: up three semitones
- Drum copy 3: up five semitones
- Drum copy 4: up seven semitones

You should now hear the drum loop increase in pitch as it's playing.

Reverse

Next, using the Razor tool, slice before and after the first snare hit. Copy the snare, before the original.

With the newly copied snare selected, use the Reverse function, found in the main Edit drop-down

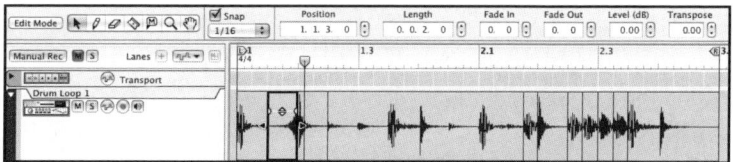

Fig. 5-18

menu. You will now have a reverse snare leading into the forward snare.

COMPOSITE EDITING

Composite editing, or comping, is the process of piecing together the best of multiple takes. This process is often used when editing a vocal track. Reason's comp editor makes the process fast and simple. In this example, you're going to comp four different drum loops together to make a new take. I used the same pattern, but selected four different kits.

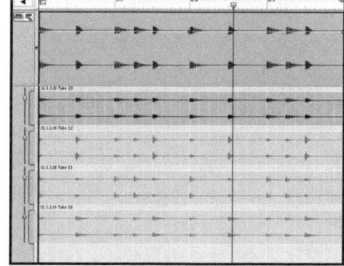

Fig. 5-19

Single Mode

Start by muting Drum Loop 1 and unmuting the second track named "Comping."

Next, double-click on the clip and the Audio editor will open. You will notice four takes labeled "Take 13," "Take 12," "Take 11," and "Take 10."

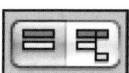

Fig. 5-20

By default, the editor is in Single mode, noted by the Single selection button shown in Fig. 5.20. In Single mode, the topmost take will play. To hear any other take, you'll have to move the take to the top.

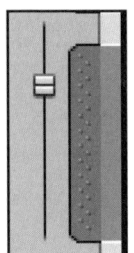

Fig. 5-21

To move a clip, grab the blue tab, next to the level slider on the left side of the clip, and move it to the top. You will also notice a red line will appear once the take has been grabbed. It will follow the clip, allowing you to better see its destination.

Comp Mode

Next, change from Single mode to Comp mode.

Select the Razor tool and make quarter-note cuts on any of the clips.

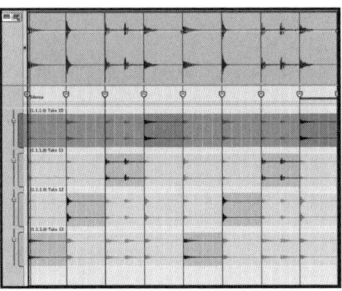

As you make the cuts, you'll find that each clip becomes active, regardless of what track it's on. You may also select a range of a clip by clicking and dragging with the Razor tool. When you're editing vocals, it may prove useful to turn the Snap function off.

Fig. 5-22

Duplicating Comp Tracks

With the Razor tool, hold down Option while selecting a new comp.

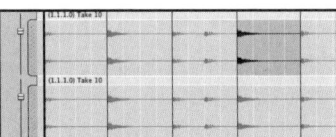

A copy of the newly selected comp will appear above the previous one. It is also possible to select Duplicate Comp Row from the Edit menu.

Fig. 5-23

Recording Offset

Another useful function is the ability to adjust the recording offset. Slide the recording forward or backward in time by simply clicking and dragging to the left or right.

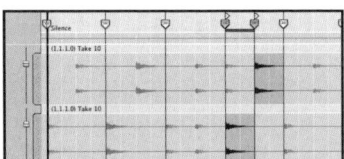

Here, I've created an additional snare hit by duplicating the comp track and adjusting the recording offset. As you can see, this technique is extremely fun and easy to do and is a godsend when editing vocal tracks.

Fig. 5-24

Now, mute Track 2 and unmute Track 3.

WORKING WITH TEMPOS

Reason has an unusual way of working with tempos, as compared with other programs. By default, when you record an audio track, Reason imprints the session tempo information into the recorded track, which allows you to adjust the tempo while both audio and MIDI tracks always stay in time. This is an incredibly useful feature if you are recording original tracks. But what happens if you import an audio file that doesn't have any tempo information imprinted?

Take a look at Track 3. I've imported a drum loop with no tempo information. The loop has a tempo of 130 bpm, but our session is set at 120 bpm.

Engage the metronome and you'll hear that it goes out of time very quickly.

Fig. 5-25

Time Scaling

Time scaling is the fastest and easiest way to wrangle the tempo of a loop. Select the Resize tag at the right side of the clip. Hold down Option and a small clock face will appear. Move the end of the clip to the desired position, in this case, Measure 3.

The loop will automatically stretch so that it ends at Measure 3. Listen to the loop with the metronome again and you will hear it is in perfect sync. Bear in mind, the loop must be perfect to begin with, for this to work. Any offsets or weird time signatures will cause this function to have unpredictable results.

Another option for getting a loop in time is to import it into the session at its proper tempo. By setting the song tempo to 130 bpm before importing, Reason will assign the current and correct tempo to the loop. Once in Reason, you can set the tempo back to its normal 120 bpm and the imported loop will automatically scale itself to the correct tempo.

Finding Tempos Manually

Unfortunately, Reason doesn't have a Find Tempo function. You either have to know it or you will have to figure it out.

Select undo from the Edit menu or use the keyboard command Command + Z if using a Mac, or Control + Z if using Windows. This should bring the time-scaled drum loop back to its original state.

Next, select the clip and from the Edit menu select Disable Stretch.

Grab the Resize tag and drag it to Measure 3. With the loop playing along with the metronome, adjust the tempo. You already know the tempo, but if you didn't, you would have to get the metronome to line up with the drum loop. Also, the waveform would move toward Measure 3 as we approached the correct tempo.

Once the loop is playing back correctly, you must use the function Bounce Clips to New Recordings from the edit menu. Now, you can Enable Stretch from the Edit menu and the loop will follow your song.

Luckily, most loop libraries have the tempo already imprinted or at least will have the tempo written in the title of the loop.

Importing .rex files on to an audio track will automatically scale the loop to your current song tempo.

Now, let's take a look at how to record or rerecord with effects. Mute Track 3 and unmute the Guitar track.

RERECORDING WITH EFFECTS

Reason records your audio files before any effects processor, yet lets you monitor with effects. What if you want to record with effect or you'd like to rerecord with effects?

The solution is quite simple!

Begin by hitting Play on the Transport. You should hear a two-bar guitar loop.

Next, select F6 and F7 simultaneously, which will bring up the sequencer and rack window together.

Fig. 5-26

Unfold the Guitar Audio Track device. You will see a Line 6 Guitar effect. Deselect Insert FX by pressing the Bypass button. The guitar loop is now being run through a Pod guitar processor.

Next, select the Rec Source button on the audio track device, located under the VU meters on the right side.

On the sequencer, create a new audio track. Because you have selected the Rec Source button, the Guitar track is now an available input.

Select Stereo and Guitar as the input.

Lastly, hit Record.

Once, you've gone through a pass, hit Stop, mute the original guitar track, and listen. You'll hear the same guitar track with effects printed. Another fun thing to try is to manipulate some of the controls while recording. For instance, you could engage the Wah on the Line 6 and adjust the knob while recording.

IN CONCLUSION

As you can see, Reason offers some great features for recording and editing. My personal favorite is the new Comp feature and one of my favorite tricks is to import several drum loops into a single track and comp them together. I'm sure you'll find new ways to inspire your creativity, and the versatility of Reason will enable you to produce as you desire. In the next chapter, you will delve into sound design.

Part Three

Sound Design and the Synthesizer

Developing a solid understanding how synthesis works during music production will help you fully unlock the true potential of not only Reason's instruments, but also its various effects and utility devices.

WHAT IS A SYNTHESIZER?

A synthesizer is an electronic device that generates waveforms. The different types of synthesizers include video synthesizers, voice synthesizers, and audio synthesizers. In this chapter, we will be focusing specifically on the types of synthesizers used in audio applications.

The advent of the synthesizer and its subsequent popularity in the late '60s and continuing throughout the '70s, forever changed the landscape of music and sound design. The concept of imitative synthesis, whereby a device is used to emulate a particular acoustic instrument, has been a huge boon for the advancement of the technology of synthesis. For instance, if you want to add the sound of a violin or oboe to a musical piece, but you neither play said instrument nor have the ability to hire someone who can, a synthesizer would prove an invaluable tool for re-creating the appropriate sounding part yourself. However, modern synthesizers have advanced well beyond the mere synthesizing of acoustic instruments, and with the vast variety of types of synthesis available today, you can now even create sounds unheard of in the natural world.

UNDERSTANDING SOUND

Before we begin discussing the components of a synthesizer, let's first reinforce our understanding of the basic elements that compose sound. Some concepts have been previously discussed, which will help you reinforce these concepts as you put them to practical use.

Basic Elements of Sound

The basic elements of sound are identified as frequency, timbre, and amplitude.

FREQUENCY

As discussed in the Sound Primer section of the previous chapter, sound waves travel in a consecutive series of peaks and troughs, with the number of cycles per second measured in units described as frequency.

For example, a waveform that has three cycles per second would be translated into written form as 3 Hz. A waveform of 1,200 cycles would be written as 1,200 Hz, or 1.2 kilohertz (kHz). Human hearing is generally thought to be in the range identified as falling between 20 Hz and 20 kHz.

TIMBRE

Most sounds can be broken up to reveal a composite of sine waves at different frequencies. Depending on the frequencies of the waveforms present, the resulting sound can be described as sounding overly bright, buzzlike, clangorous, smooth, round, or any number of similar descriptions. These terms are indicative of the quality of the sound. Often referred to as timbre (pronounced tam-ber), this is also known as the "character" of the sound.

AMPLITUDE

Amplitude is the distance between the high point of a peak and the low point of a trough within the waveform. The unit of measurement used to describe amplitude in the audio realm is called decibels (dB), and is commonly referred to as loudness. Because human hearing is logarithmic, meaning we don't hear all frequencies at the same decibel level, we are most sensitive to frequencies between the ranges of 250 Hz and 2 kHz. However, note that lower frequencies are required to have higher amplitude for our ears to perceive them at the same loudness as we do higher frequencies.

THE BASIC COMPONENTS OF SYNTHESIS

Most synthesizers use the same terminology and design to both create and shape sounds. You'll be focusing on analog subtractive synthesis as the basis for understanding the components and how they reflect the three basic elements of sound. The following circuits are used to create, shape, and even modify sounds. In addition, all the circuits are voltage controlled (CV), which allows multiple differing circuits to manipulate audio signals.

Don't worry if you find these descriptions even the least bit confusing, as you'll be looking at examples of each circuit in the following sections to provide further clarification.

VOLTAGE-CONTROLLED OSCILLATOR (VCO)

If you were to zoom in on a string of a guitar after it's been struck or plucked, you'd find the string oscillates, or visibly vibrates. The oscillation of the string forces the air molecules around it to move generating the waves that you perceive aurally as sound. The mass or thickness of the string will determine at what frequency the oscillator vibrates. Thicker strings have a lower frequency of oscillation, whereas thinner strings oscillate at a faster or higher rate.

All synthesizers use an oscillator circuit to generate sound waves. The voltage-control aspect is what determines the frequency or pitch of the oscillator, the higher-voltage settings resulting in higher frequencies. Most synthesizers are capable of generating at least four basic waveforms: sawtooth, square, triangle and sine waves. Furthermore, some or all of these waveforms are available simultaneously.

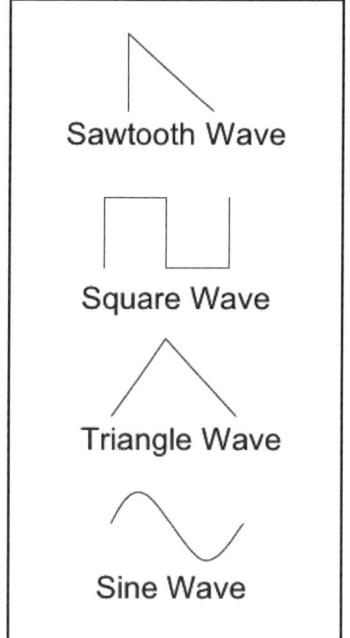

Fig. 6-1

SAWTOOTH WAVE

The sawtooth waveform is one that is rich in overtones and harmonics and is generally perceived and described as buzzy and/or bright. It is arguably the most popular of the basic waveforms and is sometimes considered the all-purpose waveform, rendering it most applicable.

SQUARE WAVE

The square waveform is often described as having a hollow quality. Like the sawtooth waveform, it contains a lot of harmonic content, yet it sounds quite different in comparison.

TRIANGLE WAVE

The triangle waveform has less harmonics and overtones when compared to the sawtooth and square waveforms. It's an ideal waveform for re-creating bass sounds as well as flute tones.

SINE WAVE

The sine waveform has no harmonics or overtones and is described as soft in comparison to the others. Sine waves are excellent for sub bass sounds and this is generally how they are applied.

VOLTAGE-CONTROLLED FILTER (VCF)

The filter circuit of an analog synthesizer is the most important circuit of all because it differentiates it from any other synthesizer. Filters are used to remove overtones as well as harmonic content.

Types of Filters

There are several filter types, including the low-pass, high-pass, band-pass, and notch filters, all with different slope attributes.

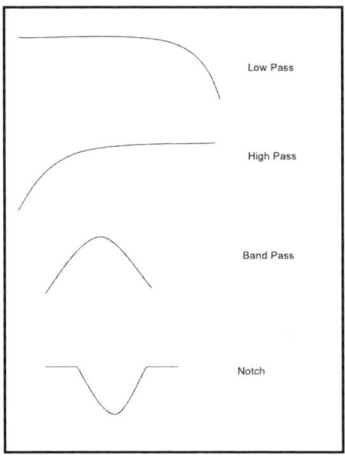

Fig. 6-2

LOW-PASS

A low-pass filter (also known as a high-cut filter) removes the higher frequencies and allows the low frequencies to pass through.

HIGH-PASS

A high-pass filter (also known as a low-cut filter) removes the low frequencies and allows the higher frequencies to pass through.

BAND-PASS

A band-pass filter combines both low- and high-pass filters to allow a central band of frequencies to pass through.

NOTCH

A notch filter works opposite of a band-pass filter. It instead notches out the central frequencies and leaves both the high and low frequencies to pass through.

Filter Slope

The slope of the filter defines how steep the filter rolls off the frequencies. Slopes are often referred to as poles, with each pole representing a 6 dB increment. For instance, the classic Moog filter contains four poles, or a 24 dB increment. The most common filter slopes are two-pole (12 dB) and four-pole (24 dB).

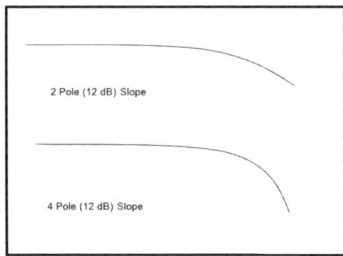

Fig. 6-3

Filter Controls

The basic controls of a filter are the Cutoff and Resonance.

FILTER CUTOFF

The Filter Cutoff control is the point at which the filter starts to remove frequencies. For instance, a low-pass filter with the cutoff set to 450 Hz will start rolling off at frequencies higher than 450 Hz.

FILTER RESONANCE

The Filter Resonance control is essentially a frequency-dependant feedback circuit. When increased, it creates an emphasis at the filter-cutoff frequency. Some filters will launch into self-oscillation when the resonance is increased enough. When using the Filter Cutoff control, this feature becomes tunable feedback. Increasing resonance on a high- or low-pass filter generally results in a thinner sound, but affords a sharper, more defined shape. When you are using the notch and band-pass filters, Resonance controls the width of the frequency band so that the higher the setting, the more narrow the frequency band will become.

VOLTAGE-CONTROLLED AMPLIFIER (VCA)

The voltage-controlled amplifier, in essence, is a preamplifier acting as a volume control. The voltage-control aspect allows for dynamic control over loudness.

LOW-FREQUENCY OSCILLATOR (LFO)

The low-frequency oscillator produces various waveforms, like a VCO, but the frequencies are well below human hearing (0.1 Hz to 10 Hz). It is used to create modulation effects, as if an invisible hand is physically moving a particular parameter at a given rate and pattern.

LFO Controls

The parameters of an LFO control the rate or frequency, and depth or amplitude.

RATE
The Rate controls the frequency of the LFO so that the higher the rate, the faster the resulting oscillation of the LFO.

DEPTH
The Depth controls the amplitude of the LFO, which in turn affects the amount of modulation sent to the desired circuit. With a lower setting, the resulting modulation is subtle; whereas a higher depth will result in a much more extreme effect.

LFO Effects

Routing the LFO signal to the voltage control of each basic circuit results in three classic effects.

VIBRATO
LFO to VCO

WAH-WAH
LFO to VCF

TREMOLO
LFO to VCA

ENVELOPE GENERATOR (ADSR)

Using an envelope generator circuit permits the shaping of sound over a period of time. Different stages of the envelope slow down or speed up various differing signals. Some synthesizers contain a dedicated envelope generator for each circuit but, at the very least, there will be one envelope routed to the VCA that controls how a sound is triggered. At its fastest settings, the sound is triggered instantly, whereas slower settings let sounds slowly fade in and out.

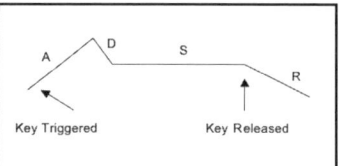

Fig. 6-5

The basic stages of an envelope generator are called Attack (A), Decay (D), Sustain (S), and Release (R). When a particular key is pressed, the level is controlled over time as the sound passes through each stage of the envelope.

ATTACK
The Attack stage commences when a key is pressed and reflects the time it takes to run upward from 0 to the Decay stage.

DECAY
The Decay stage starts from the peak of the Attack stage and continues into the Sustain stage. If the Decay and Sustain are set to the same level, there is no discernable difference between the two.

SUSTAIN
The Sustain stage is the level occurring after the Decay stage and continues until the key being pressed is released.

RELEASE
The Release stage is triggered upon release of the key and is the time taken from the Sustain stage to return back to 0.

EXPLORING THE SUBTRACTOR

The Subtractor Analog Synthesizer is a polyphonic synthesizer based on analog subtractive synthesis. It has two oscillators, two filters, three envelopes, and two LFOs.

The Subtractor is fantastic for creating any type of synthesizer sound, with a range of synth basses, pads, leads, FX, and synth percussion features.

Fig. 6-6

In the next section, you will take an in-depth look at the Subtractor synthesizer and examine how all the previously mentioned circuits work together. Every major aspect of the Subtractor will be covered, including most parameters and functions, especially those that are typically found on the majority of the synthesizers found in Reason 6. This explanation could also apply to any similar hardware or software synth being utilized.

SIGNAL FLOW

A typical synthesizer's signal flow moves from left to right on the instrument panel, and the Subtractor's signal flow is no exception.

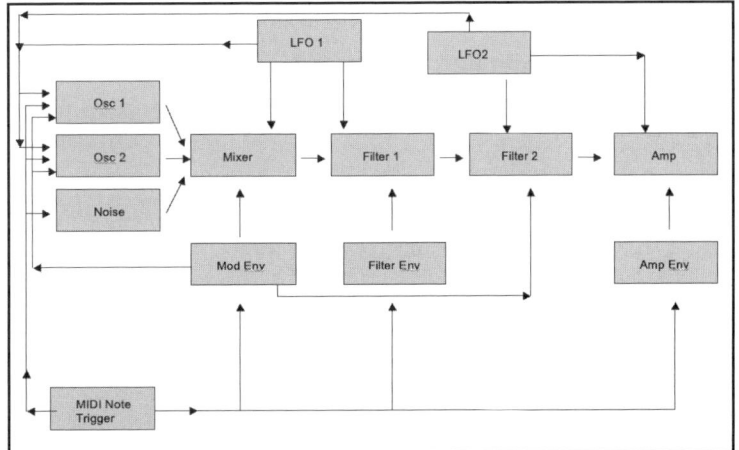

- Once a MIDI note message is received, sounds are generated via the Oscillator section, as shown the upper center section of the diagram.
- The audio signal then flows from the mix of oscillator into the Filter section.
- Once the signal passes through the Filter section, it continues into the Amplifier section.

Fig. 6-7

- LFO 1 can be routed to Osc 1 and 2, Osc 2, Freq 1 (of Filter 1), and the mixer.
- LFO2 can be routed to Osc 1 and 2, Freq 2 (of Filter 2) and the Amp section.
- There are dedicated envelopes for both the Filter 1 and the Amp section.
- The Mod envelope can be routed to Osc 1, Osc 2, the mixer, and Freq 2 (of Filter 2).

DISSECTING THE SUBTRACTOR

Begin by creating a Subtractor and then select Initialize Patch from the Edit menu.

Next, under Filter 1, drag the Freq slider up to 127. This will open up the filter and allow you to hear the oscillators unfiltered.

SUBTRACTOR OSCILLATORS I AND 2

The sounds of the Subtractor originate with the Oscillator section. The subtractor offers two oscillators as well as a noise source. Press the

Fig. 6-8

red button located in the upper left corner of Osc 2 and on the noise generator to engage their functions. Both Osc 1 and 2 exhibit identical functions.

Waveforms

By default, the selected waveform is the sawtooth. Press the upward triangle next the oscillator waveform display to scroll through all of the waveforms available for Osc 1.

Following the sawtooth waveform in order are the square, triangle, and lastly sine wave. First take a listen to the sawtooth and then compare it to the square wave, both of which, you will find, are strong in harmonic content.

Now listen to the triangle and compare it to the sine wave. The triangle waveform contains much less harmonic content than either the sawtooth and square waveforms, whereas the sine wave contains no harmonics at all.

If you keep pressing the Waveform button, you will notice it starts registering numbers (5–32). Each number represents a different variation on the waveforms. Some have bell-like qualities, rich in harmonics; others will emulate tones more suitable for brass, strings, mallets, and guitars. For a full description of all the waveforms available, refer to the "Subtractor Oscillator" section of the Reason 6 manual.

Oscillator Tune Controls

Next to the Waveform section, locate the Octave (Oct), Semitone (Semi), and Cent controls. Each is used to adjust the tuning of the oscillator.

OCTAVE
The Octave section has a range of ten octaves (0–9). Selecting higher settings will cause notes to play at higher pitches, whereas the lower settings will drop the pitch down.

SEMITONE
Semitones are equivalent to the notes on your MIDI keyboard controller. There are twelve semitones per octave.

CENTS
There are 100 cents per semitone, ranging from −50 to +50. This parameter allows you to fine-tune the pitch, thereby permittingr subtle tuning effects as minute as a half-semitone variation either up or down.

Keyboard Tracking

When engaged, Keyboard Tracking (Kbd. Track) enables your MIDI keyboard controller to control the pitch. When disengaged, the oscillator will instead maintain a constant pitch and no control will be possible via the MIDI keyboard controller. This function is particularly useful for creating percussion sounds and special effects.

Phase Control

Creates a second waveform and either multiplies or subtracts it, based on the phase offset setting.

PHASE KNOB
Controls the offset setting of the second waveform.

MODE o
No phase offset.

MODE X
Multiplies the second waveform by the first.

MODE – (SUBTRACT)
This effectively subtracts the second waveform from the first. Setting the Phase knob to 0 while in the Subtract mode causes phase cancellation and no sound will be heard. Moving the Phase knob to any other position will allow the sound to return.

The phase control may seem a little confusing, but you need not be an expert in the mathematics behind the operation to apply it well. It's quite a valuable tool for creating complex waveforms, as you will learn a little later.

NOISE GENERATOR

Fig. 6-9

The noise generator of the Oscillator section produces white noise, which is a useful sound when creating percussion and such sound effects as wind or ocean.

DECAY
The Decay knob will cause the noise to fade independent of any note or envelope controls.

COLOR
The Color knob controls the brightness of the noise. When turned to the right, it will create a full blast of white noise; turned to the left, it will cause the sound to become increasingly less bright.

LEVEL
The Level knob controls the volume level of the noise generator.

OSCILLATOR MIX

The Mix knob controls the balance between Osc 1 and 2. Moving the knob fully to the left will allow for only Osc 1 to output, whereas moving it fully to the right allows only Osc 2 to output. When the knob is left in the twelve o'clock position, both Osc 1 and 2 will mix equally. The noise source is routed to the input of Osc 2 on the Mix knob.

FM (FREQUENCY MODULATION)

This function is actually a form of synthesis known as FM synthesis or frequency modulation synthesis, which was made popular back in the mid-'80s. Functionally, it allows for Osc 1 to be modulated by Osc 2 or the noise generator, creating unique and sometimes clangorous sounds. You'll explore more about this function in a later section.

Fig. 6-10

RING MODULATOR

The ring modulator is another effect that multiplies the sum and difference of both the Osc 1 and 2. The output of this effect can be unpredictable and inharmonic, often resulting in bell-like tones.

SUBTRACTOR FILTERS

The Subtractor has two filters, which can either be linked to work in tandem or to function independently.

FILTER 1

Filter 1 is a multimode filter that permits switching between various types of filter.

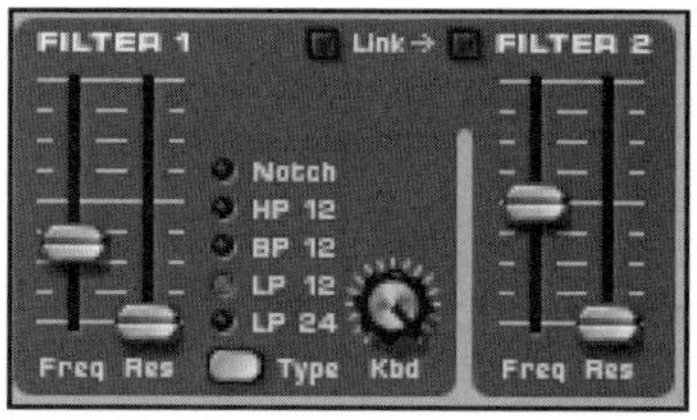

Fig. 6-11

Filter Types

The filter types offered by Subtractor's Filter 1 include notch, HP 12, BP 12, LP 12, and LP 24.

NOTCH
The notch filter works as described previously in the filter section, whereby a frequency band is removed according to the Freq slider's position. This is a subtle effect, the sound of which is similar to a phase shift.

HP 12
HP 12 is a 12 dB (two-pole) high-pass filter and will remove low frequencies based on the setting of the Freq slider. With a setting of 0, the filter is open and thereby has no effect on the sound. A setting of 127, however, will remove all the low frequencies from the signal, resulting in a tinny-sounding high-frequency timbre.

BP 12

BP 12 is a 12 dB (two-pole) band-pass filter. Working much like a combined high-pass and low-pass filter, the result is a narrow band of frequencies. (See Fig. 6.2.) This filter is an excellent choice when layering sounds, as it has proven to be quite versatile with regard to different settings of timbre within the Freq slider.

LP 12

LP 12 is a 12 dB (two-pole) low-pass filter. Setting the Freq slider to 127 will cause the filter to be open and no change in sound will be heard. As the Freq slider is brought down, you will hear the higher frequencies being removed until the 0 point is reached and there's no audible output. The Korg MS20, a popular vintage synthesizer from the 1970s, contains a 12 dB filter.

LP 24

LP24 is a 24 dB (four-pole) low-pass filter. This filter functions just like the LP 12, but has a steeper slope, which removes frequencies at a faster rate. This is a more extreme filter, especially when engaging the Res slider. The Moog Mini-Moog, from the 1970s, has a 24 dB filter and is probably, by far and above, the most popular synthesizer of all time.

Freq

As stated previously, the Freq slider controls the cutoff frequency of the filter.

Res

Similarly, the Res slider controls the resonance or the emphasis of the cutoff frequency. Increasing resonance on a high- or low-pass filter generally results in a thinner sound, but with a sharper, more defined shape. With the notch and band-pass filters, the resonance controls the width of the frequency band. The higher the setting, the more narrow the frequency band becomes.

Kbd

This knob controls keyboard tracking, a function that allows the filter to change depending on which octave of your MIDI keyboard controller you are using. This function is especially useful for creating acoustic-sounding instruments, for which higher notes are typically brighter. The Kbd knob sets the range for how much the filter opens as you play up the scale of the keyboard.

FILTER 2

Filter 2 is identical to Filter 1 set at LP 12. To engage Filter 2, first click the Filter 2 button, which illuminates red when active. The secondary filter has the ability to operate independently. It's arranged in series, which takes its input from the output of Filter 1. When linked by engaging the Link button, the Freq 1 slider will control Filter 2, but allows for an offset as determined by Filter 2's Freq setting. Having two filters permits richly complex filter effects that would be impossible to achieve with just a single filter.

Fig. 6-12

LEVEL (AMPLIFIER)

The Level slider controls the overall loudness of the instrument and, in essence, is the Amplifier section. LFO 2 also has an option for modulating the Amp to create tremolo effects.

LFO 1

LFO 1 is a low-frequency oscillator containing various waveforms. With its frequency range well below that of human hearing, the LFO is never heard, but is used as a modulation source with a variety of destinations.

Fig. 6-13

Waveforms

The Subtractor offers a variety of waveforms, including triangle, upward sawtooth, sawtooth, square, random, and noise.

TRIANGLE
The triangle is a smooth-sounding waveform that's similar to the sine wave.

UPWARD SAWTOOTH
The upward sawtooth starts low and rises up to a peak, then repeats the cycle. When set appropriately, it can afford a tape reverse or rewindlike sound.

SAWTOOTH
The sawtooth starts high and progresses into a falling effect, whereby once the waveform reaches the bottom, it repeats.

SQUARE
The square waveform creates an instantaneous change between up and down. This form is especially useful for creating pseudo-arpeggiator patterns.

RANDOM
The random waveform switches instantaneously between different values and is also known on some analog synthesizers as a sample-and-hold circuit.

NOISE

The noise waveform reacts very much like random, but instead of switching instantaneously between values, it slides smoothly into the next subsequent random value.

LFO Destinations

There are a variety of destinations for LFO 1 including Osc 1 and 2, Osc 2, F. Freq, FM, Phase, and Mix.

OSC 1 AND 2

Routing LFO 1 to Osc 1 and 2 creates a vibrato effect by modulating the pitch of both oscillators.

OSC 2

Creates the same effect as described above, but only modulates Osc 2.

F. FREQ

This modulates Filter 1's cutoff frequency, thereby creating a wah-wah sound effect.

FM

This modulates the FM (frequency modulation) knob found in the Oscillator section. Note, however, both oscillators must be engaged to activate this effect.

PHASE

This modulates the phase offset of both oscillators, but either the multiplication or the subtraction must be engaged for this function to work.

MIX

This modulates the Mix control for Osc 1 and 2.

Rate

The Rate knob controls the frequency of the LFO 1. Higher frequencies result in faster modulations.

Sync

When engaged, the Sync button causes the rate to change from a free-running oscillator (defined by Hz) to one that synchronizes with the tempo of the song. Synchronization is broken into sixteen divisions ranging from 16/4 to 1/32 notes.

Amount

Increasing the Amount knob will increase the amplitude of the LFO. On synths and effects processors, this function is often referred to as Depth. Lower settings will create more subtle effects, whereas higher settings produce more extreme results.

LFO 2

LFO 2 offers a fixed triangle waveform and there's no sync function. It is polyphonic by design, which permits each note to trigger the LFO independently and can create some interesting rhythmic effects. Most notable is the ability for the LFO's rate to track along the keyboard scale. Playing higher up the keyboard will result in a faster rate, whereas playing lower notes will generate slower frequencies.

Fig. 6-14

Destinations

The destinations for the Subtractor's LFO 2 include Osc 1 and 2, Phase, F. Freq 2, and Amp.

OSC 1 AND 2
Routing LFO 2 to Osc 1 and 2 creates a vibrato effect by modulating the pitch of both oscillators.

PHASE
This modulates the phase offset of both oscillators. Note that either the multiplication or the subtraction must be engaged for this function to work.

F. FREQ 2
This modulates Filter 2's cutoff frequency, creating a wah-wah effect.

AMP
This modulates the Amp section, resulting in a tremolo effect.

Rate

The Rate knob controls the frequency of the LFO 2. Higher frequencies result in faster modulations.

Amount

Increasing the Amount knob will increase the amplitude of the LFO. On synths and effects processors, this function is often referred to as Depth. The lower settings produce more subtle results, whereas the higher settings will produce more extreme results.

Delay

LFO 2 Delay generates a delay between the time a note is played and the modulation of the desired parameter. This is useful when playing keyboard parts because the modulation will only occur on sustained notes.

Kbd

LFO 2 Kbd (keyboard tracking) allows for the LFO to follow the keyboard with higher notes resulting in faster rates, whereas lower notes generate slower frequencies.

ENVELOPE GENERATORS

As discussed previously, envelopes allow the control of parameters over time, with Attack (A), Decay (D), Sustain (S), and Release (R) being the parameters that shape your sound. The Subtractor features two dedicated envelopes for the Amp and Filter 1 circuits. An additional envelope called the Modulation envelope (Mod env) has a number of different destinations that can result in some pretty spectacular effects.

Amp Env

The Amplifier envelope gives dynamic control over loudness. Using longer attacks and releases, you can create slowly evolving sounds that will fade in and out. The Decay adds an additional dynamic portion to the cycle; the Sustain holds its value indefinitely until **Fig. 6-15** the key is released.

Filter Env

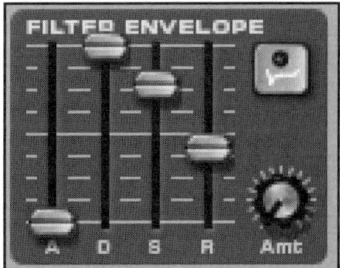

The Filter envelope provides dynamic control over the cutoff frequency of Filter 1 over time. Additional parameters include Invert and Envelope Amount.

AMOUNT
The Filter Envelope Amount makes it possible to dial in just how much the envelope will affect Filter 1's frequency cutoff. Having a lower **Fig. 6-16** setting on the Filter 1 while using the knob to increase the amount will result in Filter 1's frequency to increase dynamically over time.

INVERT
The Invert button flips the envelope so that instead of increasing Filter 1's frequency over time, it will lessen, thereby causing the filter to close.

Mod Env

The Modulation envelope allows you to control multiple destinations or parameters over time.

OSC 1
Routing the Mod Env to Osc 1 will increase the pitch dynamically over **Fig. 6-17** time. Engage the Invert button to have the pitch drop over time. This

effect has been made popular in drum and bass music, which has huge bass tones that slowly drop in pitch.

OSC 2
Functions the same as Osc 1.

FM
This is used to modify the FM (frequency modulation) parameter in the Osc section. Note that both oscillators must be active for this effect to be heard.

PHASE
Use this to dynamically change the phase offset of the Osc 1 and 2 over time.

FREQ 2
The Filter envelope allows for dynamic control over the cutoff frequency of Filter 2 over time.

AMOUNT
Amount allows you to dial in how much the envelope will affect the selected parameters. Lower settings will be subtler, whereas higher settings will result in a more extreme effect.

INVERT
The Invert button flips the envelope; instead of increasing a selected parameter over time, it decreases.

VELOCITY

Velocity by definition is the speed at something moves, happens, or is done. This this speed is often equated with the strength at which you play a note on your MIDI keyboard controller.

Fig. 6-18

The Subtractor features comprehensive control over parameters with velocity. A typical use of velocity is the control of level or volume; the harder a key is struck, the louder the sound will be generated. With the dials set at the twelve o'clock position, the function is bypassed. Moving a parameter to the right causes a positive function, whereas moving it to the left produces a negative effect.

AMP
Velocity control of the amp circuit results in dynamic control over volume. A positive setting produces the typical result in which, the harder a key is played, the louder the sound output. Negative values result in the opposite of this function, whereby the harder-pressed keys are softer in volume and softer-hit keys are played louder.

FM

Velocity control over the FM parameter of the Oscillator section results in an increase of the FM setting at a positive value. A negative value results in the opposite reaction. Note that both Osc 1 and 2 must be active, to use this function.

M. ENV

Velocity control over the Mod env results in an increase over the Mod env amount at a positive value. A negative value results in the opposite reaction.

PHASE

Velocity control over the Phase parameter of the Oscillator section results in an increase over the phase offset at a positive value. A negative value results in the opposite reaction.

FREQ 2

Velocity control over the Freq 2 results in an increase over Filter 2's filter cutoff frequency at a positive value. A negative value results in the opposite reaction.

F. ENV

Velocity control over the Filter env results in an increase over Filter 1's envelope amount at a positive value. A negative value results in the opposite reaction.

F. DEC

Velocity control over the Filter envelope Decay results in an increase over the Decay portion of the Filter 1's Decay time of the envelope at a positive value. A negative value results in the opposite reaction.

MIX

Velocity control over the Oscillator Mix parameter results in an increase over the Osc 2's mix amount at a positive value. A negative value results in an increase over the Osc 1's mix amount.

A. ATK

Velocity control over the Amp envelope Attack (A. Atk) results in an increase over the attack portion of the amp's Attack time of the envelope at a positive value. A negative value results in the opposite reaction.

PITCH BEND AND MODULATION WHEEL

Most MIDI keyboard controllers offer real-time control over pitch bend and modulation via dedicated wheels. These parameters are routed to the onscreen Pitch Bend and Modulation wheels.

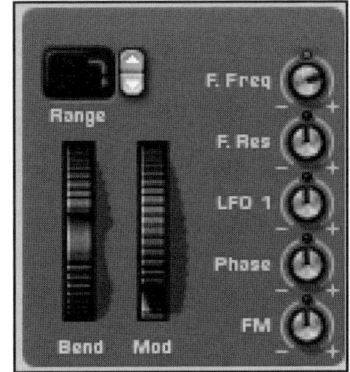

Fig. 6-19

Bend

The Pitch Bend wheel permits bending notes at set intervals.

RANGE
The Pitch Bend Range sets the range of the Pitch wheel. The maximum setting range is twenty-four semitones, or two octaves.

Mod

The Modulation wheel can be assigned to a number of parameters. Setting the knobs at twelve o'clock has no effect and causes it, in essence, to be bypassed. Moving the knob to the right will cause the function to work in a positive manner, whereas moving the knob to the left will cause a negative or inverse reaction. All functions can be assigned simultaneously, which permits complex sound manipulation with just a simple movement of the wheel.

F. FREQ
This assigns the Mod wheel to Filter 1's frequency cutoff. A positive setting causes the filter to open up, whereas a negative setting will cause the filter to close.

F. RES
This assigns the Mod wheel to Filter 1's Resonance control. A positive setting increases the resonance, whereas a negative setting will conversely decrease it.

LFO 1
This assigns the Mod wheel to LFO 1's Amount knob. A positive setting increases the amount, whereas a negative setting decreases it.

PHASE
This assigns the Mod wheel to the Phase Offset parameter of both Osc 1 and 2. A multiplication or subtraction setting must be activated for the parameter to work.

FM
This assigns the Mod wheel to the FM (frequency modulation) of the Oscillator section. A positive setting will increase the FM amount, whereas a negative setting will decrease it. Note that both oscillators must be activated for the parameter to work.

EXT. MOD

The External Modulation section allows you to control certain parameters with the use of common MIDI messages. To use this function, first select the type of incoming message the Subtractor should respond to, then set the range of parameters from the following options.

Fig. 6-20

Common MIDI Messages

There are three common MIDI messages: Aftertouch, Expression, and Breath. Once selected, these messages are routed to various destinations.

A. TOUCH

A MIDI keyboard controller typically transmits Aftertouch. Most keyboards employ monophonic aftertouch, whereby a single sensor runs the span of the keyboard. When a key is pressed with continuous pressure, a controller message is generated. The harder the key is pressed, the greater the value generated, with a range from 0 to 127.

EXPR.

Expression control (Expr.) is often employed using an Expression pedal. These types of pedals are found in most music retailers and generate a range from 0 to 127.

BREATH

A Breath controller is usually employed by use of a MIDI Wind controller with a pressure sensor. Blowing into the unit will generate a range from 0 to 127.

External Modulation Destinations

The external modulation destinations include Filter Frequency Cutoff (F. Freq), LFO 1, Amp, and FM.

F. FREQ

Positive values will increase Filter 1's frequency cutoff, whereas a negative value will invert the signal, causing the cutoff to decrease.

LFO 1

Positive values will increase LFO 1's Amount parameter, whereas a negative value will invert the signal, causing the cutoff to decrease.

AMP

Positive values will increase the volume of the instrument, whereas a negative value will invert the signal, causing the volume to decrease.

FM

Positive values will increase the FM (frequency modulation) amount of the Oscillator section, whereas a negative value will invert the signal, causing the FM amount to decrease.

PLAY PARAMETERS

Play parameters allow the user to define how the Subtractor will react to incoming MIDI messages.

Note On

The purpose of this LED is to let you know that the instrument is receiving MIDI messages.

Legato

Legato is a mode typical to analog synthesizers, especially monophonic synths. This mode prevents an envelope from retriggering unless the key is released. When using with more than one voice, it won't activate until all the allocated voices have been used.

Retrig

Retrigger has two functions, the first of which is used when playing polyphonic patches. In this situation, it retriggers the envelopes regardless of the number of keys held or voices allocated. The Retrigger's second function is designed to work like most monophonic synthesizers. If one note is pressed followed simultaneously by a second, the envelope is retriggered. When the second note is released, the first held note is retriggered.

Portamento

Portamento is a glide between notes, instead of jumping instantaneously into the next pitch. The Portamento knob is used to control how long the glide will take for it to reach the new pitch. A setting of 0 results in no portamento effect.

Polyphony

Polyphony is defined as the number of voices (or keys) that can be played simultaneously. A setting of 1 defines the synth as monophonic, or one note at a time. Settings from 2 to 99 will allow up the designated number of voices to play. Note that if Polyphony is set to 5 and six notes are played, the first note played will be stolen, or removed, to play the sixth.

Low BW

The Low Bandwidth button is designed to conserve the CPU. When activated, the high frequency of a sound is removed.

PROGRAMMING CUSTOM PATCHES WITH THE SUBTRACTOR

Now let's take a closer look at some basic programming of synth patches, using the Subtractor.

If you haven't done so already, first create a Subtractor.

Next, initialize the patch by selecting Initialize from the Edit menu and bring Filter 1's Freq slider up to 127.

Standard Effects

The standard effects found on basic effects processors are vibrato, wah-wah, and tremolo.

VIBRATO

To create a vibrato effect, route LFO 1 to Osc 1 and 2 (set by default) and increase the amount to 50. Try setting different waveforms on LFO 1 to hear how they affect the modulation.

WAH-WAH

To create a wah-wah effect, route LFO 1 to F. Freq and lower Filter 1's Freq slider to 80. Next, try raising the Res slider to 70 and test out the different types of filters available.

TREMOLO

To create a tremolo, initialize the patch and bring Filter 1's Freq slider to 127.

Set LFO 2's destination to Amp and increase the amount to 127.

PWM

Pulse width modulation (PWM) is a fantastic way to introduce motion into a static oscillator's waveform.

A standard square wave has a fifty-fifty relationship between the up and down portions of the waveform. A pulse wave is similar to a square wave, but the up and down portions' relationship is something other than fifty-fifty. By modulating the phase offset of a square wave, you can create pulse width modulation (PWM), which will then create harmonic motion by modulating the pulse of the square wave.

- Initialize the patch and bring Filter 1's Freq slider to 127.
- Begin by changing Osc 1 to a square wave and set the phase to subtraction.
- Next, set LFO 1's destination to phase and increase Amount to 87 and Rate to 52.

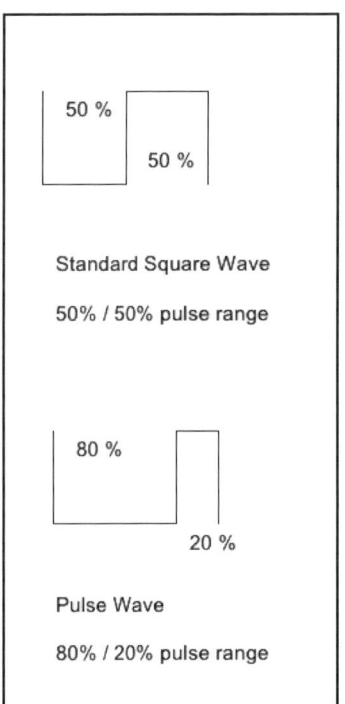

50 %

50 %

Standard Square Wave

50% / 50% pulse range

80 %

20 %

Pulse Wave

80% / 20% pulse range

Fig. 6-21

Lead

Using the PWM you just created, let's now create a lead sound.

- Turn on Osc 2 and increase the semitone to 5.
- Turn the FM knob to 24.

• Bring the Decay and Sustain sliders of the Amp envelope to 127.

Bass Drop

To create a bass drop, first initialize the patch and bring Filter 1's Freq slider to 127.

• Set Osc 1's waveform to a sine wave and lower the octave to 3.
• Set the Decay and Sustain sliders of the Amp envelope to 127.
• Lower Polyphony to 1.
• On the Mod Envelope, make sure that Osc 1 is selected.
• Set Attack to 110 and lower Decay to 0.
• Select the Invert button and increase the amount to 127.

You should now have a strong foundation in synthesis.

In the next section, you will further reinforce what you've learned while exploring the Thor Polysonic Synthesizer and the Malstrom Graintable Synthesizer.

THOR POLYSONIC SYNTHESIZER

Synthesizers, from their earliest commercial production, were produced in modular form. Moog and Buchla were among the first manufacturers to release synthesizers of this format. A modular synthesizer consists of a number of modules, each containing a circuit used to provide a specific function. Patch cables are used to route the audio and control voltage signals between the different modules. This modular approach allowed for the ultimate in expression and flexibility, enabling musicians to create and process audio in a near-infinite number of ways. However, most modular synths of this time were quite large, very expensive, and not easily transported.

In 1970, Moog developed the MiniMoog synthesizer, a more compact unit designed to target the performing musician. This synthesizer was sold preconfigured and prewired, thereby eliminating the need for patch cabling.

Another manufacturer, Alan R. Pearlman, created the Arp 2600 in the mid- to late '70s, introducing a unique semimodular design. This synth came preconfigured and prewired, but also offered patch points with which to reroute the prewired signals, thus providing the superior flexibility of the early modular synthesizers.

The Thor Polysonic synthesizer was designed as a semimodular synthesizer. It features the additional ability to swap out different modules, each containing a different and unique character. The result is a synthesizer design that is both complex and yet extremely simple to use.

The Thor is broken up into four sections: the Controller panel, the Programmer, the Modulation Routing section, and the Step Sequencer.

Fig. 6-22

THE CONTROLLER PANEL

The Controller panel contains the familiar Pitch Bend and Mod wheel controls as well as Patch selection and Master Volume control. In addition, it offers three control sections: Keyboard Modes, Trigger, and assignable controls.

KEYBOARD MODES

The Keyboard Modes section controls how Thor responds to incoming MIDI messages.

Fig. 6-23

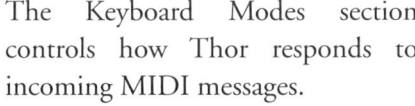

Fig. 6-24

Polyphony

This sets the number of voices (up to thirty-two) that can be played simultaneously.

Polyphony Release

This sets the number of voices that will decay following the Release section of the envelopes. As new notes are played, the previously played notes will continue to play out. If 0 is selected, the release is cut off once a new note is played.

Mono Legato

This setting prevents the envelope from retriggering when new notes are played. When selected, this function works regardless of the settings selected in the Polyphony setting.

Mono Retrigger

This causes notes to retrigger when new notes are played.

Portamento

This will cause notes to slide into the next pitch value instead of playing the new pitch instantaneously.

ON/OFF/AUTO

Portamento can be set to either On, Off, or Auto. The Auto setting will activate portamento only when more than one note is held.

Fig. 6-25

TRIGGER SECTION

This allows for sounds to be triggered by both notes and the sequencer. Both can be activated simultaneously.

ASSIGNABLE CONTROLS

These two knobs and two buttons are assignable to any parameter via the Modulation Routing section. Multiple parameters can be assigned simultaneously. The buttons offer note assignments and will act as momentary switches when notes are triggered via the MIDI controller keyboard.

Fig. 6-26

THE PROGRAMMER

The programmer serves as the heart of the instrument and features both sound creation and manipulation functionality. It contains two sections, Voice and Global.

VOICE SECTION

The Voice section generates waveforms via three oscillators.

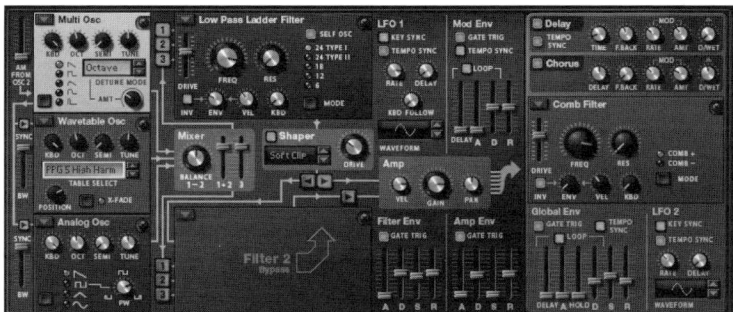

Fig. 6-27

OSCILLATORS I, 2, AND 3

The Thor offers six types of oscillators that are selectable from the downward triangle in the upper left corner of each oscillator. Each oscillator offers the same familiar controls as you're accustomed to using on the Subtractor, and includes Keyboard Tracking, Octave, Semitone, and Tune (Cents). Beyond that, each oscillator features the ability to vary drastically, thereby affording a broad tonal palette. Oscillators 2 and 3 offer oscillator sync to Oscillator 1.

Analog

This oscillator offers the same basic waveforms as found in the Subtractor. These waveforms include sawtooth, square (with PWM), triangle, and sine.

Fig. 6-28

Wavetable

Wavetable synthesis was the precursor to the advent of the sampler and was made popular by the Korg Wavestation, PPG Wave, and Waldorf Wave. A wavetable is a digital oscillator consisting of thirty-two wavetables, each with sixty-four waves, each wavetable offering a unique tonal palette.

POSITION KNOB
The Position knob allows you to dial in a specific waveform pattern within the waveform itself. You can also modulate the Position knob from the Modulation Control section, which causes the sound to sweep through the wavetable.

Fig. 6-29

X-FADE
When engaged, an X-Fade (cross-fade) is placed between each wave in the wavetable, causing the sweep to become smooth. With the X-Fade off, the sweep will instead jump to the next wave with an audible effect.

Phase Modulation

Phase modulation is also known as phase distortion synthesis. The Phase Modulation oscillator causes two waveforms to play in series, so the phase interplays between the two, thereby creating the effect of filter manipulation. When two waveforms are active, the second waveform generated is positioned one octave below the fundamental octave of the first. This technology was first pioneered by Korg, but made famous by the Casio CZ series synthesizers.

Fig. 6-30

PD KNOB
This changes the shape of the waveform.

FM Pair

Frequency modulation (FM) synthesis uses slightly different terminology but is conceptually the same as analog synthesis, in which one oscillator modulates another oscillator. In FM, the modulating oscillators are referred to as operators.

The FM pair is a scaled-down and simplified version of its larger, more complex brethren usually found on hardware/software synthesizers, such as the Yamaha DX7 and Native Instruments FM7.

In Reason, the two are referred to as oscillators, not operators.

Fig. 6-31

CARRIER
This is the first oscillator and is modulated by the modulator oscillator.

MODULATOR
This is the second oscillator and modulates the carrier oscillator.

FM KNOB
This controls the amount of frequency modulation.

Multi Oscillator

The multi oscillator has the ability to generate multiple detuned waves.

By your selecting a basic waveform and the mode of detuning, the oscillator will generate a copy and detune it in various ways. The Amount knob controls how much detuning occurs. This particular oscillator is ideal for creating bell-like tones and cymbal sounds. Check the patch library under Percussion > Cymbals for examples.

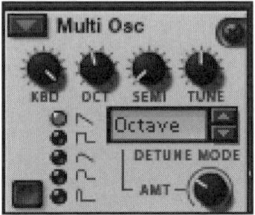

Fig. 6-32

Noise

The noise oscillator offers multiple types of noise and has dedicated controls, each having a different effect on the chosen noise selection. It can generate pure white noise or various styles of colored noise, each possessing a unique characteristic. This unit may be used as a pitch oscillator or a modulation source.

Fig. 6-33

BAND

The Band noise, with BW control, allows for the fine-tuning of the bandwidth. Positioning the knob fully clockwise allows for a wide band of noise, whereas moving the knob counterclockwise narrows the band.

S/H

Sample and Hold are found on many vintage synths and produce a type of randomization. The Rate control, when positioned fully clockwise, offers a wide spectrum of noise akin to white noise. As the knob is moved counterclockwise, you start to hear the random pulses generated from the noise. This can be used to great effect at lower rates as a modulation source for other oscillators.

STATIC

Static is exactly as it sounds. The Density knob, when positioned fully clockwise, offers a wide-range noise. As the knob is moved counterclockwise, you begin to hear the static noise breaking up. At lower settings it sounds much like a dirty stylus cracking and popping on a turntable.

COLOR

Colored noise offers a wide range of noise tones to use. The Color knob, when positioned fully clockwise, affords an emphasis on high-frequency noise, whereas moving the knob counterclockwise increasingly emphasizes the low-frequency noise.

WHITE

White noise is generated when all frequencies are positioned at the same amplitude. There is no knob for this, as all frequencies are equal.

FILTERS I AND 2

There are two identical dedicated filter slots in the Voice section, offering a total of four filter types each. The filters may be run in series or parallel. All the filters have the familiar common parameters found on most synthesizers, which include Filter Cutoff, Filter Resonance, Kbd for filter tracking, Velocity, Invert, and a Drive function that allows for the overdriving of the filter's input, which brings out more character in the filter.

It should be noted that the filter section of any synthesizer is the most important factor to consider in determining the overall character of a particular synthesizer. For example, this is what makes a Moog sound like a Moog. In fact, this element is so crucial there was a time when many manufacturers were suing one another over "stolen" filter designs.

Low-Pass Ladder Filter

This filter design was faithfully modeled after a Moog Ladder Filter, which refers to the circuit design that visually resembles a ladder. It provides a warm, musical sound and is probably the most popular filter design used today. It is capable of self-oscillation via a dedicated button, which allows for the filter to act as tuned feedback. The filter also offers four different slopes, or poles: 6 dB, 12 dB, 18 dB, and two variations on 24 dB.

Fig. 6-34

24 DB TYPE I
This sets the drive function at the filter output to before the feedback loop input.

24 DB TYPE II
This sets the drive function at the filter input to after the feedback loop.

Both types also offer unique sounds when the Self-Oscillation button is engaged. The resonance and feedback, however, are more pronounced with Type I.

State Variable Filter

The State Variable filter is modeled after the Oberheim SEM synthesizer and offers a warm, creamy sound.

This multimode filter, which will self-oscillate via the dedicated button, has LP, BP, HP, Notch, and Peak settings. Both the Notch and Peak settings offer a dedicated knob for toggling between the High-Pass and Low-Pass settings. When the knob is set to the twelve o'clock position, the filter functions as either Notch or Peak. This provides smooth transitions to different filter types and can be used as a modulation source.

Fig. 6-35

Comb Filter

This unique filter adds a series of short delays to the original signal. Each delay is a narrow band that visually resembles the teeth of a comb when viewed on an oscilloscope.

Fig. 6-36

The comb filter affords unique phasing sounds with subtle pitch variations. The filter will generate tunable feedback with high-resonance settings coupled with a low-frequency cutoff.

The Comb's – (Minus) setting can be used to cut or remove low frequencies from the signal.

Formant Filter

The Formant filter has the ability to generate vowel sounds, thus enabling the creation of talking synth patches.

Fig. 6-37

There is no filter cutoff or resonance. Instead, this filter uses a control pad with X and Y axes to control parameters. It has a frequency shift labeled Gender, which can add either female or male characteristics to the voicelike sounds it generates.

SHAPER

The shaper circuit takes input from Filter 1's output and is designed to enable reshaping of the incoming signal.

Fig. 6-38

Subtle amounts of shaping will add warmth, whereas the extreme settings will generate heavily distorted sounds. Following the signal flow, the shaper can either be routed to Filter 2, which allows for the filters to be run in series, or routed to the Amp section.

AMP

The Amp, or amplifier, section receives sounds exiting the Filter section before the signal enters the Global section.

Fig. 6-39

The Amp has a dedicated Gain knob as well as a Velocity (VEL) knob for controlling how the amplifier responds to incoming velocity information. The Amp section also contains a dedicated Pan knob that moves the sound to different points within the stereo field. It is possible to modulate this parameter to cause different voices to sound as if they are moving about dynamically within the stereo field.

LFO I

LFO 1 functions just like the LFO on the Subtractor, with additional waveforms.

Fig. 6-40

However, this LFO is polyphonic, which means it will generate a new cycle with each voice triggered (up to the maximum number afforded by the Polyphony setting). It has the same basic controls, such as Waveform selection, Rate, and Tempo Sync; in addition, it also offers Keysync, Kbd Follow, and Delay controls.

KEYSYNC
This forces any new cycle of the LFO to begin at the start of the waveform. When disengaged, the LFO is free running and might initiate anywhere within the cycle of the waveform.

KBD FOLLOW
This function allows the LFO to track the keyboard. The higher the notes are played on the MIDI controller keyboard, the faster the rate will become.

DELAY
Adds a delayed response from the triggered voice and when the LFO begins modulating. This is great for adding motion effects on sustained notes, whereas shorter notes are left unaffected.

ENVELOPES

There are three envelopes available in the Voice section of the Thor programmer. Its dedicated Filter and Amplifier envelope function just as do the ADSR parameters of the Subtractor. By default, these envelopes are triggered by Note On messages. But they can also be triggered by any other parameter by disengaging the Gate Trigger button and assigning the envelope trigger to another source via the Modulation Routing section.

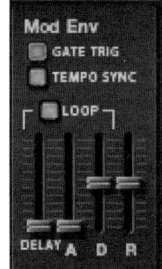

Fig. 6-41

The third envelope, called the Mod env, is only assigned from the Modulation Routing section and can be set to control any assignable parameter. It includes the standard ADSR controls, but also has some additional parameters, such as Delay, Loop, and Tempo Sync.

DELAY
This controls the time before the envelope will affect the desired parameter.

LOOP
This causes the Delay to the Decay to loop, or repeat, indefinitely.

TEMPO SYNC
When activated, this setting allows for each stage of the envelope to lock to the global tempo of the song. The Sync setting ranges from 1/32 to 4/1.

GLOBAL SECTION

The Global section of the Thor synthesizer adds a third filter, a second LFO, an expanded envelope, and two effects processors.

The Filter and LFO both afford the same functionality as the other filters and LFOs discussed previously in this chapter.

The Effects section offers a dedicated Delay with Tempo Sync, Modulation, and Rate controls, as well as a dedicated Chorus effect.

The Global envelope offers some additional controls beyond the standard ADSR. Just like the Mod envelope, the Global env offers Delay, Loop, Tempo Sync, and Gate Trigger with an additional Hold stage within the envelope, which holds for a predetermined amount of time before continuing on to the Decay stage of the envelope.

Fig. 6-42

MODULATION ROUTING SECTION

This section serves as the nerve center of the instruments, which allows you to route audio and CV signals to various destinations. It's broken up into three main sections.

SOURCE →		AMOUNT	→ DEST	AMOUNT	SCALE		CLR	SOURCE →		AMOUNT	→ DEST 1	AMOUNT	→ DEST 2		AMOUNT	SCALE		CLR
LFO 1	▼	15	Osc2 Pitch ▼	0		▼		Mod Wheel	▼	-88	Filt1 X	56	Filt1 Y	▼	0		▼	
Button1	▼	56	Del DryWet ▼	0		▼					0	0			0		▼	
Button2	▼	56	Crs DryWet ▼	0		▼					0	0			0		▼	
Rotary1	▼	-62	Filt3 Freq ▼	0		▼		SOURCE →		AMOUNT	→ DEST	AMOUNT	SCALE 1		AMOUNT	SCALE 2		CLR
LFO 2	▼	50	Filt3 Freq ▼	100	Rotary2	▼			▼	0		0			0		▼	
	▼	0		0		▼			▼	0		0			0		▼	
	▼	0		0		▼			▼	0		0			0		▼	

Fig. 6-43

On the left side, you'll see seven rows of five columns. The title of each column appears at the top as shown:

Source > Amount > Destination > Amount > Scale

Let's look at a simple example of routing.

Start by creating a Thor Synthesizer. Initialize the patch by selecting Initialize from the Edit menu.

Next, in the Modulation Routing section, select LFO 1 under the Source column. Then, under the Destination column, select Filter Frequency.

Finally, after setting the amount to 100, play a note on your MIDI controller keyboard. You will hear the filter being modulated by LFO 1.

Now, under the Scale column, select Performance > Mod Wheel and increase the amount displayed to 100. The Scale function allows you to control the depth, or amount of the LFO, using the Mod wheel. Play a note and raise the setting of the Mod wheel to hear the modulation increase as the Mod wheel is moved. Next, drag the amount of the Mod wheel down to –100. This inverts the Mod wheel setting so that as it this number decreases, the less LFO 1 is sent to the filter.

Let's now take a look at the two other modulation sections. These work the same as explained the previous section, with the notable exception of additional columns.

The section located on the upper right offers four rows of seven columns:

Source > Amount > Dest 1 > Amount > Dest 2 > Amount > Scale

This section allows you to modulate two destinations from a single source. The Scale function affects both destinations simultaneously.

The section located on the lower right offers two rows of seven columns:

Source > Amount > Dest > Amount > Scale 1 > Amount > Scale 2

This section allows for two scale functions to control the amount of the source being routed to the destination simultaneously.

STEP SEQUENCER

The design of Thor's Step Sequencer harks back to the days of the classic analog sequencers. It features sixteen steps with a variety of output data that can be generated simultaneously. When combined with the Modulation Routing section, it becomes a veritable powerhouse of creativity.

Fig. 6-44

Let's jump right in with a quick tutorial to get things up and running. This will be followed by a deeper explanation of all the individual controls available.

- To activate the sequencer, first make sure to engage the Step Seq button in the Trigger section of the Controller panel.
- Next, select Repeat from the Run Mode options on the left side of the interface and click the Run button.
- The sequencer will start running and you should hear a constant sixteenth-note pattern.
- The right side of the sequencer is the Step Edit section, which contains sixteen knobs and buttons. The knobs allow you to dial in specific note values; whereas the buttons, when deactivated, create rests.

Fig. 6-45

- Create rests at Steps 4, 8, and 12.
- Set knobs 2, 6, 10, and 14 to G2. Then set knob 16 to C#3.
- You should now have a sequence that looks like this:

Now that you have a basic sequence running, let's examine some of the other options available on the Step Sequencer.

Run Mode

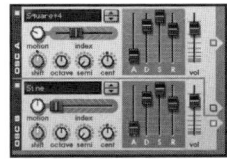

Run Mode controls how the sequencer operates. Options include Repeat, 1-Shot, and Step.

Fig. 6-46

REPEAT
Selecting this option causes the sequencer to play indefinitely.

1 SHOT
Selecting this option will cause the sequencer to play through once and stop.

STEP
Selecting this will cause the sequencer to play each step with a corresponding Incoming Note message.

Direction

The Direction function controls whether the sequencer runs forward, backward, randomly, or in a pendulum motion.

FORWARD
The sequence will run from left to right.

REVERSE
The sequence will run from right to left.

PENDULUM 1
This helps keep the sequence locked into its intended grid value. The sequence will run from left to right and right to left. The first and last steps will play twice.

PENDULUM 2
This is almost the same setting as Pendulum 1, except that the first and last steps are not repeated.

RANDOM
This setting creates random jumping around throughout the sequence.

Rate

The Rate section can be set to run freely or lock to note values ranging from 1/64 to 16/4.

Edit

The Edit section allows for the sequencing of multiple types of data. Editing is directly related to the sixteen knobs in the Step Edit section. The types of data sequencing include Note, Velocity, Gate Length, Step Duration, Curve 1, and Curve 2.

Note sequencing contains an Octave switch for scaling knob values to two octaves, four octaves, and full range.

Curve 1 and 2 offer similar controls to those found in the Matrix pattern sequencer curve controls.

Edit selections are available from within the Modulation Routing section of the Thor sequencer.

Steps

The Thor sequencer offers up to sixteen steps per sequence, but that number may be further decreased to create shorter sequences. This is achieved by clicking on the LEDs above the knob in the Step Edit section.

NOTE TRANSPOSING SEQUENCE

One of my favorite uses for the Step Sequencer is to control the transposition via incoming MIDI notes. Use the following steps to try this out.

- First, lower the Polyphony setting to one voice.
- In the left section of the Modulation Routing section, select MIDI Key > Gate from the first row of the Source column. Increase the amount to 100.
- In the destination column, select Step Sequencer > Trigger
- Next, in the second row, select MIDI Key > Note from the Source column and increase the amount to 100.
- In the destination column, select Step Sequencer > Transpose.
- Now, the sequencer is triggered and transposed by any note selected on the MIDI keyboard controller.

MALSTROM GRAINTABLE SYNTHESIZER

The Malstrom synthesizer is considered wholly unique due to its implementation of a new type of synthesis called Graintable. This effectively combines both granular and wavetable synthesis to create a sound that is far more than the sum of its parts.

Granular synthesis is incredibly complex and involves the generation of grains of sound by either mathematical formula or sampled waveforms. The individual grains are manipulated by changing the pitch, order, speed, and formant of each grain.

Wavetable synthesis, as discussed in the Thor Oscillator section, consists of banks of short sampled waveforms that contain various types of harmonically rich tones, which are all sweepable by means of various modulation sources.

By combining the simplicity of wavetable selection and the complexity of sound manipulation from Graintable, you are able to create unique sounds that cannot be produced by any other type of synthesis.

By now, you should have a solid understanding of synthesis and how all the circuits and parameters involved interact with each other. Therefore, rather than rehash a description of each individual component of the instrument interface, let's instead explore the unique aspects of the synthesizer.

OSCILLATORS A AND B

The heart and soul of the Malstrom is the Oscillator section. Each of the two oscillators contains the already familiar pitch adjustment parameters, including Octave, Semitone, and Cent, as well as dedicated amplifier envelopes.

Each oscillator may be switched on or off by simply selecting the square in the upper left corner. To select a wavetable, either click on the name of the waveform in the drop-down box, or use the up/down arrows to select the desired waveform. The variety of available waveforms is quite extensive and ranges from Bass, FX, Guitars, and Percussion to Synths, Voice, Waves, and Wind.

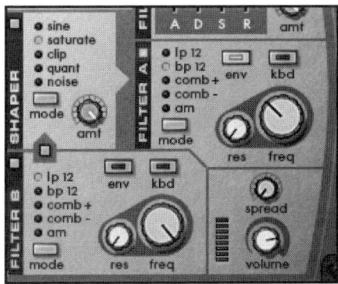

Fig. 6-47

Once a desired waveform is selected, there are three Granular controls—Index, Motion, and Shift—to further manipulate the sound.

Index

The Index control allows you to select a specific point within the graintable to initiate the sound. At the left side of the slider, the sound begins with the first grain and moves towards the right. Simply adjust the index slider to select a different starting point. This really comes in handy when utilizing complex waveforms that can drastically change the mood and feeling of your patch.

Motion

Each graintable has a preprogrammed motion pattern that moves either forward only or forward and backward. The patterns are predetermined for each graintable and cannot be edited, however, the Motion knob can be used to control how quickly the sound cycles through the index. At the twelve o'clock position, it runs at its normal rate, whereas moving the knob to the right increases the speed, and moving it to the left decreases the speed. If the knob is rotated all the way to the left, the waveform becomes static. You'll also notice that the speed of motion will track across the keyboard so that higher notes will have faster speeds.

Shift

The Shift knob, much like the Formant filter of the Thor, controls the formant of the sound and can dramatically alter its harmonic content. It essentially adjusts the pitch of each individual grain, not the pitch of the overall graintable.

ROUTING OSCILLATORS

There are triangular points located on the right side that indicate routing on the Malstrom. These, coupled with the ability to bypass any circuit, allows for easy-to-follow, yet very flexible routing capabilities.

Osc A is routed through the Wave Shaper circuit and then onto Filter A. Osc A can also be routed through Filter B, a final destination, or through the Wave Shaper and Filter A.

Osc B is routed through Filter B, but can be routed through the Wave Shaper and Filter A as well.

By disengaging the routing buttons, it is possible to route the sound directly to the output, bypassing all available circuits.

FILTERS A AND B

Both Malstrom filters are multimode and contain LP 12, BP 12, Comb +, Comb –, and AM, the functions of which were explained previously in the Thor section.

These filters contain the usual Freq Cutoff and Resonance controls, as well as dedicated buttons for keyboard tracking and for engaging the dedicated Filter envelope.

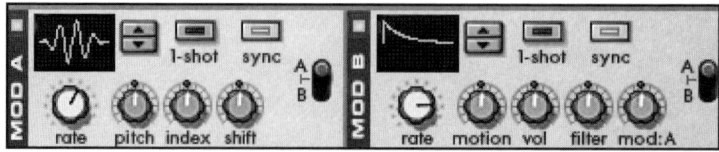

Fig. 6-48

MODULATION (MOD A AND B)

The Mod A and B section, which is essentially the LFO section, is used to create modulation effects.

Both sections contain a vast array of waveforms, well beyond the standard sawtooth, square, triangle, and sine. Both sections also have the ability to synchronize to the tempo of a song. The 1-Shot button allows the Mods to cycle through the given waveform once, effectively engaging them for use as pseudo-envelopes. Mod A or B can modulate the oscillator and filter A and B either together or separately by setting the A/B selector switch.

Mod A

Mod A contains destinations to Pitch, Index, and Shift.

Mod B

Mod B contains destinations for Motion, Volume, Filter, and Mod A.

PERFORMANCE CONTROL

This is same already familiar type of interface that you've seen on both the Subtractor and Thor synthesizers. It contains the usual assortment of controls with additional dedicated options for Polyphony and Portamento.

Fig. 6-49

Velocity

The Velocity section offers control over the levels of both the A and B sections, as well as the Filter envelope. In addition, there is independent control over the A and B sections for the Attack (Amp envelope), Shift, and Modulation settings.

PITCH BEND AND MOD WHEEL

The Pitch Bend range can be set up to twenty-four semitones, spanning a total of four octaves.

The Mod wheel maintains independent control over the A and B sections for Index, Shift, Filter, and Modulation.

WOBBLE BASS PATCH

Let's take a closer look at how to program a wobble bass, which is a popular sound often used in dubstep, crunk, drum and bass, and other forms of bass culture electronic dance music.

- Start by creating a Malstrom and select Initialize from the Edit menu.
- Next, turn on Osc B.
- From the Osc A graintable section, select SweepingSquare from the list of available waveforms.
- Set the Index of Osc A to 38.
- Set Osc A Shift to –4.
- Set the Release of both Osc A and B to 83.
- Set Osc B Octave to 3.
- Engage the Shaper circuit, select Saturate, and increase the amount to 127.
- Set the Freq knob to 46 on Filter A and select BP 12.
- Finally, set the waveform in Mod B to a triangle and increase the Filter knob setting to 47.

The Wobble Bass patch created should look like the image shown. Save this patch for now so it can be utilized later during in the advanced sequencing chapter.

ADDITIONAL THOUGHTS

It is my belief that much of the creation in sound design is effectively, and often simply, done through careful and repeated experimentation. Once you fully understand the basics of synthesis and grasp its function, it won't be long before you'll be able to imagine or hear a sound in your head and replicate it, using the synthesizer. Another great method of learning synth programming is to study other presets and apply a similar programming to your own custom patches.

In the next chapter, you will explore sampling and the application of the NN-19 Digital Sampler and the NN-XT Advanced Sampler.

Sampling

7

WHAT IS A SAMPLER?

A sampler is, in essence, a synthesizer that utilizes recorded samples of audio instead of using oscillators. As a production tool, the sampler offers an unprecedented amount of creative freedom. With it, you can record, process, and play any sound within the confines of an instrument, thereby affording unlimited sonic possibilities.

Samplers and sample playback devices add a new level of realism to music production. Instead of using a synthesizer to approximate the sounds of strings, brass, pianos, bass, or any other acoustic instrument, you instead use recorded waveforms of those actual instruments.

A BRIEF HISTORY OF THE SAMPLER

The earliest-known samplers were keyboard-driven tape instruments. The most popular of these was the Mellotron, which gained notoriety in the late '60s. This sampler used prerecorded material recorded onto magnetic tape. These units were fairly expensive and fragile, and required a lot of maintenance due to the eventual and ever-constant need to replace the recorded tape.

The mid- to late '70s ushered in the first commercially released samplers manufactured by Fairlight and Synclavier. Although highly advanced, these units were very expensive and thus simply out of reach for the average musician.

By the '80s, samplers had reached a price point at which the average person could afford them. In 1987, E-mu Systems released the SP1200, a sampling drum machine, which was and still is regarded as one of the best instruments used in hip-hop production to date. Akai released its S1000 series sampler in 1988, which became the industry standard, with CD-quality resolution.

In the '90s, several manufacturers started production on sample-based instruments called workstations. These had samplers built within them, but also came preconfigured with a massive sound library.

By the late '90s, computer software engineers began working on developing software versions of samplers. In the last ten years, these software samplers became extremely popular, as there were few limitations when compared to their hardware counterparts. Today, faster computers, ever-faster amounts of RAM, and direct disk streaming have taken this concept to even new heights.

HOW A SAMPLER WORKS

Sampling involves recording a portion of audio. It may be a drum loop, an individual tone, or even your washing machine on the spin cycle! Anything can be used as fodder for sound design when utilizing a sampler.

Sample Editor

Most samplers include a built-in editor, helps you prepare and add effects to your newly recorded sample.

START AND END
A common edit that is routinely performed is the removal of empty space before and/or after the sample. These areas are referred to, respectively, as the Start and End points of the sample.

CROPPING
Cropping examines the Start and End points of the sample and then deletes any undesired information before or after the sample itself.

LOOP
There may be instances when you wish to extend the duration of the sample. This is achieved by setting loop points. Consider a loop to be like adding an additional Start and End point for the sample. When you trigger a sample, the original attack or transient is played, followed by the designated loop section, which is looped for as long as the trigger, or key, is held. Setting the Release portion of the Amplifier envelope to a longer duration will cause the looped sound to continue after the release.

CROSS-FADE
This function creates smooth transitions between the Start and End points of the loop cycle. Some samplers will also allow for cross-fading between multiple samples.

FADE-IN/FADE-OUT
This introduces a fade-in at the beginning of the sample or a fade-out at the end of the sample.

REVERSE

This reverses the audio waveform, which results in the sample's being played backward.

NORMALIZE

This function increases the amplitude, or loudness, of the sample by finding the loudest point within the sample and increasing the overall sample to a designated level, such as 0 dB.

Key Zone

Once the sample has been edited and is ready to play back, it is loaded into a key zone. The key zone defines where the sample is placed on the keyboard. You may have a single key zone with a range that could span the entire keyboard, or you may have multiple key zones, each being assigned to a single key on your keyboard. By default, a single sample is loaded into one key zone, the range of which covers the entire span of the keyboard. As you play higher or lower on your MIDI controller keyboard, the pitch of the sample is either increased or decreased.

Key Map

A key map is a collection of several key zones.

Root Note

The root note sets where the sample plays back at its original pitch on the keyboard.

MULTISAMPLING

Multisampling is the process of using several samples within a single key map to create a realistic-sounding instrument that seems to be playing at different octaves.

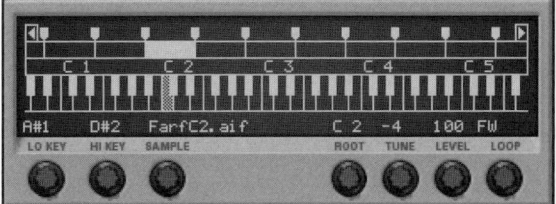

Fig. 7-1

Consider sampling a vocalist singing the phrase, "Love is all you need," at middle C. If you were to play back the sample an octave above the original pitch, your singer would sound like a Chipmunk. And if you were to play the sample one octave lower, the voice would likely be described as sounding demonic.

To achieve realism across the entire range of your keyboard, you would need to record multiple samples at different pitches and map them accordingly.

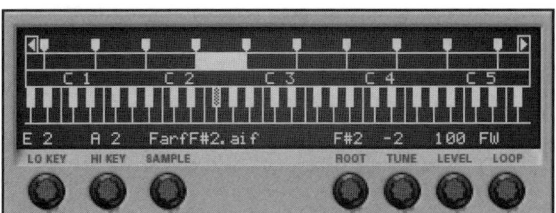

Fig. 7-2

In Fig. 7.1, you see the key map of a Farfisa organ. The current selected key zone shows a range from A#1 to D#2, with the root note set at C2. Also notice that the name of the sample indicates what key was used to record the original sample. In this case, as is shown, it's C2.

Fig. 7.2 shows the same key map of the Farfisa organ with the next key zone selected. Notice that the range displayed is now E2 to A2, with the root note set at F#2. This key zone starts picking up where the previous key zone ended.

SAMPLING IN REASON

Sampling in Reason 6 is fairly straightforward. This process can accomplished using the Song Sample tab in the Tool window or by sampling directly into certain instruments, such as the NN-19, NN-XT, ReDrum, and/or Kong Drum Designer.

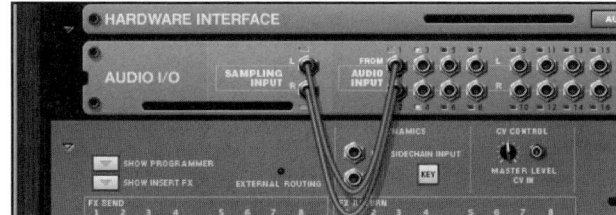

PREPARING TO SAMPLE

You'll need to review a few settings and the available options before diving into the actual process.

Fig. 7-3

Setting Up the Recording Formats

Whenever you are recording into Reason 6, the software will examine your audio preferences to determine the quality required. Reason will record files in WAV format at various bit depth and sample rate resolutions. The software will provide any conversions necessary to keep playback consistent and smooth.

The lowest settings that I recommend using are a sample rate of 44.1 KHz and a bit depth of 16 bits. This is the standard for producing CD-quality sound. Whenever possible, try to record at 24 bits.

Setting Your Inputs

The type or kind of sound you are sampling will determine how the signals are routed to the Sampling Input.

In Fig. 7.3, the Audio Input 1 and 2 are routed to the Sampling Input on the Hardware Interface. This is the default wiring and is set up to record samples from the microphone or line inputs connected to your physical audio interface.

It is further possible to record an instruments output, which allows for some creative sound design with resampling capabilities.

SAMPLING INTO THE SONG SAMPLE TOOL WINDOW

In this tutorial, you will learn to sample a drum loop from the ReDrum drum machine. I've gone ahead and programmed a four-bar drum loop to use for this process, but feel free to create your own loop if you choose, and follow along.

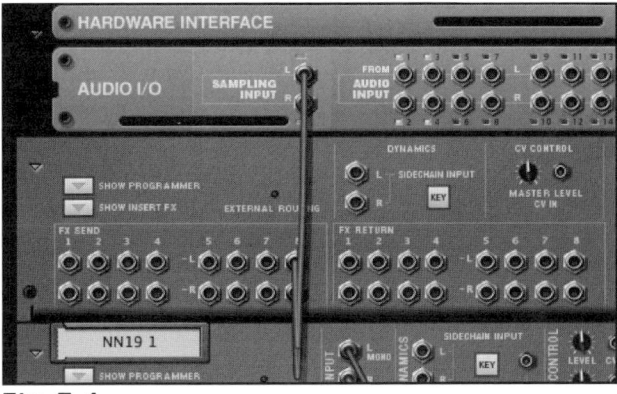

Routing the ReDrum

Fig. 7-4

By default, when you created the ReDrum, it was automatically cabled to the Mix Track device. You can either route the output of the ReDrum directly into the Sampling Inputs, or if you are planning on also sampling multiple instruments and effects, you can use an Aux send on the mixer.

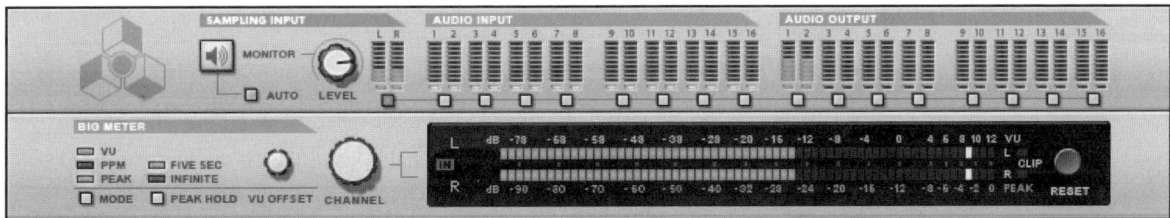

Fig. 7-5

In this case, I've decided to use an Aux 8 send to route the signal into the Sampler inputs. By doing so, Aux 8 can route any additional instruments I wish to sample, without needing additional cabling.

Make sure the Big Meter is engaged and that the focus is positioned on the Sampling input, as indicated by the red LED located just underneath the vertical meters on the Hardware Interface.

With the ReDrum playing, engage the FX Send On button on the mixer channel strip and increase the setting of the Aux 8 knob to 0 dB. The idea is to get a loud signal without clipping. If the Clip Indicator lights up, try lowering the Aux send.

Please note that if you engage the Monitor button, you'll hear both the original ReDrum and the signal coming through the Sampler input. This is normal and will not affect the quality of your sample.

Fig. 7-6

OPEN THE SONG SAMPLE TAB FROM THE TOOL WINDOW

Once the Song Sample tab is open, you will find three sample folders: Assigned, Unassigned, and Self-Contained.

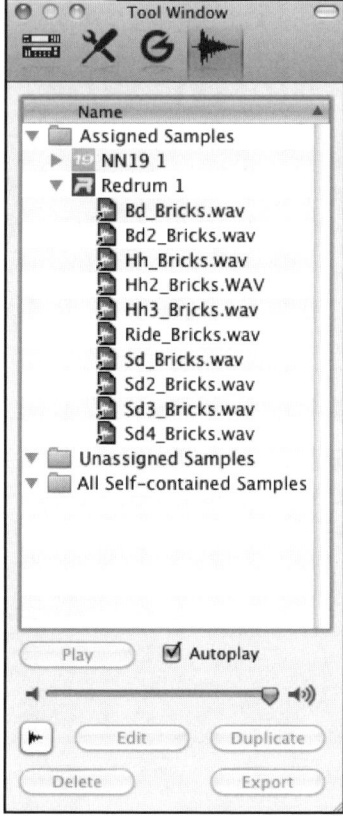

Fig. 7-7

Assigned Samples

This folder contains any samples used by any of the available instruments. In this case, you have an NN-19 and the ReDrum. The ReDrum folder unfolds to show the ten samples used in the kit.

Unassigned Samples

This folder contains any samples that have not yet been assigned to an instrument. This may be samples that were included in the Factory Sound Bank or samples that have been recorded.

Self-Contained Samples

This folder contains any samples you've recorded. All self-contained samples are saved within the Reason song. This helps immensely with the file maintenance because you never have to worry about samples used in a particular song getting lost or misplaced.

Fig. 7-8

SAMPLING THE REDRUM

Since the levels are already set, let's proceed with the recording of your drum loop.

With the sequencer stopped, press the Record button on the Song Sample window transport (see Fig. 7.8).

Once the Sample Record window is open and recording, click Play on the sequencer.

You will now see the waveform displayed in the Recording window. Once the entire drum loop has played through one time, click the Stop button on the Song Sample window transport.

Fig. 7.10 displays the newly recorded sample, named Sample 1, in both the unassigned and self-contained folders. Notice the icon in the unassigned folder contains a small arrow in the bottom left. This indicates that it has been designated as an alias file, which points to somewhere else in the system. In this case, the alias is pointing to the self-contained Sample 1 file.

If you were to look at the samples in the assigned sample folder, you would find that all of these samples are alias files with their actual files permanently located within the Reason Factory Sound Bank. This measure prevents your mistakenly deleting or modifying any sample content within the factory settings. Any editing of samples taken from the Factory Sound folder automatically re-creates a new file, so that the original data are never modified.

Edit Samples

Select Sample 1 and click the Edit button at the bottom of the Song Sample transport window.

- The first thing you want to do is to set the Start and End times and select the loop sample to be used for your drum loop.
- Select the Forward Loop setting, which is the center button located under Loop Mode.
- Next, click the Snap Sample Start/End times to the Transient option.
- Press the Play button and move the End time so that it will complete one full loop.
- Finally, click the Crop button to remove the recording data left outside the designated Start/End time.
- Then click the Normalize button to increase the level of the sample.
- Now let's change the name of the sample from Sample 1 to Drum Loop 1.
- The final step is to click the Save button to exit out of Edit mode.

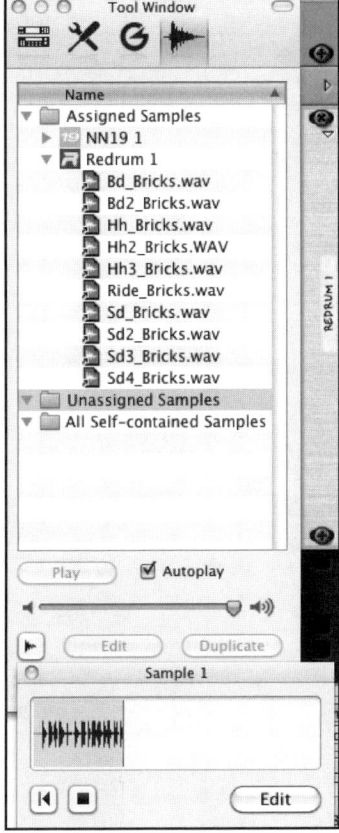

Fig. 7-9

The new sample Drum Loop 1 can now be assigned to any device capable of loading samples. Now let's take a look at the NN-19 Digital Sampler.

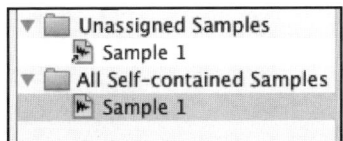

Fig. 7-10

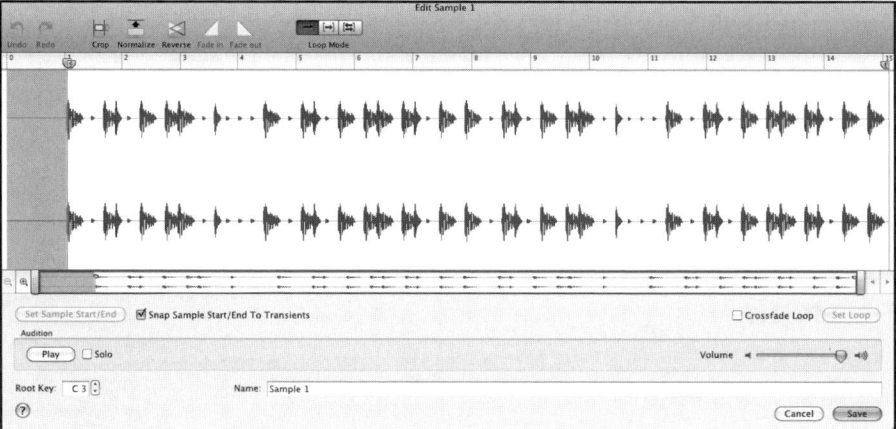

Fig. 7-11

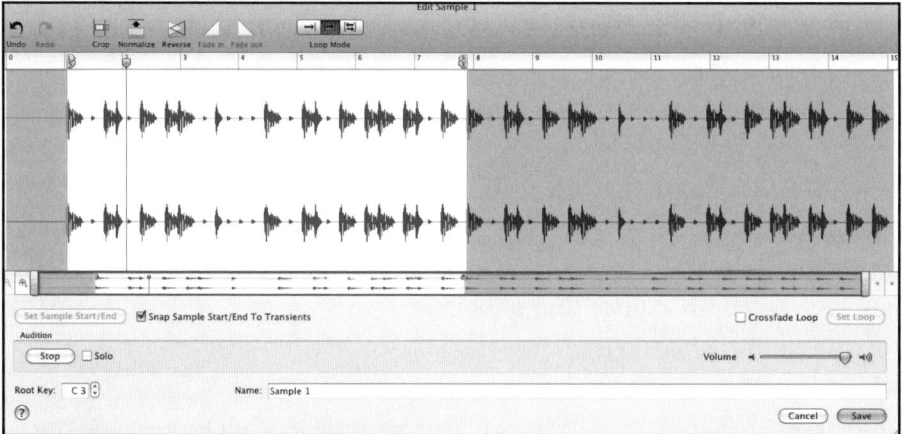

Fig. 7-12

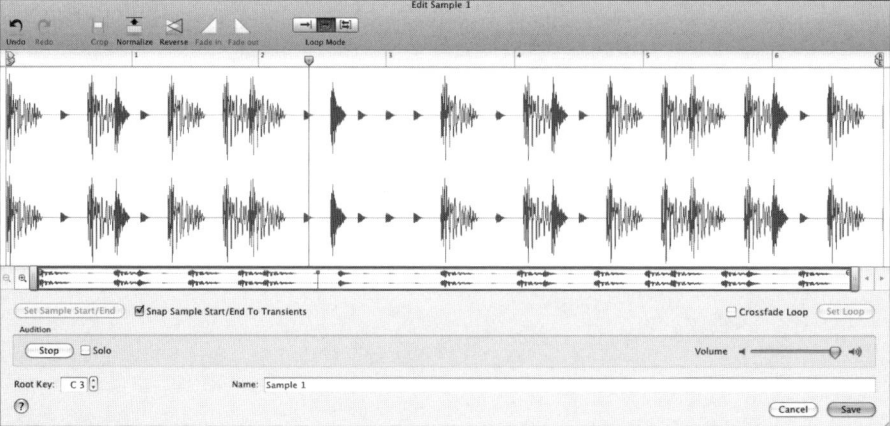

Fig. 7-13

NN-19 DIGITAL SAMPLER

The NN-19 is a fantastic instrument to use. Reason ships with a comprehensive library of ready-made presets for the NN-19.

But this instrument is also ideal for use in loading or recording your own sounds. It can be loaded with

Fig. 7-14

up to 127 samples, one for every key on the keyboard, and the key zones do not overlap.

Loading Patches

The presets for the NN-19 are loaded just as any other instrument in Reason 6, by using the Browse Patch function.

I chose the Raw_MM_Sqr1 patch found in the Synth Raw Elements folder within the NN-19 Sampler patches.

This particular patch has two samples loaded into two key zones.

Selecting the Select Zone via MIDI button allows you to watch the zone automatically update as you play up the keyboard. You will learn how to create and apply a custom patch in a later section.

Keyboard Window

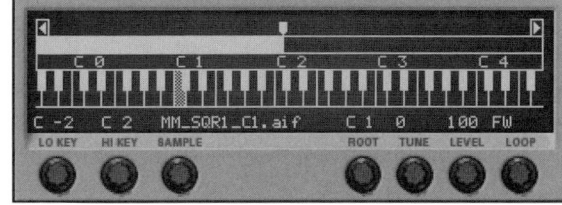

The keyboard window displays the entire key map currently being used. In this case, there are two distinct key zones. Each key zone displays settings across the bottom that define its programming.

Fig. 7-15

LO KEY
The Low key establishes the lowest note of the key zone. Turn the knob to adjust the key.

HI KEY
The High key establishes the highest note of the key zone. Turn the knob to adjust the key.

SAMPLE
The Sample diplays the name of the sample file currently loaded into the key zone. Turn the knob to scroll through any loaded samples.

ROOT
The Root knob establishes the root note by designating a key on the MIDI controller keyboard to play back the sample at its original pitch.

TUNE

The Tune knob allows for control over the tuning or pitch of the sample. This provides a range of +50 to –50 cents.

LEVEL

The Level control adjusts the volume of the sample.

LOOP

The Loop knob selects whether the current sample will loop. The three modes available are Off, Forward, and Forward/Backward.

Synth Parameters

The Synth parameters are used to shape and modulate the sounds produced by the sample. The original sample is left intact while all processing is made to the playback of the samples.

Osc

The Oscillator section controls the pitch of samples. All controls are global and affect every sample within the patch.

SAMPLE START

This knob causes the sample to begin at a later point. This is helpful if you're using custom samples that contain a bit of air at the beginning or if you want to modify how the sample starts.

OCT

The Octave knob increases or decreases the pitch range twelve semitones at a time.

Fig. 7-16

SEMI

The Semitone knob changes the pitch up to twelve semitones.

FINE

Fine, also known as cents, allows you to precisely change the pitch between semitones. There are 100 cents per semitone.

Fig. 7-17

ENV AMT

The Envelope Amount controls how much effect the Filter envelope will have on the pitch of the instrument. This is great for shaping the pitch over time.

KBD TRACK

When engaged, this button will allow the sample to change pitch according to what keys are pressed on your MIDI controller keyboard. Disengaging this parameter will cause the sample to play from its designated root note anywhere on the keyboard. This is useful for nonpitched samples such as drums, where it isn't ideal for the pitch to alter.

Filter

The NN-19 is equipped with a multimode filter with cutoff and resonance. It contains the same filter types found on the Subtractor: Notch, HP 12, BP 12, LP 12, and LP 24.

KBD

The Keyboard knob controls how the filter tracks across the keyboard. When turned fully clockwise, the filter cutoff will increase as you play up the keyboard.

Filter Envelope

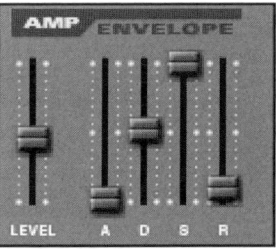

The Filter envelope allows you to shape the filter over time.

Amp

The Amplifier section controls the level of the instrument. There is a dedicated Level control and a dedicated Amp envelope.

Fig. 7-18

LFO

The LFO section contains the usual assortment of waveforms for use as a modulation source.

The Rate knob controls the frequency or speed of the LFO. It features a Sync button, which forces the LFO to work in musical increments such as eighth or sixteenth notes.

The Amount controls how much LFO is sent to the set destination, with options including Oscillator, Filter, and Pan.

Fig. 7-19

PLAY PARAMETERS

The Play parameters are designed to help with expression by controlling or modifying incoming MIDI messages.

Fig. 7-20

Portamento

This knob controls the glide function. Instead of the notes changing instantaneously to the next note or pitch, the sound instead glides into the new pitch.

Polyphony

This parameter controls the number of voices the sampler will play at once. A Polyphony setting of 1 is essentially the same as a monophonic setting.

Spread

This dynamically changes the panning of voices. The Spread knob controls how much spreading occurs.

KEY

Key spreads the sounds across the stereo field. Lower notes on the keyboard appear left in the stereo field. As you play higher, the stereo field tracks across the keyboard with higher notes appearing in the right side of the stereo field.

KEY 2

Key 2 spreads the pan position from left to right in eight steps, as each consecutive higher note is played on the keyboard. Once eight steps have been reached, the cycle is then repeated.

JUMP

Jump will alternate between the left and right stereo fields with every note played.

Legato

This style of playing, triggering a new note without releasing the previous note, will not trigger a new envelope.

Retrigger

This mode forces the envelopes to retrigger, regardless of the playing style.

Controller

This parameter designates which incoming MIDI controller will have control over the Filter Frequency, LFO, and Amplifier amounts. The MIDI controllers that the NN-19 will respond to include Aftertouch, the Expression pedal, and the Breath controller.

Fig. 7-21

Pitch Bend

This setting affects the range of the pitch bend. The range can be set from +24 to –24 semitones, to cover a total of four octaves.

Mod Wheel

The Modulation wheel can be programmed to control Filter Frequency, Filter Resonance, Filter Envelope Decay, Amplifier, and LFO amounts. All controls can be set to positive or negative values and can all be controlled simultaneously.

Fig. 7-22

Velocity

This setting controls what parameters will respond to incoming Velocity messages. The available parameters are Filter Envelope Amount, Filter Envelope Decay, Amplifier Level, Amplifier Envelope Attack, and Sample Start.

CREATING CUSTOM PATCHES

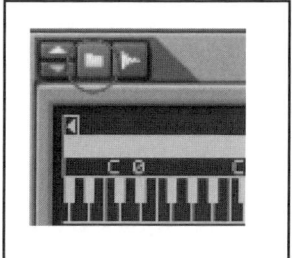

With the NN-19 selected, click Initialize Patch from the Edit menu.

Next, click the Browse Sample button, located above the keyboard display.

From the Browse Sample window, select MM_Saw_C1 and MM_Saw_C3 from the MiniMoog Samples folder, found in the Synth Raw Elements folder located in the NN-19 Sampler Patches.

Fig. 7-23

Keyboard Display

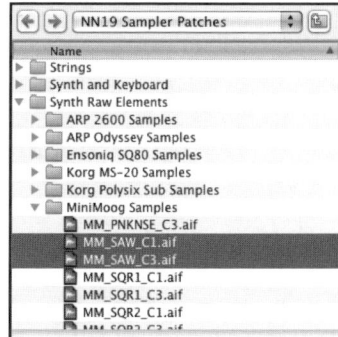

When initializing a patch, only one key zone is created, which spans the entire range of the keyboard. The solid light blue line shown above the keyboard denotes this.

The first sample you selected from the browser is selected automatically, regardless of how many samples you've loaded. In this case, you've loaded a total of two samples.

If you turn the Sample knob, you can switch between the two loaded samples.

To play both samples, you need to create a new key zone by selecting Split Key Zone from the Edit menu.

Fig. 7-24

Another useful function found in the Edit menu is the Automap Samples function. This works especially well if the sample contains pitch information. Most samples can contain pitch data, which the NN-19 can read and assign to the appropriate key zone and root note. The C1and C3 parts of the title let you know that these samples contain this information.

In Fig. 7.26, the Keyboard window now displays both of the key zones.

Fig. 7-25

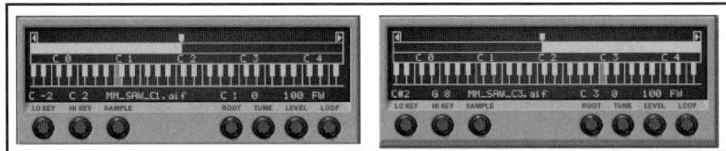

Fig. 7-26

The key zone on the left has its Lo key and Hi key set to C–2 and C2, respectively. The sample is set to MM_Saw_C1.aif, the root note to C1 and the loop mode is set to Forward. Note the correlation between the C1 in the name of the sample with the root note.

The key zone on the right has its Lo key and Hi key set to C#2 and G8, respectively. The sample is set to MM_Saw_C3.aif and the root note is set to C3. Again, note the correlation between the C3 in the sample name and the root note.

SAMPLING INTO THE NN-19

Now let's take a look at how to sample directly into the NN-19 sampler.

First, initialize the instrument by selecting the Intialize Patch function found in the Edit menu.

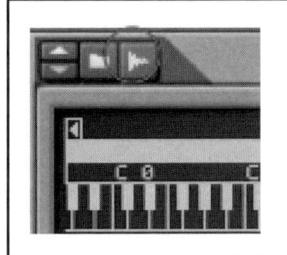

Fig. 7-27

Once it's initialized, first confirm your connections are set up properly. Earlier in this chapter, you sampled the ReDrum via FX send 8 on the mixer. You may use the same drum loop via this setting or you might try sampling via any physical input on your audio interface. A microphone, instrument, or line level device will do. Just make sure you've assigned the proper inputs to the sampling inputs on the Hardware Interface and check the levels.

Once the levels are set, click on the Sample button and play the proposed sample.

The now familiar Recording window opens, displaying the recorded waveform. Press the Stop button to assign a key zone for the sample that spans the entire keyboard.

Fig. 7-28

Next, let's add another sample.

First, create a new key zone by selecting Split Key Zone from the Edit menu. Note that the new key zone is created with no sample loaded.

Now follow the same procedure for recording a sample. You can repeat this process as many times as you like. Also remember that the samples can be edited using the Song Sample tab of the Tool window.

NN-XT

The NN-XT was initially released as the successor to the NN-19, but was never intended to replace it. Both samplers feature the same core structure, which allows you to assign samples to key zones with multiple key zones available per patch. Both have similar Synth parameters used to shape and modulate the sounds, but the NN-XT takes things to the next level with the added features providing the ability to program layers and enable velocity-controlled switching and cross-fades.

Fig. 7-29

The setup of the NN-XT is simple yet has such added features as Duplicate and Copy parameters from a key zone, Auto-zone mapping, and Pitch Detection for assigning root notes.

MAIN PANEL

In Fig. 7.29, you see the main panel features global control over the Filter and Amp envelope parameters, including the Decay for the Modulation envelope and a dedicated Master Volume.

The familiar Pitch and Mod wheels are accompanied by an additional X wheel, which is used for generating Aftertouch, Expression, or Breath controller messages. This feature provides added sound-shaping control, in the event your keyboard controller is not capable of transmitting these messages.

REMOTE EDITOR

Along the bottom of the main panel is the NN-XT Remote editor. Fig. 7.30 shows the Remote editor unfolded with the CrickleWood patch selected from the Synth Lead folder for the NN-XT sampler.

The main section of the editor is the Key Map display, which shows the loaded samples and key zones grouped together. In this particular patch you see two zone groups layered together in the same key map, which will result in both sounds' playing together as one.

Just below the Key Map is the Sample parameter bar, which gives you independent control over settings for each key zone or sample.

Fig. 7-30

Group and Synth parameters are located on the left and along the bottom of the editor.

KEY MAP DISPLAY

The Key Map display of the NN-XT is very similar to the one featured in the NN-19, but includes some additional enhancements and features.

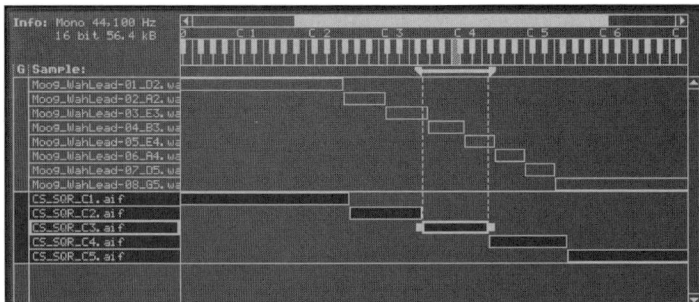

Fig. 7-31

The Info bar located in the upper left corner of the window displays a detailed breakdown of the currently selected sample. The info shown comprises the Mono or Stereo designation, Sample Rate, Bit Depth, and Size settings.

The keyboard display is positioned on the right side of the window. The solid light blue bar at the top is the scroll bar, which permits a view of the entire keyboard range by clicking and dragging the scroll bar left to right.

The left column, just below the Info bar, displays the Sample list. Fig. 7.31 shows the CS_SQR group, which is denoted by the vertical running bar situated next to the collected list of samples. Clicking on this vertical group bar selects all samples and key zones in the designated group.

To the right of the sample list column under the keyboard display are several horizontal bars, indicating the range for each key zone into which individual samples are loaded.

The centered sample has an Edit Focus, as indicated by the light blue handles appearing on either side of the key zone and dotted lines running up toward the tab bar. Select either the handles or the Tab bar to adjust the key zone's Hi and Lo parameters. Remember that it is possible to select and edit multiple key zones at once.

SAMPLE PARAMETERS

The Sample parameter section allows detailed control over each sample or sample grouping.

Fig. 7-32

The M depicted on certain parameters denotes the particular samples within the group that have different settings.

Root

This control determines at what note the sample will play back in at its original pitch.

Tune

This control allows for fine-tuning of the sample in Cents. There are 100 cents per semitone, with a designated control range of +50 to −50.

Start

This control determines the Start time of the sample.

End

This control determines the End time of the sample.

Loop Start

This control determines the Loop Start point within the sample.

Loop End

This control determines the Loop End point within the sample.

Play Mode

This control determines the loop mode.

F W
This loop mode plays the sample forward. The sample will play through once and then stop.

F W - L O O P
This loop mode also plays the sample forward, but in this case, the sample will loop continually between the loop's Start and End times. This loop will continue to play even after the key is released.

F W - B W
This loop mode plays the sample forward to Start but once the sample reaches the Loop End point, it plays backward to the Loop Start point and then repeats the cycle continuously.

F W - S U S
This loop functions like the FW-Loop, only once the key is released, the sample plays through the remainder of the sample outside the designated Loop End point. This allows samples to retain their natural decay.

B W
This loop mode plays through once only in reverse.

Lo Key

This control determines the lowest key in a key zone.

Hi Key

This control determines the highest key in a key zone.

Lo Vel

This control determines the lowest Velocity message the sample will trigger.

Hi Vel

This control determines the highest Velocity message the sample will trigger.

Fade-In

Used for velocity fades and cross-fades, this control determines the velocity value for establishing a fade-in effect. Values above the Fade-In level will play at full velocity.

Fade-Out

Used for velocity fades and cross-fades, this control determines at what setting the velocity value will establish a fade-out effect. Values up to the designated Fade level will play at full velocity. Once this value is reached, the levels will then fade out.

Alt

When enabled, this control will alternate through any number of specified samples. To use this function, first set the key ranges to an exact or partial overlap. Then, select all the samples you wish to alternate and enable the Alt function so that each time the key is pressed, it will randomly switch between the selected samples.

Out

This control determines the output for a group or sample. There are sixteen outputs arranged in stereo pairs. To gain access to sixteen individual outputs, select two samples and route them to a Stereo Pair output. Then, hard pan each sample and route each output to its own channel on the mixer.

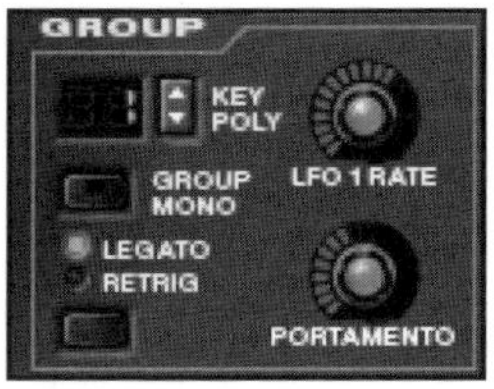

Fig. 7-33

GROUP PARAMETERS

Group parameters affect all samples assigned to a group and typically affect the style in which the samples are played.

Key Poly

This parameter affects the number of keys that can be pressed. The range is 1 to 99, with a setting of 1 equal to monophonic playback.

Group Mono

This parameter overrides the Key Poly setting and allows only one sample in the group to be triggered at a time. However, if the Key Poly is set to any value over 1, then that particular sample may be retriggered polyphonically. It's only when switching between two or more samples that the Mono function will take effect.

Legato/Retrig

Legato is a playing style that prevents the envelopes of a new sound from being triggered when you are holding down the key of a previous note. For example, with this setting engaged, play and hold one key on your keyboard and trigger a second note without releasing the first note. The pitch of the note will change, but the envelopes will not be triggered.

LFO I Rate

This is a group override that takes precedence over the LFO 1 settings in the Synth Parameter section.

Portamento

This function will cause notes to glide between note pitches, as opposed to jumping instantly to the next pitch value.

SYNTH PARAMETERS

The NN-XT features the all the typical Synth parameters used for sound shaping and modulation.

Modulation

The Modulation section features control parameters for Filter Frequency, Filter Resonance, Modulation Envelope Decay, Level, LFO 1 Amount, and LFO 1 Rate.

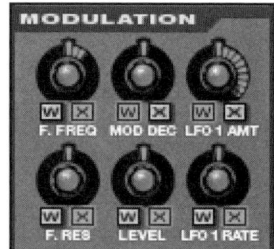

Fig. 7-34

Each control is assigned to either the Modulation wheel (W) or External control (X). Each parameter can be set to positive or negative, affording a wide variety of tone-shaping control, all simultaneously.

Velocity

The Velocity section offers control over the Filter Frequency, Modulation Envelope Decay, Level, Amplifier Envelope Attack, and Sample Start settings.

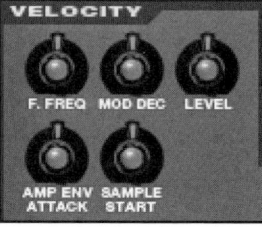

Fig. 7-35

LFO 1

LFO 1 offers the same type of waveform shapes as any other synthesizer in Reason 6. The available destinations are set as Pitch, Filter, and Level.

The Rate knob offers settings for Group Rate, Tempo Sync, and Free Run.

It also features a Delay knob, which will delay the onset of the LFO 1 en route to its destination.

A Key Sync feature is also available, which will cause the LFO to retrigger with each new note.

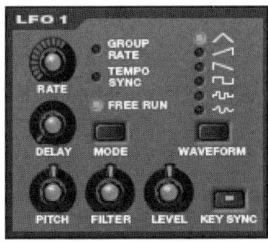

Fig. 7-36

LFO 2

LFO 2 has a set triangle waveform with destinations for Pan and Pitch.

The Rate control is set to free run.

It also offers a Delay knob, which, the same as with LFO 1, will delay the onset of the LFO en route to its destination.

Mod Envelope

The Modulation envelope offers the standard ADSR with a Hold function that grabs the Decay portion for a set time before continuing on to Sustain.

It offers destinations to both Pitch and Filter Frequency.

The Delay knob will delay the onset of the envelope to its destination.

It also offers Key to Decay, which forces the Decay portion of the envelope to track across the keyboard. When at a positive setting, the Decay will increase as you play higher up the keyboard.

Fig. 7-37

Pitch

The pitch section offers control for the pitch bend. The range can be set from +24 to –24 semitones, to cover a total of four octaves.

Three knobs offer dedicated tune controls for Octave, Semitone, and Fine (Cents).

The final control knob is the Key Track that, when turned fully counterclockwise, will cause the pitch to remain constant. Turning the knob fully clockwise will increase the pitch by one octave.

Fig. 7-38

Filter

The NN-XT multimode filter offers a variety of filter types, including Notch, HP 12, BP 12, LP 6, LP 12, and LP 24.

Fig. 7-39

The filter controls include Frequency Cutoff and Resonance, as well as Key Track, which, when enabled, will cause the Frequency to follow the keys on the keyboard. A positive setting will result in the Filter Frequency's opening up as you play higher notes on the keyboard.

Fig. 7-40

Amp Envelope

The Amplifier envelope offers the same controls as the Modulation envelope, including ADSR with the Hold function, as previously described.

There are also a Delay function and a Keyboard to Decay function, as described in the "Modulation Env" section.

In addition, the Amp envelope offers a dedicated level control and a comprehensive Pan section.

The Pan section has controls for spread with mode settings of Key, Key 2, and Jump.

Fig. 7-41

KEY

This control causes the sound to pan from left to right, based where you play on the keyboard. Playing in lower octaves will pan the sound to the left, whereas playing higher will cause panning to the right.

KEY 2

This will cause the sound to pan from left to right in an eight-note cycle.

JUMP

This control causes the sound to alternate left and right with each key pressed.

VELOCITY SWITCHING

Now let's examine a preset that offers velocity switching.

Click the Browse Patch button on the main interface and select Brush Kit from the Drums and Percussion folder.

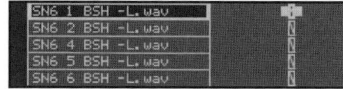

Fig. 7-42

Click the Select Zone via MIDI button located at the top of the Editor window.

Next, play D1 on your MIDI controller keyboard. Notice how each strike of differing velocities will trigger one of six different snare samples. This adds an element of realism because the sound of a genuine snare drum will vary when struck at different velocities.

Some drum sample libraries offer over fifty levels of velocity switching, each with a different sample assigned to it.

CREATING A CUSTOM PATCH

Now let's examine the process of creating a custom patch.

Programming Custom High Hats

- Start by initializing the NN-XT, by selecting Initialize Patch from the Edit menu.
- Next, use the Browse Sample button to select a high hat sound. I have selected Hat3-03 from the Click House Dub Samples folder, found in NN-XT Sample Patches > Drums and Percussion > Drums and Kits.
- Once loaded, select Automap Chromatically from the Edit menu. This will set the key range and root note to C1.
- Next, with the sample selected, click Duplicate Zones from the Edit menu. Repeat this a second time to create a total of three duplicates of your high hat.

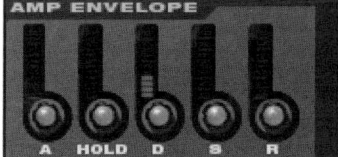

Fig. 7-43

- Then select Solo Sample at the top of the Eemote editor. This enables you to hear only the selected sample.
- Now, change the Amp env to reflect the settings shown in Fig. 7.43, with the Decay setting set to 60 ms. Then repeat this procedure for all three samples.
- On each sample, first vary the filter cutoff and resonance slightly and then adjust the pitch plus or minus four semitones.
- Then, select the group of samples and engage the Alt function.
- Lastly, turn off the Solo Sample function and play your high hat. You will notice that with every hit of the key, the samples triggered will alternate to allow for a different sample to play each time.

ID8 INSTRUMENT DEVICE

Although the ID8 doesn't sample, it is considered a sample playback device that uses prerecorded samples to generate tones.

Fig. 7-44

A general MIDI (GM) device, it is the default instrument when importing standard MIDI files (SMF). For every track in the standard MIDI file, a different instance of the ID8 will be loaded with the appropriate sound.

The ID8 has a very simple interface, featuring Pitch and Modulation (vibrato) wheels on the left, patch selection in the center, and two parameter controls on the right.

The types of sounds available are selected by clicking the large blue LCD screen to reveal nine categories. Four variations can be selected, using the four buttons labeled A, B, C, and D located to the right of the LCD.

The nine categories available are:

- Piano: Grand, Upright, Dance, and Vibes
- Electric Piano: Mark II, Wurly, Digital, and Clav
- Organ: Rock, Perc, Combo, and Pump
- Guitar: Ac Steel, Clean Electric, Jazz Semi, and Dulcimer
- Bass: Finger, Pick, Upright, and Synth
- Strings: Orchestral, Arco, Small Section, and Choir
- Brass, Wind: Fat Brass, Brass Section, French Horn, and Flute
- Synth: Saw Lead, Big Square, Analog Pad, and Crystal Pad
- Drums: Acoustic, Rock, Hip Hop, and Electronic

The ID8 offers a great way to select sounds very quickly. Although there may be better-sounding options available using other instruments, the ability to switch quickly between several sounds is a very convenient, strong point.

Reason Drum and Percussion Instruments

DR. OCTOREX

The Dr. OctoRex Loop Player is a loop playback device that uses .rex files for content. The .rex files are loops that have been processed by Recycle, a utility program created by Propellerhead. This program analyzes the loops and breaks them up into slices based on the transient of each sound within the loop. The Recycle file also generates a MIDI file that allows the loop to be played as originally produced. A huge benefit of using this technology is that you can play virtually any loop at any tempo without affecting the pitch.

Before the advent of Recycle, manually slicing loops and programming MIDI sequences was a tedious, time-consuming task, usually taking several hours to process a single loop. Recycle, however, does all the work for you instantaneously.

If you are creating your own loops and wish to use them as Recycle files, then purchasing Recycle is a must. Do note, however, that Reason ships with a stocked library of .rex files. The available loops range from drum and percussion loops to instrument and effects loops.

DR. OCTOREX INSTRUMENT PANEL

The main interface across the top of the device as shown contains the familiar Pitch Bend and Mod wheel, eight Loop Slot selector buttons, Master Volume, and Global Transpose settings.

Fig. 8-1

When Enable Loop Playback is engaged, clicking the Run button will cause the loop to start playing. This function is completely independent of the Transport control.

The current default preset is Acoustic Drums—College 130. Selecting any of the loop slots will switch between variations on the Acoustic Drum loops.

Global Transpose

This changes the pitch globally by semitones. The parameter settings from +12 to −12 provide a total range of two full octaves.

Trig Next Loop

This designates the time division at which a new loop will start. The default setting of Bar waits until the currently playing loop reaches the end of a bar, before triggering the new one. This proves to be a handy function for keeping everything in time.

SHOW PROGRAMMER

Once the programmer is unfolded, you will find the Loop Slot selection and Slice editor positioned to the left and the familiar Synth Parameter controls located to the right.

Select Loop and Load Slot

The eight buttons in the programmer coincide with the main loop selector at the top of the instrument panel. Each slot holds an individual loop. Selecting the Loop Browser button imports new .rex files into the selected slot.

COPY LOOP TO TRACK
Copy Loop to Track generates a MIDI file and places it on the Dr. Octo Rex track in the sequencer window.

SLICE EDITOR
Below the loop slots is the Slice editor. A red line placed at the beginning of each transient denotes each slice. You may select a slice by either clicking on it or using a MIDI note. (Make sure the Select Slice by MIDI setting is activated.)

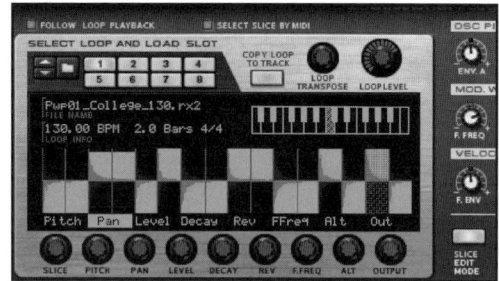

Fig. 8-2

Each slice has independent control over Pitch, Pan, Level, Decay, Reverse, Filter Frequency, Alternate Group, and Output.

There are also Loop Transpose and Loop Level settings that can affect the currently selected loop in the Loop editor.

Selecting the Slice Edit Mode button, shown in the lower right corner of Fig. 8.2, allows fast programming of slices by drawing in desired values with the Pencil tool.

Notice that here I have panned each drum hit opposite the other.

ALTERNATE OUTPUTS

Press Tab to toggle to the rear of the device and note that the Dr. OctoRex has four stereo outputs in addition to the main output.

Next, cable Outputs 7 and 8 into mixer Channel 2.

Press Tab to return to the front of the interface and select Slot 2 on the main interface.

Using Slice Edit mode, select the Out setting on the Slice editor.

Fig. 8-3

Route every snare hit to Out 7 and 8. Then select Run and notice how the snare is now routed to a separate channel on the mixer. This enables extra creative processing, such as adding reverb or delay to just the snare hits alone, among other techniques.

Synth Parameters

The synth parameters of the Dr. OctoRex are global, and as such, will affect the instrument as a whole.

There are dedicated control sections for Osc Pitch, Modulation wheel assignment, Velocity, Multimode Filter, LFO, and its dedicated Filter and Amp envelopes.

Fig. 8-4

LFO EFFECTS

The LFO has the destinations Osc, Filter, and Pan. Experimenting with these effects during production can really breathe new life into a static drum loop.

ENVELOPES

Increasing the attack of either envelope can lead to pseudo-backward effects.

REDRUM DRUM COMPUTER

The ReDrum drum computer's design is based on the vintage drum machines released in the early '80s by Roland. Since their release, the TR-808 and TR-909 models were targeted toward professional musicians. Unfortunately, however, they sounded completely unrealistic when compared to a standard acoustic kit and the line was, at last, discontinued.

In spite of this, with the emergence of modern electronic music as a genre throughout the '80s, these drum machines eventually became a staple of the sound. The TR-909 became the quintessential sound associated with house music, while the TR-808 was responsible for spawning the sounds of early hip-hop and Miami bass.

Still highly coveted today, these unique machines still have a huge following with many producers, some of whom are willing to pay prices considerably higher than what the units originally sold for.

Luckily for producers like us, Propellerhead developed a software program known as ReBirth in 1996. A precursor to Reason, ReBirth featured software emulations of both the TR-808 and TR-909.

When Reason was first released in 2000, it included another emulation component called the ReDrum drum computer. This sample-based drum machine came equipped with a sixty-four-step sequencer, which was also modeled after the early Roland machines.

Fig. 8-5

The ReDrum instrument interface consists of three primary sections: Global section, the Drum Sound parameter, and the sequencer. Entire kits can be loaded or individual drum sounds into each of the instruments' ten channels.

GLOBAL SECTION

The Global section is where you can save and load kits via the Save Patch and Browse Patch buttons.

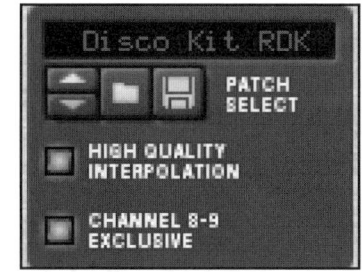

Fig. 8-6

High-Quality Interpolation

When engaged, this will trigger an advanced algorithm to interpolate samples, which produces higher-quality results. This function, however, requires more processing power and it is recommended for use only when deemed necessary. The best way to determine this need is to audition the parameter within the context of other tracks.

Exclusive 8 and 9

This option, when engaged, forces each channel to behave monophonically. For example, if Channel 8 is triggered, followed by Channel 9, Channel 9 will cut off the sound of Channel 8, rendering it exclusive to Channel 9.

Master Volume

This knob, located on the upper left side of the interface, controls the overall level of the main outputs.

DRUM SOUND PARAMETERS

Common Drum Parameters

The Drum Sound parameters found in each channel share some commonality.

Fig. 8-7

The Mute, Solo, and Play buttons are located on the top of the display. Below is the name of the sample being used, loaded onto the specific track. The sample browse functions are available underneath.

A dedicated Sample button is located to the right of the Browse Sample button. This allows for the recording of samples directly into the interface. Refer to chapter 3 for details on the full procedure for recording samples.

S 1 and S 2, Stereo, and Pan Controls

S 1 AND S 2

When connected to the mixer, Send 1 and Send 2 route their respective signals to the Channel Aux input, thereby allowing any channel direct access to effects connected to the mixer.

Fig. 8-8

STEREO SAMPLE

When illuminated, the two cojoined circles displayed between S 1 and S 2 indicate the currently located sample is set to stereo.

PAN

This knob controls the left and/or right balance of the sound within the stereo field.

Level, Length, and Decay

LEVEL

The Level knob controls the amplitude of individual sample. The accompanying Velocity knob controls how the level responds to Velocity messages.

Fig. 8-9

LENGTH

This knob controls the length of the sample. When positioned to the right, the sample is played in its entirety, but when positioned to the left, the sample is shortened.

DECAY

The Decay switch acts as an envelope and controls how the sample ends. The triangle shape will produce a natural-sounding decay, whereas the square creates an abrupt cutoff.

Pitch, Tone, and Sample Start

Fig. 8-10

The following controls will vary depending on which channel is being utilized.

Channels I, 2, and 10

PITCH

This knob controls the pitch of the sample, plus or minus one octave. When centered, the LED is not illuminated and the sample is played at that sample's original pitch. Moving this knob to the right raises the pitch, whereas moving it to the left lowers the pitch.

TONE

This knob controls the brightness of the sound. When centered, the sound is unaffected, but moving it to the right increases the brightness, whereas moving it to the left decreases it.

The Velocity knob controls how the Tone knob reacts to the note velocity.

Channels 3, 4, 5, 8, and 9

PITCH

Control is the same as for Channels 1, 2, and 10.

Fig. 8-11

START

This knob controls the start of the sample. The default setting is at the hard left and plays the sample from its beginning. Moving the knob to the right shifts the Start time, thereby cutting off the sample start. This can be a useful function for removing dead space from a sample. Likewise, it can also be used to soften the attack.

The Velocity knob controls how the sample start reacts to incoming note velocity.

Channels 6 and 7

PITCH WITH BEND

These channels offer pitch control, with the ability to bend the pitch either up or down relative to the pitch setting.

The Rate controls how quickly the bend occurs.

Fig. 8-12

The Velocity knob controls how the pitch/bend reacts to incoming note velocity.

THE SEQUENCER

The sequencer features four banks, each consisting of eight patterns, for a total of thirty-two patterns per instrument.

Each sequence can have up to sixty-four steps, with a different resolution setting for each pattern.

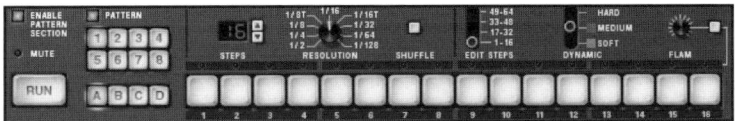

Fig. 8-13

To program the sequencer, first click on a Select button at the bottom of the Drum Parameter window. This notifies the sequencer that this is the particular sound you wish to sequence.

Next, click on a Step button wherever you wish to hear the desired sound.

Sequence Programming

Now let's re-create the steps involved in programming a simple house music pattern.

HOUSE PATTERN
- First, select House Kit 7 from the Patch Browser.
- Next, click the Run button to activate the sequencer. The red LED will begin to cycle. Maintain the resolution at the default setting of a sixteenth note to establish a one-bar pattern.

Fig. 8-14

- Now, select Channel 1. This channel is typically assigned to a kick drum sound.
- Select Steps 1, 5, 9, and 13. This will set up a quarter-note kick, which is a familiar pattern widely utilized in house and techno music.

Fig. 8-15

Fig. 8-16

- Next, select Channel 9, which is set to an open high-hat sound.
- Then select Steps 3, 7, 11, and 15.
- The open high hat in this particular preset has a very short-length set. By changing this setting to 63, you will be able to hear more of the sample.

- Last, select Channel 2, which is a handclap sample, and click Steps 5 and 13.
- Congratulations! You've just created a simple house beat.
- Now, let's change the number for steps from sixteen to thirty-two and produce some variations to your house pattern.

Fig. 8-17

- To program Steps 17 through 32, first move the Edit Steps switch to position between 17 and 32.
- Follow the same programming you used previously in Steps 1 through 16.
- This should result in a two-bar sequence that sounds exactly the same.

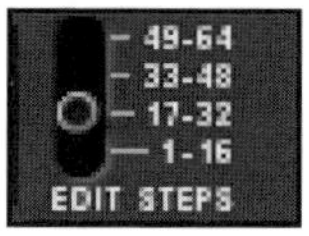

Fig. 8-18

- Next, between Steps 1 and 16, add a kick to Step 16.
- Then, between Steps 17 and 32, add a kick to Step 15.

COPY PATTERN

Click on the Pattern 1 button and use the Copy keyboard command (Command + C if using Mac, Control + C if using Windows) to copy.

Next, select Pattern 2 and use the Paste keyboard command (Command + V if using Mac, Control + C if using Windows) to paste.

Select Channel 8, a tambourine sample, and then click and drag from Steps 1 through 16. This method is a very quick and effective way of adding a sixteenth-note pattern to your sequence without having to select each individual step. This method is also useful for removing sounds from a pattern.

Do this for both sections 1 through 16 and 17 through 32.

Note how the sixteenth-note tambourine pattern sounds very mechanical. A great way to modify this to create some rhythmic variation, is to alter the dynamics of every other note, as described next.

Fig. 8-19

Fig. 8-20

Move the Dynamic switch setting to Soft.

Click on every even-numbered step in the sequence. This will create some dynamic variation, thereby infusing a little more feeling into the sequence.

SHUFFLE

Adding a shuffle to a pattern changes the rhythmic timing by moving every even-numbered step a little closer to the odd-numbered steps.

To achieve this, first engage the Shuffle button on the ReDrum interface. Immediately, you should hear the pattern alter slightly, with more of a swing feel to the rhythm.

Next, click the ReGroove Mixer button located at the bottom right of the Transport window.

On the bottom left side of the ReGroove Mixer is the Global Shuffle knob. This will adjust the overall shuffle of any device capable of the shuffle function, including the Matrix Pattern Sequencer and the RPG-8 Arpeggiator.

The valid parameters range from 50to 75 percent, with 50 percent providing no effect.

A setting of 66 percent for this will create a perfect sixteenth-note triplet.

Fig. 8-21

Fig. 8-22

USING THE REDRUM AS A SOUND MODULE

You've already worked with the ReDrum in this manner in chapter 4. However, there are some additional functions you've not yet explored, such as triggering mutes and solos from your MIDI keyboard controller.

Fig. 8-23

Triggering Sounds

Octave C1 triggers individual notes, enabling a MIDI controller to play and record sounds into the Reason sequencer.

Triggering Mutes

Octave C2 acts as a momentary mute on each drum sound and allows you to play the mutes in a musical way, as well as to record these effects into the sequencer window.

Triggering Solos

 Octave C3 acts a momentary solo of each drum sound and allows you to play the solos in a musical way, as well as to record these effects into the sequencer window.

KONG DRUM DESIGNER

The Kong Drum Designer is a sixteen-part multitimbre instrument capable creating a variety of drum and percussion sounds.

The interface contains sixteen pads, reminiscent of many hardware drum machines, most notably the Akai MPC series.

The three main sections of the Kong Drum Designer are the Pad section, the Drum control panel, and the Drum and FX programmer.

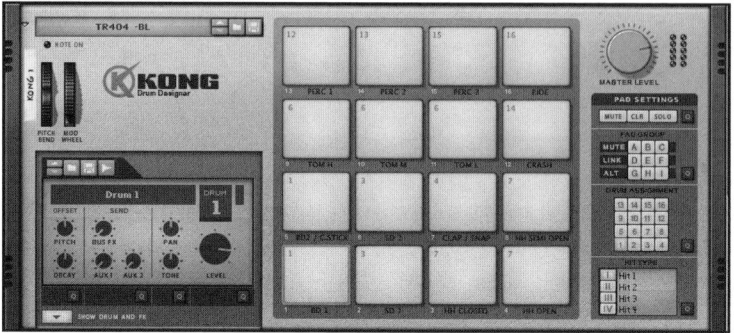

Fig. 8-24

Triggering Pads

The MIDI notes that trigger the pads can be easily played via any MIDI controller. Keyboard controllers are fine, but you may find, as I do, that a dedicated MIDI pad controller, such as the M-Audio Trigger Finger or the Akai MPD series, may offer a greater degree of control.

The C1 octave of your keyboard will trigger each sound in an ascending order (e.g., C1 triggers Pad 1, C#1 triggers Pad 2, etc.),

The C3 octave assigns each pad to every three keys on your keyboard (e.g., C3, C#3, D3 trigger Pad 1; D#3, E3, F3 trigger Pad 2; etc.). This is useful when triggering the same pad in rapid-fire procession, which is normally a difficult task when using only one key on your MIDI controller.

The pads on the instrument interface itself are velocity sensitive. Clicking at the bottom of a pad generates a lower velocity, whereas triggering at the top of a pad triggers the maximum velocity. This can be a useful tool when you are programming sounds.

Loading Sounds

Located in the upper left corner is the Kit Patch selection, with the familiar Browse and Save Patch buttons. This will load entire kits with sounds allocated to each of the sixteen pads.

To load or save an individual drum patch, select a drum pad and use the Browse or Save Drum Patch section in the upper left corner of the Drum control panel. This section also offers direct sampling into each of the sixteen pads. Refer to chapter 3 for more details on the process of recording samples.

Fig. 8-25

DRUMS AND FX

Before you look at how to create custom sounds, first let's examine the signal flow process of the Kong.

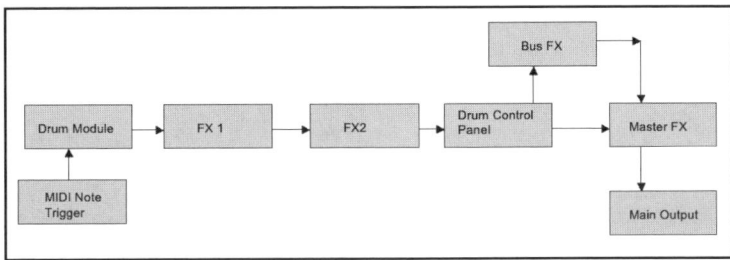

Fig. 8-26

- First, a MIDI note triggers the Drum module.
- From the Drum module, the signal is passed through Insert FX 1 and Insert FX 2 serially.
- From FX 2, the signal is passed into the Drum control panel.
- The Drum control panel then routes the signal to the Master FX section.
- The Drum control panel also offers an effects send to the Bus FX.
- The Bus FX output is routed through Master FX.
- The Master FX then routes the signal to the main outputs of the instrument.

There are variations possible whereby the output of the control panel may be routed through the Bus FX or directly into either the main or individual outputs.

Drum Modules

The Drum modules available in the Kong Drum Designer are nothing short of spectacular. Each module offers unique ways to tailor your sound, using samples, .rex files, physical modeling, and analog modeling. Depending on the type of module used, the Hit Type under Pad Settings will re-create a different effect. Let's first look at the available modules and then explore the Hit Type settings and how each affects performance.

Fig. 8-27

NN-NANO SAMPLER

The NN-Nano Sampler takes its cues from the NN-XT sampler. It contains four hit slots, each with multiple layers.

Loading multiple samples per hit slot enables you to achieve sophisticated velocity switching between samples, a function that is quite useful for creating highly realistic sounds.

The Nano Sampler also features the usual assortment of sound-shaping capabilities, including parameters for precise control over Mod wheel, Velocity, Pitch, Osc, and Amp envelope settings.

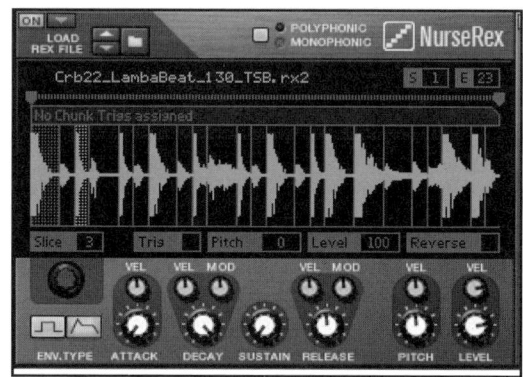

Fig. 8-28

NURSE REX LOOP PLAYER

The Nurse Rex Loop Player utilizes the same Rex player technology employed by the Dr. OctoRex Loop Player.

The Rex file will respond to various Hit Type settings, thereby providing some really creative ways to manipulate the loop, including Loop Trigger, Beat Juggling, and Individual Slice Triggering settings.

Also included with the Nurse Rex are the usual synth controls, including velocity-controlled envelope stages (ADSR), as well as Pitch and Level control settings (also controlled by velocity).

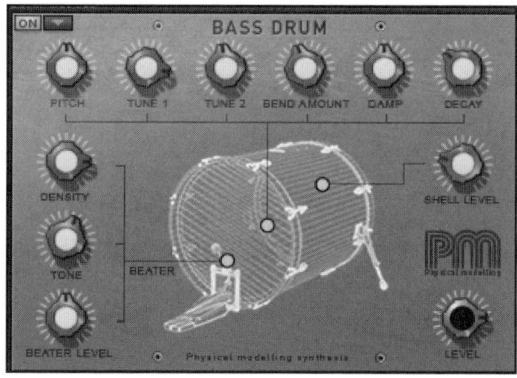

Fig. 8-29

PHYSICAL BASS DRUM

Physical modeling synthesis provides unprecedented control over sound-shaping capabilities, which far exceeds the control of a sample playback device.

The Bass Drum physical modeling module offers control over the Beater, Drumhead, and Shell settings, each containing a variety of parameters.

PHYSICAL SNARE DRUM

The Physical Snare Drum offers control over the Shell and Snare, Drumhead, and Edge Tuning settings.

The assignment of different hit types gives you independent and precise control over the Center, Position, and Edge settings.

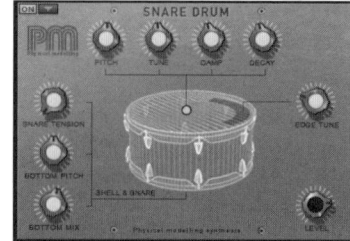

Fig. 8-30

PHYSICAL TOM TOM

The Physical Tom Tom drum offers control over the Drumstick, Drumhead, and Shell settings.

SYNTH BASS DRUM

Analog modeling synthesis, much like physical modeling, affords an unprecedented level of control over sound-shaping capabilities, which far exceeds the control offered by a sample playback device.

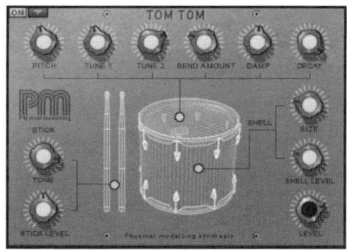

Fig. 8-31

Fig. 8-32

The Bass Drum offers control over the Pitch, Tone, Click, and Envelope settings.

SYNTH HIGH HAT

The Synth High Hat offers control over the Pitch, Decay, Level, Click, Tone, and Ring settings.

Fig. 8-33

Fig. 8-34

Hit Type control further offers four types of high-hat sounds: Closed, Semi-Closed, Semi-Open, and Open.

SYNTH SNARE DRUM

The Snare Drum module offers control over the Pitch, Decay, Level, Harmonics, and Noise settings.

SYNTH TOM TOM

The Synth Tom Tom module provides control of the Pitch, Click, Level, Decay, and Noise settings.

Fig. 8-35

FX

The effects available include FX 1, FX 2, Bus FX, and Master FX.

COMPRESSOR

The compressor affords control over dynamics by rendering the louder sounds softer and the softer sounds louder.

The compressor settings comprise the Compression Amount, Attack, Release, and Makeup Gain.

FILTER

This resonant multimode filter offers both standard cutoff and resonance control with LP, BP, and HP settings. Also included is a MIDI-triggered envelope generator.

Fig. 8-36

Fig. 8-37

OVERDRIVE/RESONATOR

Providing two effects in one, the Overdrive section offers a nice assortment of distortion, whereas the Resonator section is modeled on the Body algorithms of the Scream Distortion processor.

PARAMETRIC EQ

This is a single-band parametric equalizer with frequency control and gain. The Q parameter offers the ability to shape the bandwidth of the EQ, creating a wider band when turned to the left and narrower band when turned to the right.

Fig. 8-38   **Fig. 8-39**   **Fig. 8-40**

RATTLER

Set this device to add a snare rattle to any signal produced.

RING MODULATOR

The ring modulator utilizes a mathematical algorithm that combines the sum and difference of two distinct signals.

This particular unit has a built-in sine generator that works in tandem with the incoming signal to produce wild metallic-sounding tones and effects.

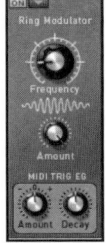

Fig. 8-41   **Fig. 8-42**   **Fig. 8-43**

ROOM REVERB

This creates a standard Room Reverb effect, which imparts the characteristics of variously sized rooms to the incoming signal.

TAPE ECHO

Tape Echo is modeled after the vintage Roland Space Echo, a highly sought-after tape delay used for dub effects.

Fig. 8-44   **Fig. 8-45**   **Fig. 8-46**

TRANSIENT SHAPER

The Transient Shaper affords the ability to change the attack of any drum hit. This can be especially useful when modifying drums to sit better in a mixer, without the use of EQ.

Support Generator Effects

These effects are only available with the FX 1 and FX 2, and are designed to add character and weight to an incoming signal. Additionally, the use of hit types allows for more precise control over when the device will generate sounds.

NOISE GENERATOR

This adds noise to the incoming signal. It also offers Envelope control with dedicated Resonance, Sweep, and Click to round out this module.

TONE GENERATOR

This will add a sine wave to any incoming signal and offers Envelope, Bend and Shape control settings.

DRUM MODULE PANEL

The Drum module panel was reviewed earlier in this section, with regard to loading drum patches. Now, let's examine the global parameters this module has to offer.

OFFSET

Pitch and Decay Offset are global controls that affect all modules used in the Drum and FX section. By adjusting pitch or decay, any applicable parameters can also be adjusted.

Fig. 8-47

For instance, lowering the Decay Offset will cause not only the decay of any drum module, but can also be applied to any FX device containing a Decay parameter.

SEND

This section controls the level of sound sent to the Bus FX module. In addition, the Kong further offers Aux 1 and 2, which allow the signal to be routed outside via Kong to other devices in Reason.

LEVEL, TONE, AND PAN

These control the overall level, tone, and pan positions of the entire Drum module.

PAD SETTINGS

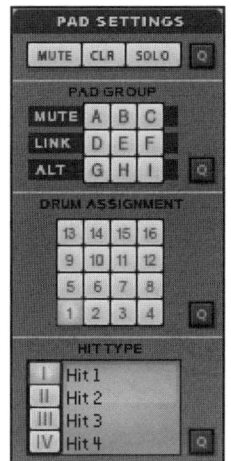

Pad settings offer control over a variety of useful functions as they pertain to each of the sixteen pads.

Mute/Solo

This setting controls the status of solo and mute for any given pad. There is also a dedicated Clear button that removes multiple soloed or muted pads simultaneously.

Fig. 8-48

Pad Groups

There are nine pad groups broken up into three categories: Mute, Link, and Alt.

MUTE

Mute groups (A, B, and C) cause any pad assigned to mute any other pad within the same group. For instance, if you assign Pads 1 and 2 to Mute Group A, hitting either Pad 1 or 2 will cause the previously triggered pad to be muted. This is useful for creating realistic high-hat patterns in which a closed high-hat sound would mute an open high-hat sound.

LINK

Link groups (D, E, and F) cause any assigned pads to trigger simultaneously. For instance, if you assign Pads 3 and 4 to Link Group D, then hitting either Pad 3 or 4 would cause both pads to trigger.

ALT

Alt groups (G, H, and I) will alternate between any pads assigned to a group. For instance, if you assign Pads 9, 10, and 11 to Alt Group G, then hitting any pad in the group would alternate randomly among any of the three assigned pads.

Drum Assignment

The Drum Assignment section allows you to trigger one drum module across multiple pads. This can prove to be quite useful, depending on the type of drum module as well as the hit type being used.

Hit Type

Depending on which drum module is utilized, the Hit Type affords the ability to trigger different samples or variations of sound, depending on the module used.

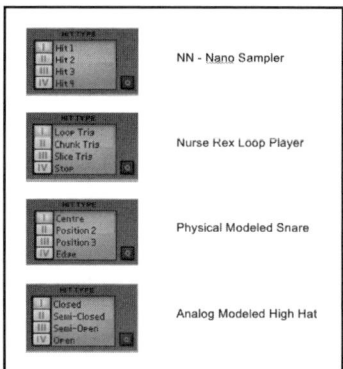

Fig. 8-49

QUICK EDIT

Located across the bottom of each section of the Drum Module control panel and the Pad Settings panel are small boxes labeled Q. When engaged, this setting affords an overhead view of the assignments of specific parameters over all sixteen pads simultaneously.

In Fig. 8.50, you see the Quick Edit mode of the Pad Drum Assignment.

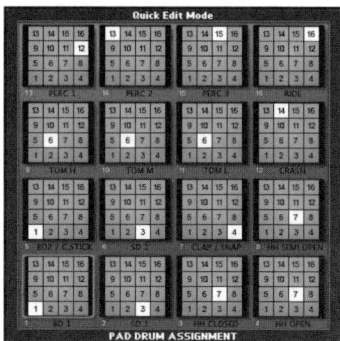

Fig. 8-50

Notice that Pad 5 is assigned to Pad 1 and Pads 3, 4, and 8 are assigned to Pad 7.

This means that Pad 1 and 5 share one drum module, while Pads 3, 4, and 8 share another drum module.

PRACTICAL USE OF PAD SETTINGS

For you to fully grasp the programming potential of pad assignments, let's take a closer look at the programming of a preset.

- Start by opening the TR404 kit from the Beyer Lekebusch folder located in the Kong Kit folder.
- Once open, click on Pad 1 and open the Show Drum and FX programmer.
- Pad 1 has an NN-Nano Sampler assigned.
- Hit Slot 1 has sample BD_Sturdy loaded into it.
- Hit Slot 2 has sample BD_404Loose loaded into it.
- Next, open the Quick Edit Drum assignment, by hitting the Q button.
- Here you will find Pads 1 and 5 have been assigned to Pad 1.
- Now, hit the Quick Edit Hit Type button.
- Here you will find that Pad 1 is assigned to Hit 1, while Pad 5 is assigned to Hit 2.
- The hit type designates which sample is triggered from the NN-Nano Sampler.

BEAT JUGGLING WITH NURSE REX

- Begin by selecting Initialize Patch from the Edit menu.
- Next select Pad 1 and open the Show Drum and FX programmer.
- Select the Nurse Rex Loop Player from the Drum Module drop-down list.
- Then select the BSQ_PhatDrumz_105.rx2 from the Beats folder, found within the Bomb Squad (BSQ) folder, which is located in the Dr. Rex Drum Loops folder.
- Engage the Quick Edit Drum Assignment button and assign Pads 1, 2, 3, 4, and 5 to Pad 1.
- Next, engage the Quick Edit Hit Type button and assign Pads 1 through 4 to Chunk Trigger.

Notice how with each assignment of the chunk trigger in the Hit Type window is reflected within the display of the Nurse Rex Slice editor.

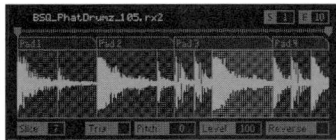

Fig. 8-51

Playing Pad 5 triggers the entire loop; Pads 1 through 4 trigger sections of the loop. By playing the sections rhythmically, you can approximate a form of beat juggling.

Reason Effects

EFFECTS PROCESSORS

Effects processors have been around since the 1940s. Originally conceived as devices for studio use, they're often large and equipped with tubes and high-voltage transformers, which made them expensive and impractical for live musicians. The earliest effects were modified tape machines creating tape loops and overdriven amplifiers to create distortion.

Another popular effect used early on was the reverb, or echo, chamber—essentially, setting up a speaker and microphone in a large, reflective room to record the ambience of the room. Some of these tactics are still worth investigating today. There's a ton of DYI information online and in books that talk about various setup and recording techniques.

By the late 1970s, the first digital effects were commercially available. In the mid 1980s , processors offering multiple effects, from reverbs and delays to modulation and dynamics, in one box became hugely popular. Some of these devices cost several thousand dollars and set the standard for high-quality effects processing.

Fortunately, Reason 6 is equipped with no less than twenty-two effects processors. They run the full gamut, offering a wide palette of sonic manipulation.

With the advent of Reason's new mixer based on the SSL9000K, complete with channel strip processors, you'll have several options of using the same type of effect. You'll learn about the SSL channel strip in the chapter on mixing.

For now, let's focus on the outboard effects offered by the Reason and gain an understanding of how best to use them.

As you move through the chapter, you'll focus separately on each effect. This will involve creating the effect, manipulating controls, and deleting the effect before moving to the next effect.

SIGNAL PROCESSORS

Signal processors are typically used as an insert effect. The audio signal is routed into the effect, processed, and passed on to the mixer. This is commonly used when the processed output signal has replaced the original sound from the instrument.

Reason ships with a vast number of effects presets, which contain several effects in a chain. You'll investigate these later in this chapter.

For now, you'll focus on creating one effect at a time.

To begin, open Chapter 9—Effects, on the enclosed DVD.

You'll focus first on two processes that are the mainstay of the mixing process; equalization and compression.

EQUALIZATION

There are several types of equalizers, each offering unique ways of shaping frequencies. You'll begin by exploring the parametric equalizer.

Reason is quite adept at auto-cabling devices on your behalf. You'll need to select the device before creating an effect.

When you select the Dr. OctoRex Loop Player, a light blue box will outline the device, denoting its selection.

From the Create menu, select Effects > PEQ-2 located at the bottom of the list.

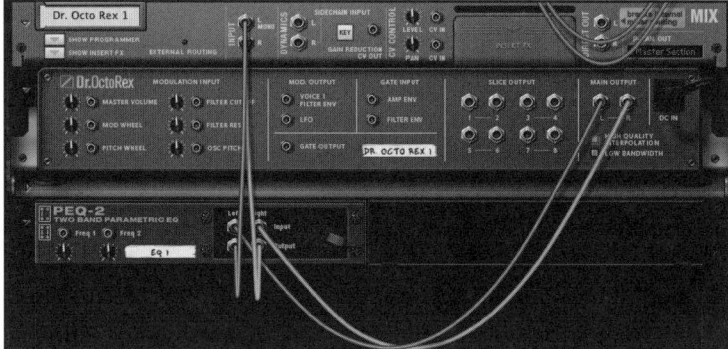

Fig. 9-1

Press Tab to view the rear of the rack and you'll discover that Reason has auto-cabled the output of the Dr. OctoRex to the inputs of the EQ and the outputs of the EQ to the inputs of the Mix Channel device above.

PEQ-2: TWO BAND PARAMETRIC EQ (EQUALIZER)

The PEQ-2 is a two-band parametric EQ (equalizer). As mentioned earlier, sound is measured by frequency and amplitude. The function of an equalizer is to correct imbalances within the audio frequency spectrum, by either boosting or cutting

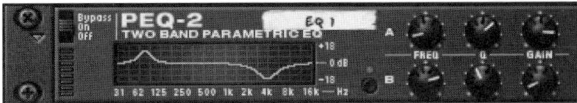

Fig. 9-2

the amplitude of specific frequencies. Each band of the EQ has a Frequency, Q, and Gain control that can be used to make adjustments.

Frequency

The Frequency spectrum of the EQ ranges from left to right, with the lowest frequencies on the left and higher frequencies to the right. Adjusting the knob allows you to zero in on a specific frequency. (Note: Unless you've boosted or cut the gain, you won't see any movement on the graphical interface.)

Gain

The Gain knob boosts or cuts from +18 to –18 dB at the frequency setting.

Q

The Q knob changes the width of the band. Moved to the left, it narrows the band of frequencies with surgical precision. When the knob is moved to the right, the width opens into a bell-like shape, affecting more frequencies.

To hear this effect, press Run on the Dr. OctoRex.

Start by boosting the Gain knob and sweeping the Frequency knob up and down the audio spectrum.

You'll explore the practical application of equalization in the chapter on mixing, but for now, feel free to explore boosting or cutting while sweeping the Frequency knob. Notice how pronounced the kick drum becomes around 62 Hz, and the high hats around 8 kHz.

The second band of the PEQ must be turned on to be used.

Before continuing, select the PEQ and delete it by using the Delete or Backspace key on your computer keyboard.

DYNAMIC PROCESSOR

Another incredibly useful device for mixing is the compressor. Initially designed to control the dynamics of sound on movie soundstages, the compressor has become an indispensable tool in audio production.

To begin, select the Dr. OctoRex and create the Comp-01 from the Create > Effects menu.

COMP-01: AUTO MAKEUP GAIN COMPRESSOR

The Comp-01 is a compressor used to control the dynamics, or amplitude, of a sound by making louder sounds softer and softer sounds louder. The overall processed signal is more even and often results in individual instruments' having more presence and longer sustain. It can help smooth out an erratic performance where the artist is playing too loudly or too softly. It can also be used to add punch to drums or change the overall perception of loudness of an entire mix. However, compression is one of the more difficult processes to use because it's hard to discern what is really happening to the signal (unlike an EQ, which is quite apparent).

Fig. 9-3

Threshold

This parameter controls at what dB the compressor circuit will start compressing.

Ratio

This parameter effects how much compression is applied to the signal. For example, a ratio of 2:1 (two to one) means for every 2 dB the signal exceeds the threshold, the circuit will output 1 dB.

Attack

This parameter affects how quickly the compressor starts working. Moved to the left, it's at its fastest setting, causing the compressor to work immediately. Moving it to the right will cause the compressor to delay before operation.

Release

The Release parameter controls how long the compressor will continue to process the signal. Moved to the left, the release is very fast, whereas moving to the right causes the circuit to sustain for longer periods.

In Use

Instead of blindly turning knobs and hoping for the best, the following approach is a great starting point when using compression.

- Start by turning the Ratio knob all the way to the right, its highest setting.
- Next, bring the Threshold to its lowest setting (to the left). This will cause the compressor to react fully.
- Next, set both the Attack and Release knobs to their fastest settings (to the left).
- Press Run on the Dr. OctoRex.

You'll notice that the sound quality may seem distorted, but ignore this for a moment. Your focus should be on the rhythm of the sound. What I like to listen for is the bounce.

- Start by increasing Attack, which lets more of the original transient through before compressing. This will result in an audible snap to the drums. Set the Attack knob to 91.
- Next, turn the Release setting all the way up. You'll hear the signal is getting squashed and sounding lifeless, as the release isn't fully resetting. Move Release toward a faster setting. Set it to 38.
- Now that you've found the rhythm, you can focus on the quality. Bring the Ratio setting back to 4:1 and raise the Threshold setting to 54.
- Bypass the compressor by moving the switch in the upper left corner. This will help you hear the compression by comparing it to the original signal.
- Reengage the compressor and adjust Threshold down for a more compressed sound.

This entire process is completely subjective, so feel free to explore different settings. However, I urge you to follow the setup procedure when setting up the compressor, as it will help you find the right balance of rhythm and sustain.

Delete the compressor before continuing.

DISTORTION

Distortion has been a staple for rock and roll, but has also infiltrated into almost all genres of high-energy music. The most common distortion we know and love is from guitar amps. Reason 6 now has dedicated amp simulators from the Line 6 Pod series. You'll investigate these processors later in the chapter, in the Specialty Effects section.

For now, let's explore two other distortion units, the D-11 Foldback Distortion and the Scream 4 Sound Destruction Unit.

Start by selecting the Dr. OctoRex and creating a D-11 from the Create > Effects menu.

D-11 FOLDBACK DISTORTION

The D-11 provides the typical array of distortion effects and is extremely simple and versatile to use, with adjustable Amount and Foldback settings.

Fig. 9-4

Amount

This controls how much distortion is added to the signal. Moving to the left subtly decreases the distortion, whereas moving right increases the distortion.

Foldback

This parameter controls what type of distortion is in use.

Moving to the left will offer soft clipping, with a softer, rounded effect.

At the twelve o'clock position (centered), the signal has morphed into hard clipping, offering a harder sound as the waveform has been squared off at the top.

Moving farther to the right causes the center of the frequency spectrum to fold in half, resulting in extreme sonic destruction.

Delete the D-11 before continuing.

SCREAM 4 SOUND DESTRUCTION UNIT

The Scream 4 is sound destruction unit that provides a vast array of distortion effects, including analog, digital, tape emulation, and ring modulation. From subtle tape compression to the sound of fully blown speaker, this effects processor will inspire you to create extraordinary sounds. It has presets that can be loaded from the Browse Patch section.

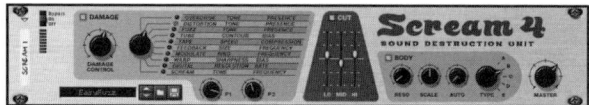

Fig. 9-5

Start by selecting the Dr. OctoRex and create the Scream from the Create > Effects menu.

Hit Run on the Dr. OctoRex and explore the sound-mangling capabilities.

The interface is broken up into three sections: Damage, Cut, and Body.

Damage

Damage offers ten different types of distortions. The Selector knob permits quick navigation. To the right of the distortion types, you find two columns of variable parameters, which differ depending on which distortion chosen. The knobs P 1 and P 2 offer control over their respective column.

The Damage control knob increases the amount of the effect as you turn it to the right.

Cut

Cut has three equalization bands (Lo, Mid, and Hi), each with a range of −18 to +18 dB.

Body

The body circuit places the sound in a resonant body.

There are five resonant bodies, selectable by type (A through F).

The Resonance knob increases the resonance of the selected body

The Scale knob increases the size of the resonance body.

The Auto knob controls the amount of the envelope follower that's connected to the Scale parameter. When enabled, the louder the signal, the higher the Scale parameter is adjusted.

The Scream processor is a sophisticated sonic destructor and worthy of additional examination. I highly recommend reading the Reason manual to learn more about this processor. Also, you'll be exploring it a bit more in the advanced routing chapter later in this book.

Delete the Scream before moving to the next section.

PHASE

A phaser is an effects processor that creates a series of peaks and troughs in the frequency spectrum, which are modulated by an LFO, creating a sweeping effect.

PH-90 PHASER

The PH-90 is a classic phaser effects production unit that shifts portions of audio out of phase and mixes is it back in with the original signal, causing a sweeping sound. This is a typical guitar or pad effect that creates movement in the sound.

Fig. 9-6

Start by selecting the Dr. OctoRex and create the PH-90 from the Create > Effects menu.

Hit Run on the Dr. OctoRex and explore the phaser in action.

The PH-90 is a four-stage phaser with a syncable LFO section.

Frequency

The Frequency knob sets the frequency of the first stage of the phaser. The other stages will adjust based on the initial frequency setting.

Split

The Split knob adjusts the distance between each stage of the phaser.

Width

The Width knob changes the width of each phase. Increasing this parameter leads to a more hollow sound.

LFO

The LFO section offers control over the frequency of the phaser. Rate controls the speed; LFO Freq. Mod controls the depth. Selecting the LFO Sync button will cause the rate to lock to the sequencer tempo and offers time division settings from four bars to a thirty-second note.

Feedback

Increases the amount of the effect, similar to resonance.

Delete the PH-90 before continuing.

TIME-BASED EFFECTS

Time-based effects are often used in conjunction with FX sends on the mixer. This type of effect is best employed with a mix of both the original, or dry, signal and the processed, or wet, signal. When using the effects via the FX sends, the effects processors will automatically be set to fully wet. It is possible to use time-based effects as insert effects. When this method is engaged, you can use the Dry/Wet knob to balance the processed and unprocessed signal to your desired taste.

REVERBERATION

Reverberation, or reverb, is one of the most widely used effects. It is essentially a room modeler, which imparts the characteristics of a room to an instrument or recorded signal and gives the impression that the tracks were recorded in the same space, offering a bit of sonic glue.

I'm a fan of reverb, but often find that less is more.

RV-7 DIGITAL REVERB

The RV-7 Digital Reverb is a simple yet effective reverb with algorithms ranging from rooms to halls, and special effects such as Echo and Gate.

Fig. 9-7

Start by selecting the Dr. OctoRex and create the RV-7 from the Create > Effects menu.

Hit Run on the Dr. OctoRex and explore the reverb algorithms.

Algorithms

The RV-7 offers ten different reverb algorithms, selectable from the up and down arrows located at the left of the interface.

HALL
A large smooth hall.

LARGE HALL
A larger hall with noticeable predelay.

HALL 2
A large hall with a brighter tone.

LARGE ROOM
A large room with hard early reflections.

MEDIUM ROOM
A smaller room with softer reflections.

SMALL ROOM
A small room, similar to a drum booth.

GATED
A reverb with an abrupt cutoff. Think Phil Collins.

LOW-DENSITY
A low-intensity algorithm with individual echoes.

STEREO ECHOES
An echo effect that alternates between sides of the stereo field.

PAN ROOM
A similar effect to the Stereo Echoes, with a softer sound.

Size

Adjusts the size of the algorithm. The middle position is the default setting of the selected algorithm.

Decay

Tailors the length of the reverb effect.

Damp

Cuts the high-frequency content of the algorithm.

Dry/Wet

This parameter adjusts the balance between the dry, unaffected signal and the wet, processed signal. If you are using the RV-7 as an insert, adjust this knob to get the correct balance. If you are using the RV-7 from an FX send off the mixer, then this parameter should be set to full wet.

Delete the RV-7 before continuing.

RV-7000 ADVANCED REVERB

The RV-7000 Advanced Reverb is a high-quality reverb with nine algorithms. The palette of available presets is vast, but further editing can also be accomplished by utilizing the remote programmer. In addition, there is also an EQ and Gate section that allows you to dial in your sound with even greater control.

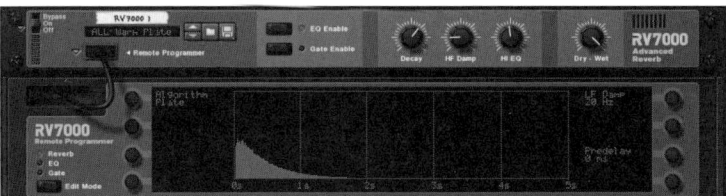

Fig. 9-8

Start by selecting the Dr. OctoRex and create the RV-7000 Advanced Reverb from the Create > Effects menu.

Hit Run on the Dr. OctoRex and explore the reverb algorithms.

The main interface offers basic controls over decay, damping, and high EQ.

The patch browser allows you to find presets quickly through the categories ALL, AMB, DRM, EFX, EKO, and VOX.

Further examination reveals that nine algorithms are used to create the presets. To edit and adjust these parameters, you'll need to engage the remote programmer, located on the lower left side of the main interface. Select the left-facing triangle and it will face down and engage the programmer.

On each side of the graphical interface, you will find four knobs (eight total). Depending on the algorithm, all or some of the knobs will be assigned to parameters.

To change algorithms, turn the knob on the upper left corner, which currently says Algorithm—Echo. As you scroll through the nine algorithms, notice how the other knobs change.

Algorithms

The RV-7000 offers nine different reverb and echo algorithms selectable from the up and down arrows located at the left of the interface.

SMALL SPACE
Creates a small space.

ROOM
Emulates a room with adjustable shape and wall character.

HALL
An emulation of a hall.

ARENA
Emulates a large arena, with predelay with left, right, and center reverbs.

PLATE
Faithful emulation of a classic plate reverb.

SPRING
Re-creates the sounds of a classic spring reverb, often found on guitar amps.

ECHO
A syncable echo effect with gradually diffusing echoes.

MULTI TAP
A four-tap delay offering temp sync.

REVERSE
Delays the dry sound until after the reverb, creating a pseudo reverse effect.

As each different algorithm has unique editing parameters, it is beyond the scope of this book to discuss each algorithm's set of parameters. Feel free to explore. For more information on these parameters, please consult the manual.

Now, select the EKO Space Echo 2 preset.

EQ

The RV-7000 offers a two-band equalizer to shape the sound of the reverb. To engage the EQ, make sure you have the EQ Enable button selected on the main interface. To access the EQ parameters, select the Edit Mode button, found on the left side of the remote programmer.

The left side of the graphical interface shows a low-shelf EQ. The second knob adjusts the frequency of the shelf EQ, whereas the first adjusts the gain.

A shelf EQ either boosts or cuts all frequencies from the low-frequency selection on down. For example, the Space Echo 2 preset has its low frequency set to 719 Hz. By scrolling the Gain knob up and down, you'll find that all frequencies from 719 Hz and down are either boosted or cut.

On the right side of the graphical interface, you'll see a parametric EQ, complete with Grain, Frequency, and Q.

Gate

To engage the gate, make sure the Gate Enable button is selected on the main interface. To edit the Gate parameters, select the Gate mode on the right side of the remote programmer.

Threshold

This parameter works when the Trig source is set to Audio. It determines the level at which the gate will open, allowing the reverb to trigger. By raising the threshold, you can set the gate to react only to the loudest signals. All other signals will be ignored.

Decay Mod

This parameter modulates the reverb decay time. At a low setting, the reverb decay will follow its normal length, which may have the reverb decay present the next time the gate is opened. With higher settings, the decay becomes dynamic and will cut the length of the decay when the gate closes, ensuring that with each new opening of the gate, a new reverb sound with decay starts.

Trig Source

Selecting Audio allows the gate to follow the audio signal. Selecting MIDI/CV forces the gate to open based on MIDI and CV signals. You'll explore this feature more in chapter 11.

High Pass

The High Pass filter will cause the gate to ignore bass frequencies, as only high frequencies will pass through and trigger the gate.

Attack

Determines how long it takes for the gate to open after a signal has breached the threshold.

Hold

This parameter is only active when the Trig source is set to Audio. It controls how long the gate will stay open after an audio signal has triggered the threshold.

Release

Controls the length of time it takes for the gate to close after the Hold parameter.

Reverse Gate

Here's a cool reverse gate reverb patch.

Start by increasing the Decay and HF Damp to full right.

Next, select the Reverse algorithm.

Set the following parameters:

• Length: 16/16
• Density: 98
• Tempo Sync: On
• Rev Dry/Wet: 95

Select the EQ mode and set the following parameters.

• Low Gain: −18
• Low Frequency: 670
• Param Gain: +11
• Param Freq: 1,414 Hz (1.4 kHz)
• Param Q: 1.0
• Select the Gate mode and set the following parameters.
• Threshold: −1.2 dB

- Decay Mod: 100 percent
- Trig Source: Audio
- High Pass: 2,968 Hz
- Attack: 3 ms
- Hold: 52 ms
- Release: 290 ms

If you like the patch and wish to recall it again, select the disk icon next the Patch Browser button and name it RevGateVerb.

Delete the RV-7000 before continuing.

DELAY

Delays are another popular time-based effect used by both audio engineers and musicians alike. Delays and echoes have become a major part of just about every genre of music. From creating a subtle slap-back echo on vocals to extreme syncopated rhythms, the delay effect has changed the way we produce music.

DDL-1 DIGITAL DELAY LINE

The DDL-1 Digital Delay Line is a monophonic delay (with stereo output) that permits the programming of precision delay lines. The unit can be configured to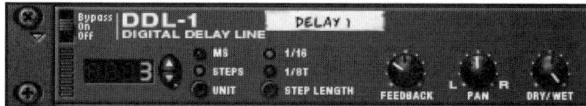

Fig. 9-9

work in Free mode with parameters set to work in milliseconds. It can also be synchronized with the Reason sequencer with up to sixteen steps at various set lengths.

Start by selecting the Dr. OctoRex and create the DDL-1 Digital Delay Line from the Create > Effects menu.

Hit Run on the Dr. OctoRex and explore the Delay parameters.

Unit

The Unit selection toggles between the tempo-based Step mode and the free-running milliseconds (ms) mode.

Delay Time

The Delay Time displays the note value steps with values of one to sixteen steps, or in milliseconds from 1 to 2,000 ms (2 seconds).

Step Length

Dictates the value of the step in either eighth notes or eighth-note triplets.

Feedback

This controls the number of repeats. When Feedback is set to full left, it will create a single echo. As you increase the feedback, the number of delays will increase. Setting Feedback to full right creates an infinite loop where the sound of the delay continues indefinitely, even after the source has stopped.

Pan

This controls the delayed signals panoramic spectrum.

Wet/Dry

The Wet/Dry knob controls the balance between the dry, unprocessed signal and the wet, processed signal. When using the DDL-1 with an FX send, set this parameter to full wet for best results.

Delete the DDL-1 before continuing.

THE ECHO

New to Reason 6, The Echo hails back to the days of analog tape delays, with some additional unique sound-shaping parameters. The unit features several presets that are definitely worth investigating.

Start by selecting the Dr. OctoRex **Fig. 9-10** and create The Echo from the Create > Effects menu.

Hit Run on the Dr. OctoRex and explore the Delay parameters.

The Echo is broken up into six segments; Mode, Delay, Feedback, Color, Modulation, and Output.

Mode

The Mode section allows you to select among three different ways of passing signal to the other sections.

NORMAL

This is the standard setting used for inserts and FX send setups. Its input continuously feeds the rest of the parameters of the delay.

TRIGGERED

This mode engages the delay effect only when the Trig button is pressed. A typical use for this is for momentary delays on specific sounds, such as every third snare hit or specific words.

ROLL

This mode allows the signal to pass until engaged by sliding the switch to the right. As you slide the switch, the dry signal is lowered while the feedback is increased. It's designed for a rolling or freezing effect, often attributed to glitch and stutter sound effects.

Delay

This section controls the time of the delay and offers control over Stereo parameters.

TIME

The parameter sets the delay time from a range of 1 to 1,000 ms. When the Sync button is engaged, it synchronizes with the song tempo and offers a range of tempo divisions from 1/128 to half notes.

OFFSET R

This parameter shifts the right delay up to 1,000 ms or half notes, creating a wider stereo delay effect.

KEEP PITCH

As you switch between different times, you'll notice the pitch is slightly changed. This sound is often heard with tape delays such as the Roland Space Echo and gives an amount of realism to the sound. However, the Keep Pitch button allows you to switch between different times without the pitch transitions.

SYNC

Engages the delay from free-running to tempo sync.

PAN

Controls the pan position of the delay.

PING-PONG

When engaged, will cause each repeat of the delay to alternate between left and right. The Pan knob determines the stereo width of the panned delays. A full left setting causes the delay to start on the left, whereas a full right setting causes the delay to start on the right.

Feedback

This section controls the amount and density of the feedback.

FEEDBACK

The Feedback setting controls the number of repeats. Full left results in a single repeat. The three o'clock position will cause the effect to continue indefinitely. Increasing the feedback full right will result in distortion, a common tape delay effect.

OFFSET R

This parameter is bipolar, meaning that at the middle position it's not affecting the signal. By shifting left or right, the feedback on the right side of the delay will increase or decrease, causing a pseudo stereo effect. This parameter works well with the R Offset parameter in the Delay section.

DIFFUSION

Diffusion will thicken up or smear the sound of the repeats. The Amount controls how much diffusion is introduced; the Spread will widen the diffusion in the stereo field.

Color

This section offers control over the delay distortion and filter effects.

DRIVE

The Drive selects the amount of the selected distortion.

TYPE

This toggle allows you to switch among various types of distortion.

- Lim: Offers the sound of tape compression (limiting)
- OVDR: Offers the sound of analog overdrive distortion.
- DIST: A thicker, heavier distortion than overdrive
- TUBE: Offers tube distortion

FILTER

The Filter section offers control over the resonant Band Pass filter.

FREQ

Controls the Band Pass filter's cutoff frequency.

RESO

Controls the resonance, or emphasis, of the cutoff frequency.

Modulation

This section controls the pitch of the delay. It offers an LFO and can vary the stereo image.

ENV
This bipolar knob has no effect when set in the middle position. Moving the knob to the right causes the pitch to increase, whereas moving it to the right will cause a decrease in pitch.

WOBBLE
This parameter creates the random sound of wow and flutter associated with analog tape.

LFO
The LFO modulates the left and right channels independently, causing a moving stereo spread.

RATE
Controls the speed of the LFO.

AMOUNT
Controls the amount of the LFO.

Output

DRY/WET
Controls the balance between the unprocessed signal and the processed delayed signal.

DUCKING
This parameter causes the delay to be suppressed until the input signal drops, allowing the delay to increase.

Breakout Jacks

The breakout jacks located on the rear of the device allow one or more effects to be inserted into the feedback loop.

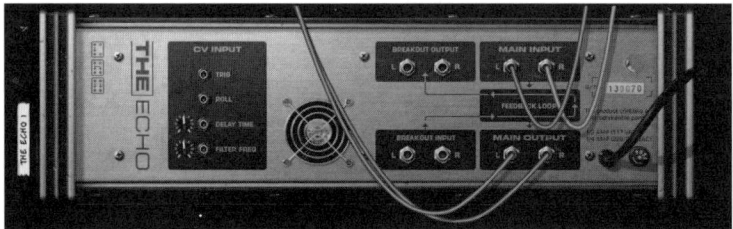

Fig. 9-11

As you can see, this Holy Grail delay offers an unprecedented amount of control over the delayed signal. I highly recommend exploring the presets. A lot of great effects can be created, especially when using the breakout jacks.

Delete The Echo before continuing.

CHORUS/FLANGER

Chorus and Flange are two effects often attributed to signal processing, but at their core, are true time-based effects. Essentially these are delay effects with very short delay times and modulation capabilities.

Interestingly, running two synchronized tape machines playing the same signal at the same time created the original flange effect. The tape operator would place his hand on one of the tape reels or flanges to slow down one tape machine, causing one machine to go slightly out of time. He would then do the same on the second tape machine, manually controlling the rate of the flange. To this day, I have yet to hear a flange effect from a processor sound as good as the original, manual analog tape flange.

CF-101

The CF-101 Chorus/Flanger creates a combined chorus/flange effect. It's a typical effect used to create movement and motion by delaying small amounts of signal and modulating the rate of the built in LFO.

Fig. 9-12

Start by selecting the Dr. OctoRex and create the CF-101 from the Create > Effects menu.

Hit Run on the Dr. OctoRex and explore the parameters.

The controls include Delay and Feedback, as well as Rate and Modulation amounts (with sequencer synchronization). The unit also features a Send mode that sets the unit to either Insert or Aux Send mode.

Delete the CF-101 before continuing.

UNISON

This is a typical feature found on analog synthesizers, where two or more oscillators are doubled and slightly detuned, creating a thicker sound.

UN-16

The UN-16 is a device that emulates the Unison mode on a synthesizer, which provides an effect of multiple voices slightly detuned.

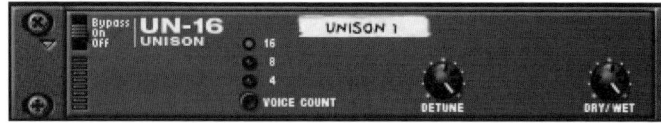

Fig. 9-13

Copying the incoming signal and then slightly delaying and pitching the individual voices create this effect. The unit has settings of four, eight, and sixteen voices with Detune and Dry/Wet controls.

The UN-16 doesn't do much with the Dr. OctoRex drum loop currently selected. It really shines with synthesizers and is worth investigating. Simply create a new synthesizer (e.g., the Subtractor) and explore.

FILTER EFFECTS

Filters effects are often associated with analog synthesizers and offer great sound design potential. By now, you should be familiar with the parameters of the filter.

ECF-42 ENVELOPE CONTROLLED FILTER

The ECF-42 Envelope Controlled Filter is a multimode resonant filter designed to create filtered envelope effects.

It features three filter types: 12 dB Band Pass, 12 dB Low Pass, and 24 dB Low Pass. The unit is designed to work with pattern devices or can otherwise

Fig. 9-14

be triggered with a MIDI signal. Controls include Frequency Cutoff, Resonance, Envelope Amount, Velocity, and the standard envelope controls Attack, Decay, Sustain, and Release.

BV512 DIGITAL VOCODER

The BV512 Digital Vocoder is a fantastic sound manipulation tool. By using two different instruments or sound inputs (Modulator and Carrier), you can create a number of

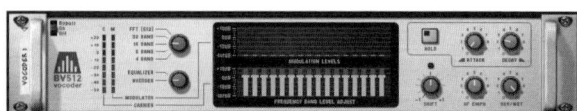

Fig. 9-15

effects, including FFT Equalization and talking drums or synthesizers. The famous Robot Voice effect can be achieved easily by using this device.

It features five different modes ranging from 4 to 512 bands. Controls include Band Selection, Equalizer/Vocoder Mode, Modulation Levels, Frequency Band Levels Adjustment, Hold, Attack, Decay, Frequency Shift, High-Frequency Emphasis, and Dry/Wet.

For additional information on the BV512, see the Advanced Routing chapter.

M-CLASS EFFECTS

The M-Class Effects suite consists of four individual processors that are designed to help finalize your mix and are an excellent choice for the master inserts on the mixer in Reason. The four processors are the M-Class Equalizer, M-Class Stereo Imager, M-Class Compressor, and M-Class Maximizer.

M-CLASS EQUALIZER

The M-Class Equalizer is a mastering grade equalizer that features two bands of parametric equalization, two bands of shelf equalization (High and Low) and a Low Cut Filter that removes frequencies below 30 Hz.

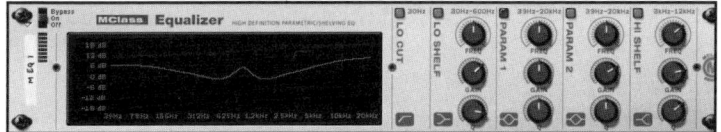

Fig. 9-16

The unit features a graphic window that shows frequency curves and displays controls for Frequency, Gain, and Q settings. The unit is designed to be a mastering equalizer on the stereo bus of the mixer, but is also extremely effective at equalizing frequencies of single instruments.

Start by selecting the Dr. OctoRex and create the M-Class EQ from the Create > Effects menu.

Hit Run on the Dr. OctoRex and explore the EQ parameters.

To enable any of the five bands on the equalizer, you must engage the button on the upper left of each band.

Lo

The Lo band cuts all frequencies from 30 Hz down. There are no additional controls, as this is a low-frequency filter, typically used to remove low-frequency rumble.

High and Low Shelf

Shelf EQs are great, general-purpose EQs that either boost or cut frequencies below or above the selected frequency. The Q function changes the slope of the shelving curve.

The Lo band has a range of 30 to 600 Hz.

The Hi band has a range of 3 to 12 kHz.

Parametric

The two bands of parametric EQ will boost or cut frequencies around the selected frequency. For more information on parametric EQ, see the PEQ-2 section earlier in this chapter.

The two bands offer a range of 39 to 20 kHz.

The best way to learn about this processor is to experiment with settings while listening to the results.

Delete the M-Class Equalizer before continuing.

M-CLASS STEREO IMAGER

The M-Class Stereo Imager is a dual-band stereo processor that splits the signal into two frequency bands and permits discrete control over the perception of width of both high- and low-frequency bands. This is a fantastic unit to use for focusing low frequencies while widening high-frequency content.

Fig. 9-17

Start by selecting the Dr. OctoRex and create the M-Class Stereo Imager from the Create > Effects menu.

Hit Run on the Dr. OctoRex and explore the Stereo Imaging parameters.

To set up the M-Class Stereo Imager, use the solo Hi and Lo band to isolate each frequency band. I usually start with the low-frequency band soloed and adjust the crossover frequency between 200 and 400 Hz.

Once the crossover frequency is set, I adjust the Lo frequency knob from the middle (original) setting toward the Mono setting.

After the Lo section is set, I solo the Hi band and adjust the Hi frequency knob from the middle (original) toward the Wide setting.

Moving the Lo spectrum toward Mono will focus the low frequencies, giving them more punch and clarity. Moving the Hi spectrum toward Wide will widen the depth of the stereo field for the higher frequencies.

Typically, this processor is used on a stereo mix to add punch and clarity. I find that a less-is-more attitude works best when adjusting it. Use is completely subjective, so let your ears guide you.

If you tab to the rear of the interface, you'll find an additional set of outputs with a Hi/Lo band switch that routes the selected option to the separate outputs, allowing the device to be used as a crossover filter.

Delete the M-Class Stereo Imager before continuing.

M-CLASS COMPRESSOR

The M-Class Compressor is a stereo compressor featuring side-chain input. Not unlike the Comp-01 compressor that controls dynamics and the perception of loudness, the M-Class Compressor adds some fantastic features, including a Soft Knee setting, side-chain input, and adaptive release. The side-chain input can be used for ducking effects and de-essing when used in conjunction together with an equalizer. The adaptive release allows for more transparent sound in your production.

Fig. 9-18

Start by selecting the Dr. OctoRex and create the M-Class Compressor from the Create > Effects menu.

Hit Run on the Dr. OctoRex and explore the compressor's parameters.

Following the same procedure discussed in the section on the Comp-01, set up the compressor to taste. You'll find usable results, and with the addition of the Input and Output gain controls you'll be able to dial in as much compression as deemed necessary.

The Soft Knee button changes the shape of the compressor to a softer slope, generally used for vocals or stereo bus compression, and offers more transparency from the effect.

The Adapt Release button makes the release of the compressor active, which will self-adjust based on the signal routed through the compressor.

There is a side-chain input on the rear of the compressor, which causes the compressor to react to a secondary source. A popular effect is to side-chain a bass from a kick drum. We'll check out the process in the advanced routing chapter.

You may also use an EQ'd signal into the side-chain input to create a frequency-dependent compressor or de-esser, great for controlling sibilance.

To be honest, since Reason added the M-Class Compressor, I've stopped using the Comp-01, as it's quite versatile and sounds amazing.

Delete the M-Class Compressor before continuing.

M-CLASS MAXIMIZER

The M-Class Maximizer is a look-ahead limiter that allows the maximization of sound levels without digital clipping. The look-ahead function gives a 4 ms period of time, so the device is able to see into the future and prevent signal amplitudes from exceeding 0 dB. The unit also features a Soft Clip option, which not only prevents digital clipping but also introduces a warm, harmonic distortion.

Fig. 9-19

The M-Class Maximizer is your secret weapon for getting your tracks LOUD! It's typically used on a stereo bus and is often last in the signal chain.

It allows you to increase the overall perception of loudness without clipping. The unit features a 4 ms look-ahead feature that provides brick wall limiting. This allows you to increase the gain while preventing digital distortion.

Start by selecting the Dr. OctoRex and create the M-Class Maximizer from the Create > Effects menu.

Hit Run on the Dr. OctoRex and explore the maximizing parameters.

With limiting turned on, you'll find a few settings worth exploring.

Look-ahead works best with the attack set to Fast and the output set to 0 dB. This setup will result in true brick wall limiting.

With the attack set to Mid or Slow, you can use the Soft Clip section to prevent digital clipping. The Soft Clip offers warm harmonic distortion, which we find pleasing to our ears. Increase the amount of the Soft Clip to engage the brick-wall limiter and prevent digital clipping.

This is another amazing processor that really helps with polishing the sound of your tracks.

SPECIALTY EFFECTS

The Specialty Effects section covers some of the newer effects introduced in Reason 6.

LINE 6 AMPS

The Line 6 amp processors are licensed from Line 6 and feature amp and cabinet modeling technology. If fact, if you are an owner of a Line 6 product with USB, you may use amp models available from the device within the Line 6 Amps. This opens up the sonic possibilities.

Fig. 9-20

I didn't include the Line 6 amps in the Distortion section as the devices offer far more than simple distortion. These devices delve into physical modeling of guitar and bass amplifiers and cabinets.

Amp and Cabinet Models

The current offerings of amp and cabinet models available from within Reason 6 include:

1964 Blackface Lux

This model is based on the 1968 Fender Deluxe Reverb. It's a versatile amp, offering clean tones to subtle crunch, a great amp for blues and pop.

1X12 1964 BLACKFACE LUX
The speaker cabinet is a single combo cabinet featuring a single 12-inch Celestion speaker.

1968 Plexi Lead 100

This model is based on the 1968 Marshall Super Lead and is considered one of the quintessential amps used for classic rock tones. It has excellent dynamic range and rich crunch.

4X12 1968 GREEN 25S
The speaker cabinet is based on a 4x12 cabinet fitted with four 12-inch Celestion Greenback speakers.

2001 Treadplate Dual

This model is based on a Mesa Boogie Dual Rectifier. This offers a modern tone capable of blistering distortion.

4X12 2001 TREADPLATE
The cabinet model is based on a classic Mesa Boogie 4 x12 with Celestion V30 speakers.

1974 Rock Classic

This model is based on the Ampeg SVT Bass Amp, a 300-watt monster capable of deafening amplitude. It's the top choice of many rock bassists.

8X10 CLASSIC
The cabinet model is based on the infamous 8x10 Classic, a cabinet with a whopping eight 10-inch speakers. Needless to say, it offers a massive sound.

1968 Flip Top

This model is based on the Ampeg B-15 Portaflex, a 25-watt combo amp often used in recording studios.

1X15 FLIP TOP

The cabinet is model is based on a closed-back design with a single 15-inch speaker. It offers a tight, solid bass tone.

Tone Controls

Both amps offer similar tone controls. The drive controls the input gain that, when increased, adds crunch and distortion to the signal.

The guitar amp offers Bass, Middle, and Treble controls for shaping the frequency range of the amps.

The bass amp offers Bass, Lo Mid, Hi Mid, and Treble for tone control. The Lo and Hi midsection gives excellent control over the midrange of bass instruments.

The Presence on the guitar amp adds high frequency, to help the signal cut through in dense mixes.

Both amps have a Volume knob to control the output of the amp.

The guitar amp offers pedal controls for volume and wah-wah, which can be interfaced via CV input or by MIDI controllers. They are designed to work with foot pedals for volume swells and wah-wah filter effects.

The bass amp offers a built-in compressor to help thicken up the sound.

Presets and Patches

All guitar and bass amps and cabinets are available in both the Line 6 Guitar and Line 6 Bass effect processors. Furthermore, you can interchange any of the cabinets and amps, giving you an immense tonal palette.

The presets available from the patch browser are designed to work with their respective devices (meaning you can't open a guitar preset in the bass amp or vice versa).

Final Thought

You can explore the amp modelers with real instruments or samplers and synthesizers. The Dr. OctoRex also offers wide selection of guitar loops, ripe for experimentation. There's also nothing wrong with running your drums through them to experiment with distorted beats!

PULVERISER DEMOLITION

The Pulveriser is a compression, distortion, and filter effects processor with a built-in LFO and envelope

Fig. 9-21

follower. Capable of subtle processing to complete decimation, it's a versatile processor suitable for any style of music or sound design.

A unique attribute to this processor is the ability to change the routing. You have the choice of Comp > Dist> Filter or Filter > Comp > Dist, located on the lower left of the interface.

Squash

The Squash parameter controls the compressor's threshold, ratio, and makeup gain from a single dial. There is a dedicated release to help with further shaping the sound.

Dirt

The Dirt parameter controls the level of distortion, while the Tone knob controls a dedicated low-pass filter. Moved all the way to the right, the filter is open, allowing all frequencies to pass.

Filter

In the center section of the interface lies the multimode filter. The different modes offered include Bypass, Low Pass 24, LP 12+ Notch, Band Pass, High Pass, and Combo.

BYPASS
This allows the signal to pass through the Filter section unaffected.

LOW PASS 24
This is a classic Moog-style filter with a 24 dB per octave slope.

LP 12+ NOTCH
This unique filter contains a low-pass filter with a 12 dB slope and combines it with a notch filter. The cutoff frequency controls both filters simultaneously. The result is a uniquely animated sound.

BAND PASS
This is a Band Pass filter, similar to the one on the Subtractor. It's like combining a Low Pass with a High Pass.

HIGH PASS
This is a 12 dB per octave slope similar to the Subtractor. A High Pass filter lets high frequencies pass through. Also known as a Low Cut filter.

COMB
The Comb filter setting is similar to the Comb+ filter found on the Malstrom.

FREQUENCY
Controls the filter's cutoff frequency.

PEAK

This controls the filter's resonance or emphasis.

Tremor

The Tremor acts as the LFO section on the Pulveriser and can be routed to either the Filter or Amplifier section. Routing is done by two bipolar knobs on either side of the Tremor section.

RATE

Rate controls the speed of the LFO. It offers a wide range, able to generate frequencies in the audible range. The Rate section can also be modulated by the envelope follower.

SYNC

This button allows the tremor to sync to the global tempo of the sequencer.

WAVEFORM

The Waveform section offers a choice of nine classic and specialty waves.

SPREAD

This unique effect doubles the LFO's output and shifts the phase of one side by 180 degrees. The result is like a rotary speaker simulation, where the sound shifts between the left and right sides of the stereo spectrum.

LAG

The Lag processor smoothes out the shaper edges of the LFO waveforms. Works well with square and sawtooth waveforms. The sine wave has no effect, as it is already smooth in nature.

The Follower

The Follower section features an envelope follower, which analyzes audio and outputs a control signal that may be routed to the filter or to the Tremor's Rate section via bipolar knobs to the left of the interface.

TRIG

The trigger button permits manual control over the envelope follower. By clicking and holding, you can cause the envelope to be triggered independent of the incoming audio signal.

THRESHOLD

This sets the level in which the envelope follower will react. At a low setting, it reacts to any incoming audio. With a higher setting, it will only react to higher audio signals or from the Trigger button.

ATTACK AND RELEASE

This knobs controls how long it takes for the envelope to react after the signal crosses the threshold and how long it takes for it to return to its 0 setting.

Blend

The Blend knob allows you to blend the processed signal with the dry signal, similar to most time-based effects. This offers the capability of parallel compression without having to create a separate channel.

Presets and Patches

The Pulveriser ships with its own bank of presets and is worth perusing. A great way to work with the processor is to find a preset and modify it. It's a great processor for any material, but really shines on drums and synthesizers.

ALLIGATOR FILTER GATE

Another new effect offered in Reason 6, the Alligator Filter Gate is a triple gate processor that injects a multitude of rhythmic effects on to the sound source.

Fig. 9-22

The unit contains three lines of resonant filters with Drive, Phase, Delay, Pan, and Volume controls, all controlled by gate signals derived from the on-board pattern generator or via MIDI or CV-Gate inputs.

Signal Flow

The Alligator is typically set up as an insert effect and can accept mono or stereo inputs; it always outputs in stereo.

Following the signal flow diagram, let's trace the signal from its input to the output.

- From the input, the signal is broken into three separate lines and passed on to the Amplifier section.

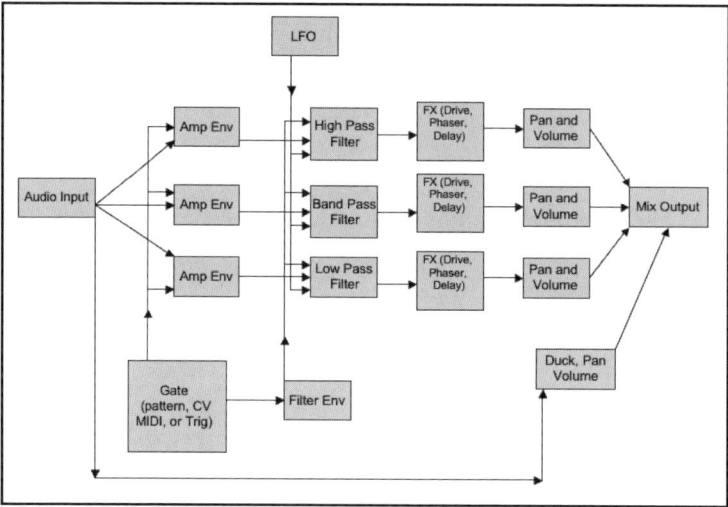

Fig. 9-23

- A gate signal is sent via the on-board pattern generator, MIDI note, or CV/Gate signal to both the audio amplifier with envelope and the Filter envelope.

- With the audio amplifier triggered from the gate and shaped by its envelope, the signal is passed through one of three filters (High, Band, or Low Pass). There are dedicated Frequency Cutoff, Resonance, LFO Amount, and Envelope Amount controls.

- From the Filter section, the signal passes through the effects. Each line has dedicated Drive, Phase, and Delay parameters.

- From the Effects section, the signal passes through the Pan and Volume section. Each line also has dedicated Pan and Volume controls.

- Additionally, a copy of the original, unprocessed signal is sent from the input to the Dry Processing section, which includes Ducking, Pan, and Volume control.

- The processed and dry signals are combined via a mixer and sent out of the unit. The final stage has a Master Volume Control output.

THE INTERFACE

The Alligator is broken up into four sections, with the Global parameters across the bottom.

Pattern

The pattern generator offers sophisticated control over gate signals that are routed to the Gate section of the effect. Each pattern contains information for each of the three Gate sections, which control the High Band and Low-Pass filter sections.

ON

This turns on the Pattern section when you want to use the on-board pattern generator. To trigger manually or use a different pattern generator, such as the Matrix or Redrum, this should be turned off.

PATTERN

The pattern selection picks one of sixty-four available patterns. To see a visual representation of them, consult the Reason 6 manual.

RESOLUTION

The Resolution knob selects a division of time based on the global tempo. The range runs from an eighth to a thirty-second note.

SHIFT

The Shift knob allows the pattern to start early or late. It permits to sixteen shift positions, with the increment of the position defined by the current selected resolution. For instance, with a resolution of sixteen and the Shift knob set to –2, the pattern would start two sixteenth notes early.

SHUFFLE

The shuffle selection will add shuffle or swing to the selected pattern. The amount of shuffle is controlled by the ReGroove mixer's Global Shuffle control.

Gate

The Gate section offers a visual feedback of the selected pattern via the three red LEDs. It also offers three manual Trigger buttons that may be used to override the current pattern.

The Gate section is tied to the Amp env and Filter env sections on the Global parameter section located at the bottom of the interface. The envelope controls allow you to shape the gate signals over time.

To manually control each of the three independent gates, turn the pattern generator off and use these MIDI notes on your controller keyboard: F#1, G#1, and A#1.

Filters and Modulation

The Filter section controls LFO amount, frequency cutoff, resonance, and filter envelope amounts for each of the three filters. The controls are identical for each of the three lines.

LFO

The LFO control is bipolar. A positive setting controls the amount of the LFO to the filter cutoff. A negative setting inverts the LFO and controls the amount sent to the filter cutoff.

FREQ
The Freq knob controls the filter cutoff of the selected filter line (High, Band, and Low).

RES
The Res knob controls the amount of resonance, or emphasis, of the filter cutoff frequency.

ENV
The Env knob controls the amount of the Global Filter envelope setting. It is bipolar, which offers the normal control at a positive setting. The negative setting inverts the envelope.

Effects

The Effects section controls the amount of drive, phaser, and delay for each of the three filter bands.

DRIVE
Drive controls the amount of distortion on each of the filter lines.

PHASER
Phaser controls the amount of the phaser effect for each filter line. The Global Phaser controls set the overall phaser settings.

DELAY
The Delay knob acts as a postfader send to the global delay. The postfader setting means that if you lower the volume of the filter line, less of the signal is sent to the Dclay parameters.

Mix Controls

Each gate/filter line has independent control over volume and pan settings.

PAN
Controls the panorama of each gate/filter line.

VOLUME
Controls the loudness of each gate/filter line.

Dry

The Dry section offers control over volume, pan, and ducking.

DUCKING
The Ducking parameter inverts the Amp env signal and applies it to the dry signal. When the Ducking setting is increased, it causes the dry signal to drop in volume when the

processed signal is present. As the processed signal drops, the dry signal is increased. Note the dry volume must be up for you to hear the ducking effect.

Master Output

The Master Output section mixes all three gate/filter lines with the dry signal. The combined output is controlled with the Master Volume knob.

Global Parameters

The Global parameters control the overall sound shaping and effects used within the effect. The controls comprise Amp Env, LFO, Filter Env, Delay, and Phaser.

AMP ENV

The Amplifier envelope is triggered from the gate signals. There are three separate amplifiers, one for each gate/filter line, but one envelope to control each separate envelope. The Amp envelope offers control over Attack (A), Decay (D), and Release (R).

LFO

The low-frequency oscillator (LFO) controls the waveform type and frequency or rate of the LFO. The LFO can either free run or be synced to the global tempo of the song.

FILTER ENV

The Filter envelope is triggered from the gate signals. There are three separate filters, one for each gate/filter line, but one envelope to control each separate envelope. The filter envelope offers control over Attack (A), Decay (D), and Release (R).

DELAY

The Delay controls the delay time with Sync, Feedback, and Pan controls.

PHASER

The phaser controls the rate and feedback of the phaser effect.

Alligator in Use

The Alligator is a powerful effect that can be used to processes individual synthesizers or drum loops, but may also prove useful as a remix tool when placed on the master output. It ships with some useful presets available from the patch browser. When it is combined with the available sixty-four patterns, you could easily spend hours tweaking it to create mind-blowing effects.

NEPTUNE PITCH ADJUSTER AND VOICE SYNTH

New to Reason 6, the Neptune offers a simple approach to a complicated task, pitch correction of vocals tracks. The unit combines a mono-phonic pitch corrector, pitch shifter, and polyphonic voice synth, to create high-quality results.

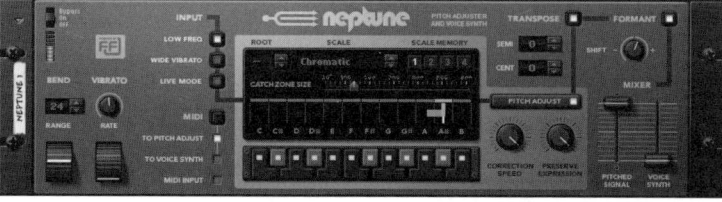

Fig. 9-24

Some uses of the effect include transparent pitch correction, hard pitch correction (T-Pain/Cher effect), octave dub, and creating backing harmonies.

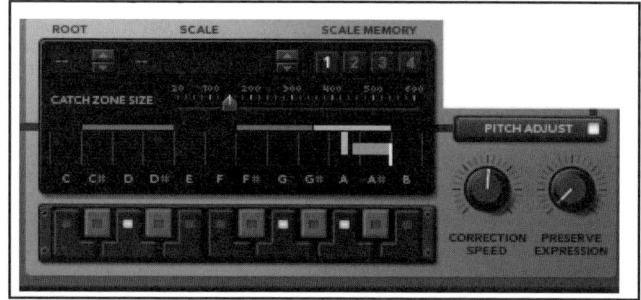

Fig. 9-25

NEPTUNE INTERFACE

Wired in series, the three main sections that make up the heart of the effect are Pitch Adjust, Transpose, and Formant.

Pitch Adjust

The main section of the Neptune is the Pitch Adjust, which you find at the center of the processor. The display shows the input pitch, target note, catch zone, and virtual keyboard.

INPUT PITCH
A yellow vertical line displays the incoming pitch of the signal above the keyboard.

TARGET NOTE
The green vertical line displays the target note of the pitch corrector.

DISTANCE AND DIRECTION
An orange horizontal line will display between the input pitch and the target note displaying the direction and distance between the two. It also gives feedback for the correction speed.

CATCH ZONE

The red horizontal bars above the selected keys on the virtual keyboard display of incoming notes fall into the pitch correction zone. When a note falls into the catch zone, it will change from red to green.

ROOT KEY AND SCALE

Above the display are options for changing the root key and scale of the pitch adjuster. By default, it's set to chromatic (shown by –), which will shift each note to the closest semitone.

To engage the Root Note and Scale parameters, you may click on the blank section underneath the words Root and Scale, or use the up and down arrows located to the right of the blank sections. By selecting a root note and scale, the virtual keyboard will automatically adjust itself by turning on and off specific notes within the selected note scale.

VIRTUAL KEYBOARD

The virtual keyboard at the bottom of the display shows the active notes within a specific note scale. You may also create custom scales by manually turning notes on and off by simply selecting them. Custom tuning may be saved in one of four slots at the upper right of the display under the scale memory. Remember to pick a new scale memory slot before making adjustments to a previously created custom scale, as it will overwrite the selected scale memory slot.

CORRECTION SPEED

The Correction Speed knob controls how quickly the note correction occurs. Fast settings are obtained by moving the knob fully to the right and will result in hard pitch correction (a.k.a. the T-Pain/Cher effect). Slow settings are obtained by moving the knob to the left and result in an almost unnoticeable process, as many of the notes will not be adjusted due to the sluggishness of the setting.

A great place to start for natural-sounding pitch correction is having the correction speed set at the middle (twelve o'clock) position.

PRESERVE EXPRESSION

The parameter controls the amount of vibrato from the original signal kept after the pitch correction.

A minimum setting is obtained by moving the knob to the left, and with a fast speed setting, the result will have very little of the original vibrato. With a maximum setting to the right and a fast correction speed, the original vibrato will result.

Transpose

The Transpose section offers pitch shifting, which is great for shifting the pitch of atonal signals. It may be used on its own or in conjunction with the Pitch Correction and Formant sections, to yield some interesting results.

The parameters offered by the Transpose section are semitone and cents, which allow you to dial in specific pitch shifting over a two-octave range.

This section on its own is great for creating demonic and Chipmunk effects.

Formant

A formant is considered the sonic fingerprint for a particular sound. All sounds have a specific formant that is imparted onto their signals via the shape of the cavity producing them. Consider the human vocal tract. The generated sound by our vocal cords is shaped by our throat and mouth, which imparts their unique character to the sound.

The Neptune is constantly analyzing the input signal and has the ability to change the formant of the signal in real time.

When the Formant knob is turned to the right, the characteristics of the formant are shifted to a higher register, which results in a formant associated with a female register.

When the Formant is turned to the left, the characteristics are shifted to a lower register, resulting in a formant with a more masculine register.

By using this feature, it is possible to create realistic vocal doubling and harmonies that sound as if they were sung by a different person all together.

IN USE

There are several ways to create usable results with the Neptune. You can set up the processor to work on prerecorded material or in a live situation, where a microphone input is routed from the Hardware Interface to the Neptune.

Automatic Pitch Correction

The basic setup procedure is to create an instance of the Neptune on a track as an insert. Once it is created, you'll need to make sure the Pitch Adjust button is active and that you've selected an appropriate root note and scale.

Next, you'll want to define the input by selecting Low Freq, Wide Vibrato, or Live Mode.

LOW FREQ
The Low Frequency setting will cause Neptune to react to lower pitches more accurately. Note that latency may be increased as the lower-frequency waveforms are longer and result in more time to process. This setting is good to bass or baritone voicing.

WIDE VIBRATO
A signal with a lot of vibrato may cause Neptune to behave erratically, with incorrect notes, wobbling, and glides. With this type of material, it's best to select the Wide Vibrato setting, which will ignore the vibrato in the incoming signal.

LIVE MODE

Live mode is best used if you are planning on using the Neptune effect in real time for live vocal processing. This will result in less latency, but also may reduce the quality of the pitch shifting.

MIDI Control

Another useful setup is to engage the MIDI to Pitch Adjust. This allows you to control Neptune via your MIDI controller. Simply create a MIDI track in the sequencer window for the Neptune and input notes on your controller to pitch correction. This may be used in conjunction with the automatic setting; MIDI to Pitch Adjust will manually override the automatic settings.

Voice Synth

The Neptune also offers a polyphonic voice synthesizer that works independently of the pitch adjust, transpose, and formant functions.

To set it up, it works very much the same way at the MIDI controller, only you select MIDI to Voice Synth on the interface.

When one or more notes are played on a MIDI controller along with the signal inputted from a microphone, the results are a natural and transparent signal with harmonies that are controlled by your MIDI keyboard.

The voice synth has its own slider in the mixer, and it is possible to use both effects simultaneously and adjust their levels via the mixer. Additionally, the voice synth has a separate output on the rear of the Neptune, which lets the signal be routed to its own mix channel for further processing.

In Conclusion

The Neptune is fantastic addition to the sonic arsenal of Reason 6. It may seem a bit complicated at first, but with some experimentation, you'll quickly get the hang of things and be able to produce perfect vocals and effects in no time.

INSERT EFFECTS: PRESETS

By now, you should have a strong understanding of Reason's effects processors and so far, you've been wiring effects inline between the Dr. OctoRex and the Mix Channel device.

There is another way to create and use effects: with the insert presets.

Selecting the Show Programmer and Show Insert FX buttons on the Mix Channel device will reveal additional options for creating effects and programming.

In Fig. 9.26, you see the programmer and the effects box.

Fig. 9-26

The programmer concept was borrowed from the Combinator interface (which you'll look at in the next chapter) and allows you to map multiple parameters from any number of devices to four knobs and buttons, which you'll see on the lower left of the programmer interface. The Modulation Routing section, where these settings are made, is located on the right.

To load an insert FX patch, click the Insert FX patch browser.

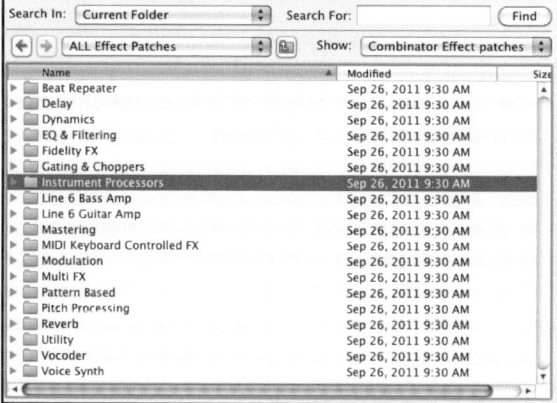

Fig. 9-27

The browser window will open and you can search through the ALL Effect Patches folder. There are nineteen categories of effects, each with a massive set of preset insert FX.

Select Instrument folder and load the preset Drum.

In Fig. 9.28, you see the entire Dr.OctoRex Mix Channel device, with four loaded effects. Notice how the knobs and buttons have been relabeled to reflect their control settings. As you adjust any of the knobs or buttons on the programmer, their respective parameters on the effects below will be adjusted.

Fig. 9-28

Let's take a closer look at the Modulation Routing section of the programmer to learn how the control knobs and buttons have been assigned.

On the left side of the Modulation Routing window, you'll find a device list that coincides with the available effects.

On the right side of the Modulation Routing window, you'll see four columns: Source, Target, Min, and Max.

Source

The Source column contains which rotary knob or button you wish to assign to a parameter on an effects device.

Target

The Target column contains the assignment for source.

Min and Max

The Min and Max columns allow you to scale the assigned parameter. This lets you set a minimum and maximum value. The default is a minimum of 0, with maximum of 127, but you may set any value in between. It is also possible to inverse the scale by assigning the minimum to 127 and the maximum to 0.

Also, you may assign multiple parameters to the same rotary knob or button, which is an excellent way to morph between two different settings.

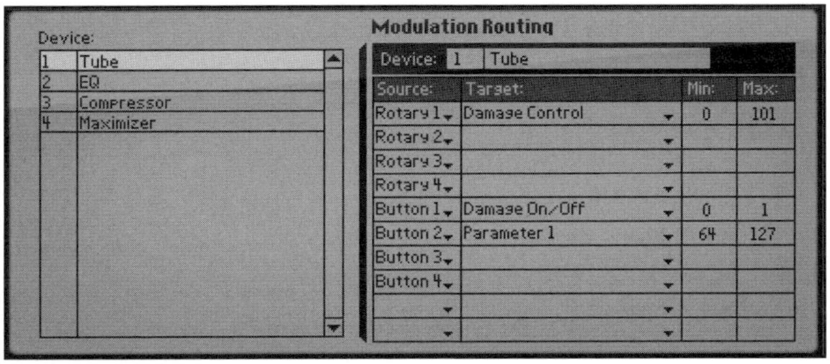

Fig. 9-29

In Fig. 9.29, you'll find the Scream 4 (labeled Tube) is currently selected.

Rotary 1 has been assigned to Damage Control, with a minimum value of 0 and maximum value of 104.

Moving Rotary 1, labeled Tube Amount, will cause the Damage Control knob on the Scream 4 to be adjusted.

Button 1 is assigned to the Damage button on the Scream, which turns the effect on or off.

Additionally, you'll find that Button 2 has been assigned to the P1 knob on the Scream.

Exploring Other Device Settings

Feel free to explore the other devices in the Device list to see what parameters are assigned to the controls on the programmer interface.

Keep in mind, you may assign multiple parameters from any and all devices to the same controller on the programmer interface.

FINAL THOUGHTS

As you can tell, the effects processors offered by Reason 6 range from the simple to the highly complex. Coupled with Reason's instruments and content, the sound design capabilities of Reason 6 now rival those any other audio system, hardware or software. Add the ability to load preset FX and control multiple parameters simultaneously, and you'll be able to create any sound you hear in your head.

In the next chapter, you'll discover the rest of the Reason devices, which will get you to the next level in regard to understanding this outstanding software package known as Reason 6.

Utility Devices

What are referred to here as utility devices are actually found in a part of the submenu labeled Other, located under the Create menu. This range of devices includes mixers, merger/splitters, and pattern generators. Often overlooked, these utility devices can add a whole new dimension of functionality to Reason.

MIXERS

All mixers share one common, most basic purpose: to blend multiple streams of audio into a stereo pair.

Reason's original mixers were simple yet effective, but with the advent of a new mixer modeled after an SSL9000K, Propellerhead has raised the bar with regard to mixing capabilities.

You will thoroughly investigate the new mixer's robust feature set in chapter 13, but for now, let's start by looking at the other mixer options offered by Reason.

Before the advent of the newly modeled SSL mixer, Reason utilized two mixers, the 14:2 and the 6:2, both of which, while still available, are now resigned to the duties of submixing.

MIXER 14:2

The Mixer 14:2 is a stereo mixing device that allows the merging of up to fourteen stereo or mono signals into a stereo output. Each channel features a Volume Fader; Pan Pot, Mute, and Solo buttons; two-band High and Low Shelf equalizers; and four Auxiliary sends. The Master

Fig. 10-1

**Fig.
10-2**

section, which is displayed on the right, contains four dedicated auxiliary returns and a stereo master fader, to control the overall output of the session. This device serves as an excellent submixer for combining multiple instruments and effects. It is also possible to chain several mixers together to obtain higher track counts.

Channel Strip

Let's begin by taking a closer look at an individual channel on the mixer.

- Aux: 1–4
- 2-band shelf EQ
- S: Solo
- M: Mute
- Pan Pot: Left, Center, and Right
- Volume Fader: Loudness control
- Channel Label: Name of instrument assigned or connected to track.

   All fourteen channels on the mixer essentially do the same thing. It doesn't matter whether the mixing board has 14 tracks or 144. Every channel strip serves the same primary function. Learn to use one, and you know how to use them all. The only other section of the mixer you must become familiar with is the Master section. Fortunately, the 14:2 has a very simple and easy-to-use Master section, featuring a Master Fader that controls the overall loudness of the mix. It also contains dedicated Aux returns for time-based effects.

Master Section

**Fig.
10-3**

AUX RETURNS
 These interact with the Aux sends on the channel strip. For every Aux send, there's a dedicated Aux return.

MASTER FADER
This is the level control for the main mix, or stereo master fader.

LINE MIXER 6:2

The Line Mixer 6:2 is a mixing device that features six stereo inputs and one stereo output. Each input module on the mixer features a Volume Fader; Pan Pot, Mute, and Solo buttons; and a single Aux send.

Fig. 10-4

The Master section features a Master Volume knob used for controlling the overall volume of mixed signals, and a dedicated Aux return. This is yet another great mixer for connecting devices together to create a submix.

MIX CHANNEL

The Mix Channel device offers the same feature set as an Audio Track device. As discussed in the chapter on recording, these devices serve as the rack connection to Reason's main mixer.

Fig. 10-5

The option of generating a Mix Channel device permits the creation of additional channels for use with instruments with additional outputs. You'll be using several mix channels in conjunction with the 14:2 mixer to create a submix for drums in chapter 13.

MERGER AND SPLITTER

Reason offers a unique method of interconnecting instruments and effects via Control Voltage (CV) and Gate signals on audio signals. Two devices that aid in these interconnections are the Spider Audio and CV Merger and Splitter.

SPIDER AUDIO MERGER AND SPLITTER

The Spider Audio Merger and Splitter is a device that merges or splits audio signals. The unit features four stereo inputs connected to a single stereo output.

While this function is not unlike that of a mixer, it contains no Gain or Pan controls. It also has the ability to split a stereo input into four separate stereo outputs, making this a superior utility used to great effect for advanced routing capabilities.

Fig. 10-6

SPIDER CV MERGER AND SPLITTER

The Spider CV Merger and Splitter is a device that merges or splits Control Voltage (CV) and Gate signals. The unit features four CV/Gate inputs to one CV/Gate output. It also has two single CV/Gate inputs to four CV/Gate output.

Fig. 10-7

For added flexibility, one of the split signals is inverted (labeled Inv), allowing for the inversion of the incoming signal. This is a great utility for routing a pattern generator to multiple devices. It also aids in the creation of complex LFOs.

PATTERN GENERATORS

Before the advent of the digital synthesizer and MIDI, all controls for synthesizers and sequencers were in the form of analog control voltages (CV). Even though Reason 5 is completely digital, Propellerhead has adopted both the architecture and nomenclature of this bygone era, which gives you the simplicity of physically routing cables between a device's CV inputs and its outputs.

In the next section you'll explore how to set up and program both the Matrix Analog Pattern Sequencer and the RPG-8 Monophonic Arpeggiator.

THE MATRIX PATTERN SEQUENCER

Begin by creating a Subtractor synthesizer.

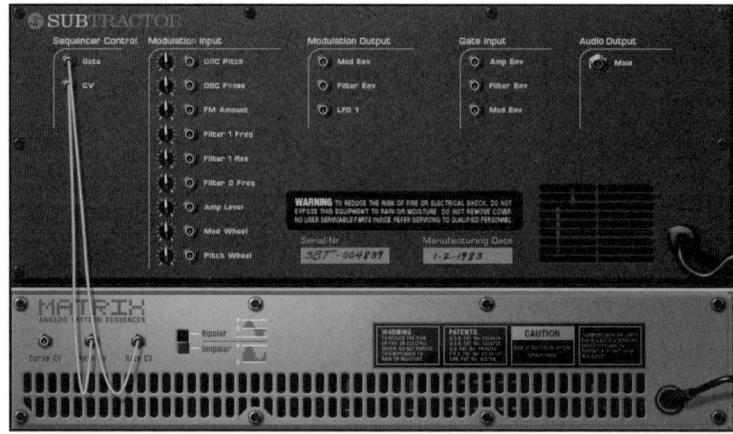

Fig. 10-8

On the Subtractor, click the Browse Patch button and select the Fat VeloBass patch from the Bass folder.

Select the Subtractor synthesizer and then from the Create > Other menu, click Matrix Pattern Sequencer.

The Matrix Pattern Sequencer is loaded into the rack just under the Subtractor. Now, press Tab to toggle the view around to the rear of the rack and take a closer look at the cabling.

In addition to the normal Audio routing that connects the Subtractor to the mixer, you'll find two more cables running from the Note CV and Gate output of the Matrix to CV and Gate inputs of the Sequencer control of the Subtractor. The Note CV contains the pitch information, while the Gate controls the duration of the note.

Press Tab again to return to the front of the rack so that you can explore the Matrix interface.

The Matrix is divided into two main sections: the Pattern Control section and the Sequencer Control section.

Fig. 10-9

THE PATTERN SECTION

The Pattern section is divided into four banks (A through D) with eight patterns per bank, yielding a total of thirty-two patterns per device. Switch between the banks and patterns simply by selecting their respective controls. While it is possible to record an automated pattern selection onto a pattern lane, you may also use Copy Pattern to Track, which will print the currently selected pattern onto a track between the L and R locators. You'll explore the different ways to record and arrange with patterns in the next section, but first, let's learn how to program in the Sequencer Control section.

Types of CV Data

The Matrix sequencer is capable of generating three types of data: Note CV, Gate CV, and Curve CV.

NOTE AND GATE CV

This is the default setup used when working with the Matrix and is a great means of generating synth lines.

The main part of the sequencer is designed in a Matrix format, with individual horizontal blocks representing notes. There is a one-octave piano keyboard located on the left side of the sequencer, with a five-way switch to toggle between octaves, 1 being the lowest octave and 5 the highest. By default, the Octave switch is set to 3.

The vertical blocks displayed at the bottom of the sequencer window control the Gate information for each note. Velocity for each note is controlled by the height of each vertical Gate block.

CURVE CV

Curve CV is used to control parameters other than Note and Gate CV. To engage this, click the switch above the Octave selection switch. Switching from Keys to Curve changes the setting to a secondary sequencer that allows the sequencing of CV Curve data.

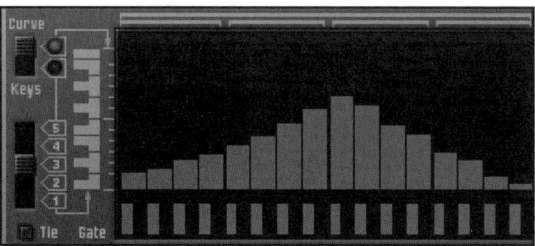

Fig. 10-10

Figure 10.10 shows a simple up–down curve programmed into the sequencer. Notice how the sequencer window has changed from Note CV blocks to vertical lines, which provides smoother, more precise control over the desired parameter setting. Note that even though the Gate sequencer data are still visible, they have no bearing on the control of the Curve CV.

MATRIX SEQUENCER PROGRAMMING

Now we will try programming the Matrix.

Note CV and Gate Programming

First, switch the Curve setting back to Keys and program in a bass line.

The sequencer resolution and number of steps are set by the controls on the left side of the device. By default, the Resolution is set to sixteenth notes, while the Steps are set at 16, giving you a one-bar sequence. You will maintain the default settings for your sequence.

Next, change the Octave Switch setting from 3 to 2.

Now program the sequencer so that it resembles the image in Fig. 10.11. To

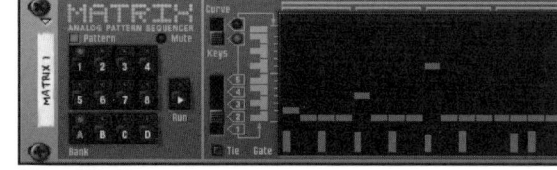

Fig. 10-11

remove the Gate data, simply click and drag down on the vertical bar until it disappears. With no Gate information, the step now acts as a rest and no audio will be produced.

Press the Run button, to listen to the sequence produced.

Now, let's create a variation on the sequence by pressing Command + C if using a Mac or Control + C if using Windows to copy. Then, select Pattern 2 and press Command + V if using a Mac or Control + V if using Windows to paste the data.

Fill in any unused Gate slots with a low-velocity Gate bar. Pattern 2 should be set to look like Fig. 10.12.

Select Pattern 3 and press Command + V if using a Mac or Control + V if using Windows.

This should paste the copied pattern from Pattern Slot 1 into Pattern Slot 3.

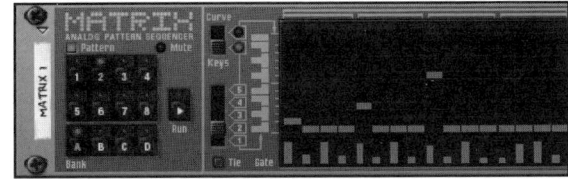

Fig. 10-12

Just below the Octave Switch control, you'll find a button labeled Tie Gate. When enabled, any selected Gate data will appear to have a fatter bar and will create the effect of a longer note. Here you are using a sixteenth-note resolution, so if you tie two notes together at the same pitch, they are effectively played as eighth notes.

If you tie two gates together at different note pitches, it creates a portamento effect in which the first note slides into the second note. This effect was made popular in the acid style of bass line often produced by a TB303.

With the Tie Gate button enabled, now re-create the sequence pattern shown in Fig. 10.13.

Curve CV Programming

Copy Pattern 2 to Pattern 4 by using the same keyboard command method used before.

By default, the Curve CV output is not cabled to anything, so to program the effect, you must first decide what parameter you wish to control with the Curve CV. Let's control the Modulation wheel.

Tab to the rear of the rack and now cable the Curve CV output to the Mod Wheel input. Turn the dial located to the left of the Mod Wheel input all the way to the right, to maximize this effect.

Tab back to the front of the rack and change the Keys switch to Curve. Next, re-create the sequence pattern shown in Fig.10.14.

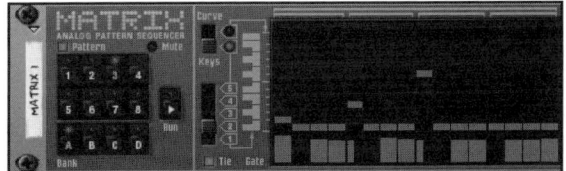

Fig. 10-13

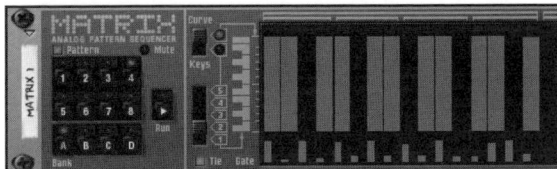

Fig. 10-14

RECORDING PATTERNS TO THE SEQUENCER WINDOW

There are two ways to work with patterns created with the Matrix Pattern Sequencer. The first is by recording the pattern in real time and the second is by using the Pencil tool to draw in the desired pattern information.

Recording in Real Time

To record pattern information, you first need to create a Pattern Lane for the data.

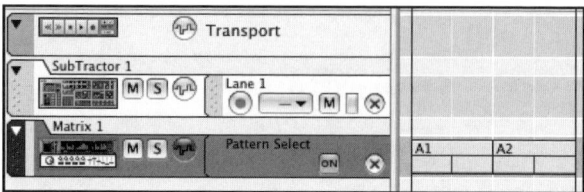

Fig. 10-15

The easiest way to do this is to right-click on the Pattern section of the Matrix and select Edit Automation.

The same results can be obtained by selecting the Matrix track in the sequencer window and selecting Create Pattern/Loop Lane from the Edit menu.

Once the pattern lane has been created, set the SPL to Bar 1, located on the sequencer page.

With Pattern 1 selected, click the Record button on the Transport. As the SPL approaches Bar 3, select Pattern 2. Stop recording when the SPL reaches Bar 7.

You should now find Patterns A1 and A2 recorded onto the Matrix track on the sequencer page.

Drawing Patterns

From the Tool Palette, select the Pencil tool. With the Pencil tool, click and hold while dragging from Bar 5 to Bar 7.

Again, click and hold while dragging from Bar 7 to Bar 9.

Note that the new patterns are set to Pattern A1.

Next, select the arrow from the Tool Palette and select the third pattern. Once it is selected, a downward-facing arrow will be displayed in the middle of the pattern. Click and hold on this and then select Pattern/Loop 3.

Do the same for the fourth pattern and name-select Pattern/Loop 4.

CONVERT PATTERN AUTOMATION TO NOTES

Another way of working with the patterns generated by the Matrix is to convert the patterns into a MIDI clip.

With the Matrix track selected on the sequencer page, select Convert Pattern Automation to Notes from the Edit menu.

Notice how the Pattern button on the Matrix has been turned off and the notes of the patterns have been replaced as MIDI clips on a newly created lane. If you were to hit Play, you wouldn't hear anything, because the Matrix doesn't produce any sounds. It can only generate patterns. So you now have to move the new MIDI clip onto the Subtractor track.

One minor drawback to this feature is the Curve CV data are not converted; only Note CV and Gate data are converted.

COPY PATTERN TO TRACK

Another option of working with the Matrix is to use the function Copy Pattern to Track from the Edit menu. This works just like the same option found on the ReDrum Edit menu.

First, select the pattern to be copied.

Set the L and R locators to specify the desired range.

Then, select Copy Pattern to Track from the Edit menu.

THE RPG-8 MONOPHONIC ARPEGGIATOR

The RPG-8 is a pattern generator, but unlike the Matrix, it requires MIDI note data and does not offer the ability to store preset patterns. It is what I call a live performance tool and is capable of creating complex rhythms and patterns on the fly.

Because the RPG-8 doesn't generate sounds on its own, you'll first need to create an instrument and cable it to the RPG-8.

Before you begin, first select the Matrix and hit Delete.

From the Subtractor's patch browser, select Acid Saw 2 from the Monosynths folder.

Next, with the Subtractor selected, select RPG-8 Monophonic Arpeggiator from the Create menu.

Tab to the rear of the rack and confirm how the cabling works.

Similar to the Matrix, the Note CV Out and the Gate CV Out of the RPG-8 are connected to the Note and Gate input of the Sequencer Control of the Subtractor.

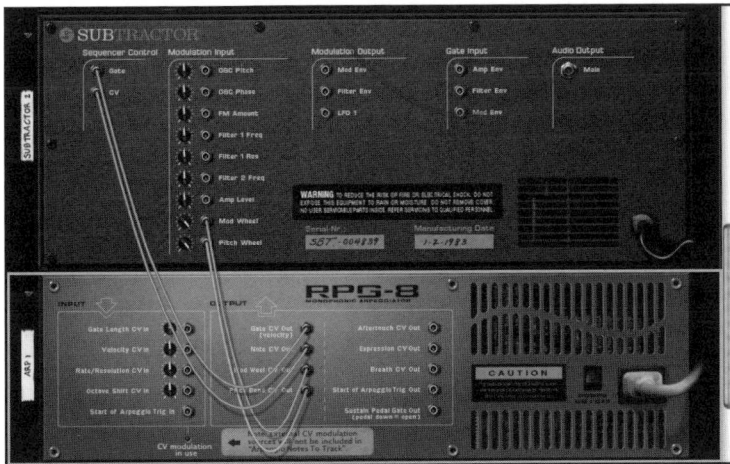

Fig. 10-16

Note that the Mod Wheel CV Out and the Pitch Bend CV Out are connected to the Mod Wheel and Pitch Bend inputs of the Modulation Input section of the Subtractor. This lets the Modulation wheel and Pitch Bend data pass through the RPG-8 from your MIDI keyboard controller to the Subtractor.

THE RBG-8 INTERFACE

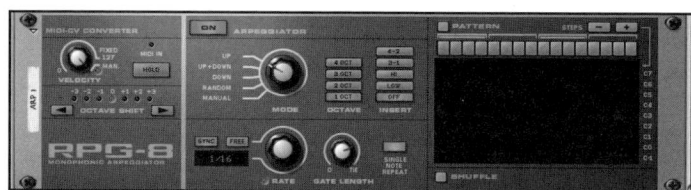

The RPG-8 interface is divided into three main sections: MIDI-to-CV Converter, Arpeggiator, and Pattern.

Fig. 10-17

MIDI-TO-CV CONVERTER

The MIDI-to-CV Converter section, located on the left side of the interface, takes incoming MIDI messages and converts them to CV and Gate messages.

Velocity

The Velocity dial provides control over how the RPG-8 interprets incoming velocity information. By default, the Velocity dial is set to Manual, which passes the incoming data through to the synthesizer. This enables you to easily change the velocity response according to how hard (or quickly) you strike a key.

Changing from Manual to Fixed lets you set a constant velocity value independent of how you play your keyboard controller. Values for this setting range from 0, which outputs no sound, to 127, the loudest possible velocity setting.

Hold

The Hold button will latch onto any MIDI notes played and continues to run. You can change the sequence by pressing a new MIDI note or chord (several notes played simultaneously).

Octave Shift

The Octave Shift section shifts the incoming MIDI data up or down over three octaves, regardless of which octave was used to generate the original data.

ARPEGGIATOR

The Arpeggiator section is located in the middle of the interface and is used to control the generated patterns.

Mode

The Mode section controls the direction of the pattern, based on the notes played.

The Pattern section displays a visual representation of the patterns being generated. Try hitting three notes at once and switching among the different modes.

UP
This generates an upward pattern, playing the lowest note first and continuing up the scale.

DOWN
Conversely, this generates a downward pattern, starting from the highest note and continuing down the scale.

UP + DOWN
This generates a pattern that starts with the lowest note played and continues up to the highest note, and then plays back down to the first note.

RANDOM
Set this to randomly select the order of the notes played.

MANUAL
Notes are played strictly in the order they are inputted.

Octave

The Octave section sets the range for how many octaves the pattern will scale.

OCTAVE 1
Selecting this will cause the notes to play within the same octave played.

OCTAVE 2
Selecting this will cause the notes played to play in the same octave and then repeat one octave above. A random setting will further cause the generated pattern to alternate between the two octaves randomly.

OCTAVE 3
Selecting this will have the same effect as Octave 2, but increases the range to three octaves.

OCTAVE 4
Selecting this will have the same effect as Octave 2 or 3, but increases the range to four octaves.

Insert

This section is used to create variations by repeating certain notes in a predetermined order.

OFF
No change.

LOW
The lowest note is repeated between every second note.

HIGH
The highest note is repeated between every second note.

3-1
The generated pattern plays three notes forward and steps one note back, and then repeats.

4-2
The generated pattern plays four notes forward and steps two notes back, and then repeats.

Rate

This controls the speed of the Arpeggiator.

SYNC
When engaged, the Arpeggiator speed is locked to sync with the song tempo as determined by note value (e.g., sixteenth note, eighth note).

FREE
When this is selected, the Arpeggiator runs freely within a range of 0.1 to 250 Hz.

Gate Length

This determines the length of each note. The default duration is dependent on the Rate selected. Turning the dials to the left shortens the duration, whereas turning them to the right increases it. A setting of 0 has no output, whereas a setting of 127 ties the durations together.

Single Note Repeat

This determines how the Arpeggiator responds to single notes. When engaged, a single note is repeated. When disengaged, single notes will not trigger the Arpeggiator, only two notes or more.

PATTERN

The Pattern section is located to the right of the interface and provides visual feedback of the pattern being generated by the Arpeggiator.

Pattern Editor

Engaging the Pattern Editor button provides more control over the generated pattern, with the ability to create rests within the Arpeggiator.

Steps + or −

This setting allows you to modify the number of steps within the pattern. By default, the pattern is set to its maximum of sixteen steps. Pressing the + or − button will increase or decrease the number of steps, respectively.

Shuffle

The Shuffle button engages a global swing, which can add a nice rhythmic effect to the patterns generated.

USING THE RPG-8

Putting the RPG-8 to use is quite simple. Just cable it to an instrument, adjust some of the parameters to your liking, and then play your MIDI controller.

Let's take a look at some ideas for generating patterns.

My favorite modes to generate patterns are with the Random and Manual modes. I'm also a huge fan of the Insert section, with the 3-1 and 4-2 settings.

In this patch, I have set up the RPG-8 to generate a bass line. Using two octaves limits the range so that it stays in the low-frequency area. The random setting ensures that the bass line mutates every bar.

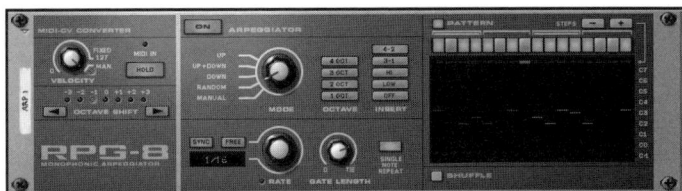

Fig. 10-18

With the Pattern section, I chose the random pattern feature found in the Edit drop-down menu.

To use this, first make sure to have the RPG-8's Pattern editor turned on. In the Edit menu, you'll find several options that can be used to affect the pattern.

EDIT MENU OPTIONS FOR PATTERN EDITOR

For the Edit functions to have any effect, there must be a pattern in the Pattern editor. Note that some functions will not have an effect if all the steps are either active or deactivated.

Shift Pattern Left or Right

As the functions suggests, this will shift the current pattern one step either to the left or right.

Randomize Pattern

This will randomize the pattern currently in the Pattern editor. Selecting this function repeatedly will result in a different outcome every time it is used.

Alter Pattern

This will alter the current pattern and is a great way to quickly modify patterns. However, note that this is not as extreme an effect as using the Random function.

Invert Pattern

This turns all notes to rests and all rests to notes.

Arpeggiator Notes to Track

This is one of my favorite features because I prefer to work with MIDI clips when arranging. To try this out, first you'll need to record a MIDI clip onto the RPG-8 track.

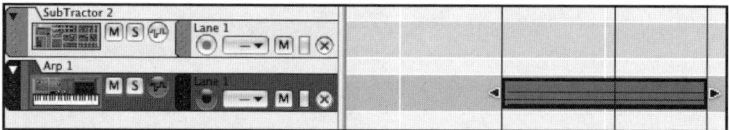

Fig. 10-19

To start, I have recorded a two-bar loop of a C-minor chord (C2, D#2, G2).

Next, select the target track on the sequencer page. This is where you want the arpeggiated sequence to be directed.

This destination is normally the instrument cabled to the RPG-8, and in this case would be the Subtractor with the Acid 2 patch.

Now, select the RPG-8 from the rack and click Arpeggio Notes to Track from the Edit drop-down menu.

A new MIDI clip is created from the output of the RPG-8 onto the Subtractor track.

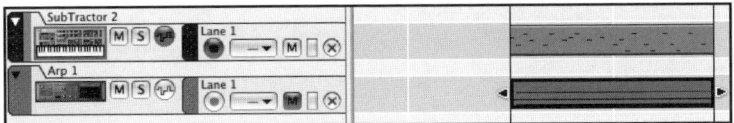

Fig. 10-20

Be sure to mute the RPG-8 track from the sequencer track list, to avoid double triggers.

ADDITIONAL THOUGHTS

As is evident, the Matrix Pattern Sequencer and RPG-8 Monophonic Arpeggiator are incredibly powerful tools to have in your programming arsenal. Spending some time experimenting with these devices can inspire you to create new and different types of patterns quickly and efficiently.

REASON REBIRTH INPUT MACHINE

The ReBirth input machine is a device that allows you to connect Propellerhead's Rebirth to Reason. ReBirth was the precursor to Reason and featured two TB303s, a TR-808 Drum Machine, and a TR-909 Drum Machine.

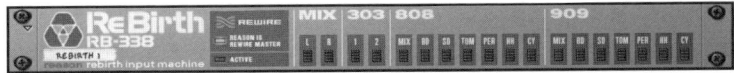

Fig. 10-21

ReBirth, a fantastic computer software for creating electronic music, was discontinued and is now only available for use on the PC. Currently, however, a version is being offered as an application for the iPhone and iPad.

THE COMBINATOR

The Combinator is a unique device that allows for multiple instruments, effects, pattern generators, mixers, and so on, to be nested inside it. This nesting of devices allows for extremely complex routing capabilities that can be saved and recalled at will, which can translate into a huge time-saving technique.

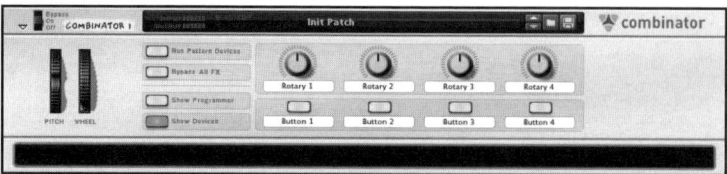

Fig. 10-22

The Combinator is by far the most complex and creatively useful device offered by Reason 6. This device permits the saving and recalling of any number of devices, including instruments, effects, mixers, and pattern generators. Once saved, the patch (or Combi) can be recalled, no matter how complex the setup used to create it.

Imagine spending hours crafting a sound that includes a mixer, several layered synthesizers, and multiple effects. And now imagine having to re-create the same patch all over again in a different song. Using the Combinator saves you all that effort.

Beyond sound creation, there are a number of dedicated multieffect Combis, including the Mastering Combi, with all the requisite M-Class Mastering effects. Each mastering Combi offers a different type of preset setup. The Combinator nests all the devices within the box located at the bottom of interface. Selecting Show Programmer enables you to route any button or knob of any instrument or effect to the four knobs/buttons located on the Combinator. Several parameters can then be controlled from a single knob or button.

When asked what my favorite instrument is in Reason 6, my answer is consistently and without hesitation, the Combinator. Let's explore some of the presets of the Combinator and get a feel for how to build a simple instrument.

EXPLORING COMBINATOR PRESETS

Let's begin by selecting Combinator from the Create menu.

From the patch browser, navigate to Combinator Patches > Performance Patches > Arpeggiated folder and select As Falls Victoria Falls patch.

LAYERS

Play a few notes and you'll hear a complex, layered patch with multiple synthesizers, arpeggiators, and effects. Feel free to adjust some of the knobs and buttons to hear how the sound changes. More noticeable changes can be heard by engaging the Arp Mute and Pad Mute buttons, or by turning the knobs on the Pad Timbre and Arp Speed.

I chose this patch to demonstrate how complex a Combinator can be.

Fig. 10-23

Now, let's take a closer look to see just how it was created.

SHOW DEVICES

If it is not already displayed, engage the Show Devices button located on the bottom left of the Combinator interface.

Next, hold down the Option/Alt key on your computer keyboard while clicking the unfold triangle of any device within the Combinator device window.

This is a quick way to unfold all the devices at once, as opposed to the tedious task of unfolding each instrument individually. Incidentally, you can do the same from the rack to fold and unfold all of the devices for a real-time and space-saving technique.

Within the Combinator, you'll find three synthesizers, two arpeggiators, and multiple effects all being routed through a mixer and compressor before connecting to the Combinator output. Tab to the rear view of the rack and take a look at the complex routing.

Next, tab to the front view of the Combinator and press the Show Programmer button on the Combinator interface, located just above the Show Devices button.

SHOW PROGRAMMER

The programmer interface is divided into the two main sections: Key Mapping and Modulation Routing.

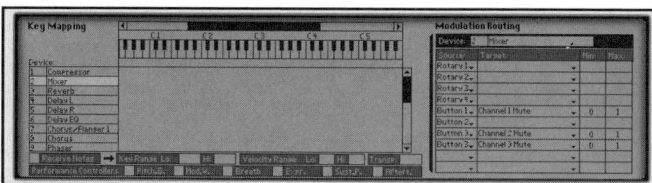

Fig. 10-24

KEY MAPPING

Displayed under Key Mapping is a list containing each of the twenty devices within the Combinator.

Drag down the vertical navigation bar, located on the right side of the Key Mapping section, to view all the devices.

Next, select Joy Pad (Device 10) from the device list on the left. Once selected, the horizontal bar on the Joy Pad plane becomes highlighted and all the parameters located at the bottom of the Key Mapping section become active.

Note Data

This group of parameters controls how the incoming note data are recognized and processed.

Receive Notes

This setting determines whether the current instrument will recognize incoming note data.

KEY RANGE LO
This sets the lowest key on your controller keyboard in which this device will play.

KEY RANGE HI
This sets the highest key on your controller keyboard in which this device will play.

VELOCITY RANGE LO
This sets the lowest range of velocity in which the triggered note will play.

VELOCITY RANGE HI
This sets the highest range of velocity in which the triggered note will play.

TRANSPOSE
This setting offers a transposition offset of the device.

Performance Controllers

Performance Controllers allow sound to be manipulated in real time.

PITCH BEND

Check this to have the device respond to Pitch Bend data.

MODULATION WHEEL

Check this to have the device respond to Modulation wheel data.

BREATH

Check this to have the device respond to Breath controller data.

EXPRESSION

Check this to have the device respond to Expression controller data.

SUSTAIN

Check this to have the device respond to Sustain Pedal controller data.

AFTER TOUCH

Check this to have the device respond to Aftertouch messages. Only keyboard controllers with Aftertouch will generate this type of message.

MODULATION ROUTING

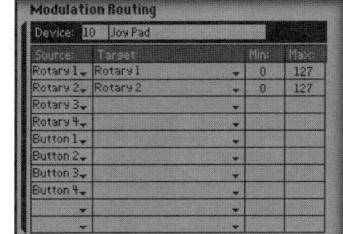

On the right side of the Show Programmer window, you'll find the modulation routing. This is where you can assign any number of parameters to be controlled by a number of sources, including the four on-board knobs and buttons found on the Combinator interface.

Fig. 10-25

With the Joy Pad device still selected, note in the Modulation Routing window that Knobs 1 and 2 are routed to the Timbre and Drive knob on the Thor synthesizer. If you were view the Thor while moving the Pad Timbre and Drive knob on the Combinator interface, you'd see the Thor knobs being adjusted.

Ten slots are available in the Modulation Routing section of the programmer.

SOURCE

The Source column contains any number of controller types. Pressing on the downward triangle of each slot reveals an extensive list of possible controls.

TARGET

The Target column has any number of destinations where the Source control is routed. Pressing the downward-facing triangle reveals an extensive list of destinations.

MINIMUM AND MAXIMUM

To the right of the Target column are the Minimum and Maximum slots, which are used to set a range of scalable values.

SPLITS

Another popular use for a Combinator is the ability to program a split. Whereas a layer has two or more instruments playing simultaneously, a split divides the keyboard controller into two or more parts, each playing a single instrument.

Let's take a look at a split preset.

Navigate to Combinator Patches > Performance Patches > Splits and select the patch Ac Bass & Vibraphone Split

This is patch contains a line mixer, two NN-XT Samplers, an EQ, and an RV7000 reverb unit.

Open the programmer and note that the Bass Instrument Key range has been set from C–2 to C3 on the key mapping, while the Vibraphone is mapped from C#3 to G8.

Notes played below C3 will produce bass sounds, whereas notes played above C#3 will trigger the sounds of the vibraphone.

The modulation routing is set to control the room settings of the RV7000 reverb unit.

SONG STARTERS

Another really fun type of preset are the Song Starter, also found the Performance patches.

Navigate to Combinator Patches > Performance Patches > Song Starters and select Ecstatic Salvation.

This Combinator even offers directions on how to play the instrument, as displayed on the right side of the interface.

Press Run and have fun!

As you can see, Combinators are incredibly powerful and indispensable devices. They allow you to tap into the ability to play multiple instruments at once and give you dedicated control over crucial sound-shaping controls and parameters.

Fig. 10-26

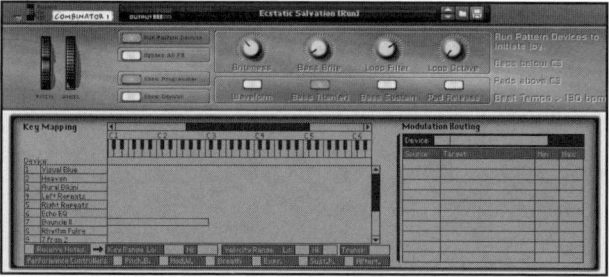

Fig. 10-27

FINAL THOUGHTS

The Combinator offers up a simple solution to the complex task of controlling multiple devices. Featuring the ability to nest any of Reason's instruments, effects, and utility devices into a single entity, the Combinator truly shines as a beacon of innovation.

Part Four

Advanced Routing

One of them most fascinating and exhilarating aspects of Reason is the reverse side of the rack. As a teaching tool, it offers a glimpse at how to wire up a physical rack and connect analog synthesizers and sequencers.

Reason offers an unprecedented amount of control in an easy-to-understand format. Other programs offer similar types of control, but you need a degree in computer science to program them. With the basic understanding of control voltage and gate signals and a spirit for experimentation, you will be able to create sophisticated sounds and processors.

You'll also work with the ReGroove mixer, a MIDI processing tool for timing, velocity, and duration.

AUDIO AND MIX CHANNEL DEVICES

If you examine the back of the either an Audio Channel or Mix Channel device in the rack, you will find CV inputs for both Pan and Level control.

Auto-Panning

The Subtractor offers no control for creating an auto-pan effect, as it only offers a Mono output, but with the use of the Pan CV input on the Mix Channel device, it is completely possible.

Begin by creating a Subtractor synthesizer and selecting the Omenous patch from the Pads folder.

Tab to the back of your rack and cable LFO 1 from the Modulation output to the Pan CV input for Channel 1.

Use the knob just below the Pan CV input to control the width of the pan. Moving the knob to the left decreases the width; to the right, it increases the effect.

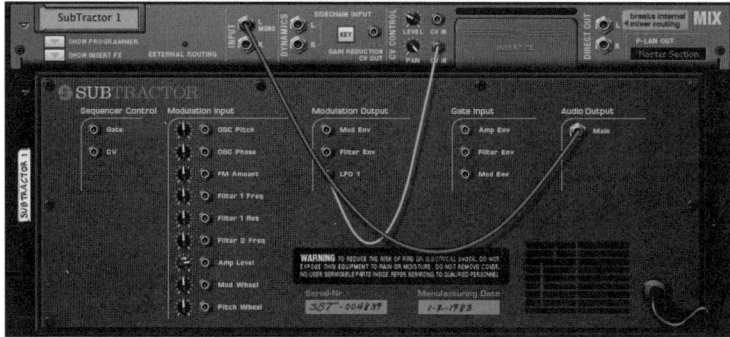

Fig. 11-1

You can adjust the waveform and rate of the pan via LFO 1 control parameters, as you normally would. Note that you don't have to increase the amount of the LFO, because the Pan CV knob on the rear of the Mix Channel device controls that.

Auto-Leveling

This creates a tremolo effect by modulating the level, exactly like modulating the amplifier on the Subtractor. Only LFO 2 has the ability to modulate the Amp circuit, but is somewhat limited, with a fixed waveform and no sync.

Use the same instrument and setup you used previously for the auto-pan, only wire LFO 1 from the Modulation output to the level CV input.

Try experimenting with different patches and different waveforms.

A favorite patch for this type of effect is the Outer Mongolia from the Pad folder.

Set LFO 1 to sync at sixteenth note with a square waveform.

Incidentally, it is possible to create this on the Subtractor itself by cabling LFO 1 from the Modulation output to the Amp Level input of the Modulation Input section.

COMPLEX LFO

This is a useful patch that combines the signals of different LFOs to create a modulation truly unique and unpredictable.

Begin by selecting patch Wheel Wah Lead from the Monosynth folder for the Subtractor.

Holding Shift while creating an instrument prevents any auto-cabling and will result in the creation of an instrument or effect without a Mix Channel device.

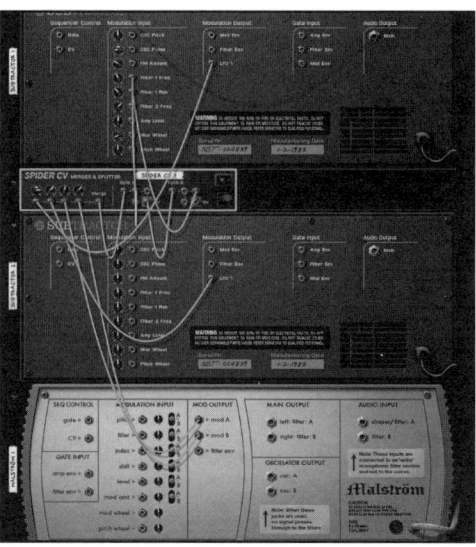

Fig. 11-2

Hold Shift while creating a Spider CV, Subtractor, and Malstrom.

 Next, cable LFO 1 from the Wheel Wah Lead to the first input of the Spider CV Merge section.

Next, do the same for the Subtractor 2 to the second input.

Finally cable both Mods A and B from the Malstrom to the third and fourth inputs of the Spider CV.

Cable the Merge output to Split A input of the Spider CV.

Now cable from Split A output to the Filter 1 Freq input of the Wheel Wah Lead Subtractor.

Also cable the Inv output of Split A to Filter 1 Res.

In Fig. 11.2, I cabled the Inv out to Split B input and then routed a Split B output to the Filter 1 Res. This gives you multiple outputs of the inverted signal to route to other parameters or additional devices. You could create an additional Spider CV device for additional splits to route to other devices and instruments.

If you like this patch and wish to be able to access the setup quickly, try combining everything into a Combinator.

Simply Shift + click each instrument and device, and select Combine from the Edit menu.

Be sure to not have the Mix Channel device selected when trying to combine, as the Menu item will be unselectable.

Save the Combinator as a custom patch. It's now a sonic tool in your arsenal.

TUNABLE FEEDBACK

Sometimes you may be looking for not-so-pretty sounds, such as the sound of an electric guitar's feeding back. This particular patch emulates the scraping of the pick on a guitar string and is followed by feedback, which can be played by your MIDI controller keyboard.

Start by creating a Subtractor and selecting the Bass Guitar patch.

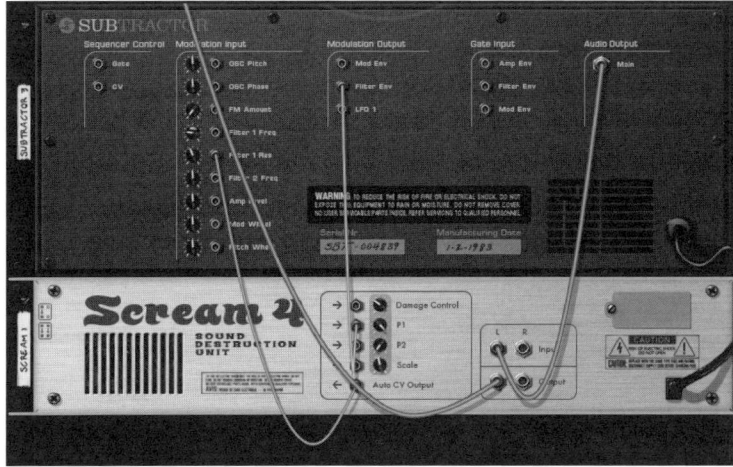

Fig. 11-3

Next, create a Scream 4 Sound Destruction Unit. The auto-cabling should have cabled the output of the Subtractor into the Scream 4 and from the Scream 4 into an available channel on the mixer.

On the Scream 4, select EasyFuzz from the Instrument Tweaks folder. Next, adjust the Damage Type to Modulate.

On the rear of the rack, cable the Filter env from the Modulation Output to the P 1 input of the Scream. Turn the P 1 knob all the way to the right.

Next, route the Auto CV output of the Scream 4 to the Filter 1 Res of the Subtractor.

SEQUENCED STUTTER VOCAL SAMPLE

Any vocal sample will do. I chose a simple two-syllable sample Bad Bwoy to work with. You will find this sample available in the chapter 11 folder on the encoded DVD or available as a download from the Hal Leonard website.

Create a NN-XT Sampler and initialize from the Edit menu.

From the Remote editor, click the Browse Sample button and select the vocal sample.

Next, open the Song Sample tab from the Tool window.

Fig. 11-4

Select the sample from the Assigned > NN-XT and click Duplicate.

Next, hit Edit on the original. Once the Edit window is open, click the Snap Sample Start/End to the Transient selection and move the End position of the sample so that it ends before the Bwoy portion. Rename the sample Bad and hit Save.

On the duplicate sample, move the Start position **Fig. 11-5**
so that it starts with the Bwoy portion.

You should now have two samples labeled Bad and Bwoy.

On the NN-XT, click the Bad sample zone and select Duplicate Zone.

Click the Browse Sample button and navigate to the Song Sample section and select Bwoy.

Next, click the Sample Zone group so that both samples are selected.

With both samples selected, turn the Alt knob to On. Now, as the keys are pressed, the sample alternates between Bad and Bwoy.

With the NN-XT selected, create an RPG-8.

Set the Mode to Random, the Octave to 2, and the Rate to eighth notes.

Tab to the rear of the rack.

Cable the Aftertouch CV output to the Osc Pitch input.

Play C3 on your MIDI keyboard controller. You will hear the Bad Boy sample play randomly at different octaves.

If your keyboard has Aftertouch, pressing harder will cause the pitch to increase. By pressing rhythmically, you can create glitched vocals sounds.

If you wish to save this patch, you must detach the samples.

To do this, select the Song Self-Contain Settings from the File menu and deselect Bad and Bwoy from the sample list.

BV512 DIGITAL VOCODER

Vocoders, or voice encoders, were developed in the 1930s. During WWII, they were used widely to help with communications over long distances, thanks to their ability to encrypt messages.

Their application to music was first attempted in the mid- to late '50s, but didn't reach mainstream consciousness until the late '60s/early '70s by way of electronic musicians such as Kraftwerk.

The most famous sound of the vocoder is the talking synthesizer, or robot voice, but many unique sounds are possible.

The technology involves a carrier and modulator signal. The carrier is the base of the sound, while the modulator acts as an envelope follower, controlling several multiband filters. The more bands available, the more intelligible or precise the vocoding will be.

Let's begin by creating a Malstrom synthesizer and a Dr. OctoRex Loop Player, while holding Shift to prevent auto-cabling.

Sounds with lots of harmonic content and rhythm really help when making an interesting and effective patch. Choose the Screech MW from the Monosynths folder for the Malstrom and the KLB Percussion/ BongoBoom patch found under the Dr OctoRex Patches > Percussion > Keith LeBlanc folder.

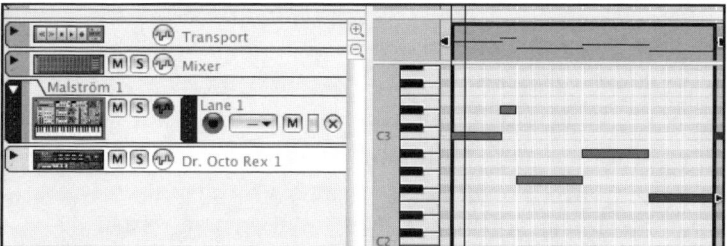

Fig. 11-6

In Fig. 11.6, I recorded a simple sequence with the notes C3, D#3, G2, A#2, and F2. Feel free to use any sequence that works for your production.

Next, with the Malstrom synthesizer selected, create a BV512 Digital Vocoder. The Malstrom will auto-cable itself to the carrier input of the BV512, while the BV512 cables itself to the Mix Channel input.

Tab to the back of the rack and route the left side of the Main Out of the Dr. OctoRex to the Modulation input of the BV512.

Tab to the front of the rack. You'll now explore some parameters on the BV512.

The two LED meters represent the Carrier signal (C) and the Modulation signal (M).

The knob on the upper left permits band selection, with a range of 4, 8, 16, 32, and 512 (FFT).

The 512 (FFT) uses a different method of analysis called fast Fourier transform, which works at a much higher resolution and offers the best intelligibility when synthesizing vocals. It does tend to be slower than the other band settings and is not as ideal for processing drums and rhythmic content.

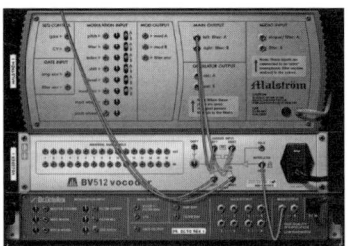

Fig. 11-7

The knob below the band selection changes from Vocoder mode to an Equalizer mode. This is not a high-fidelity EQ, but one that offers some harsh tonal adjustments.

The center section offers a visual graph of the modulations levels on the top portion, while the frequency band levels may be adjusted along the bottom. The number of bands selected will be reflected in the number of frequency band levels one can adjust. The 512 (FFT) selection gives you 32 bands, but each band represents sixteen bands per level adjustment in a linear fashion. The lower frequencies are on the left side of the interface, increasing to higher frequencies as you move to the right.

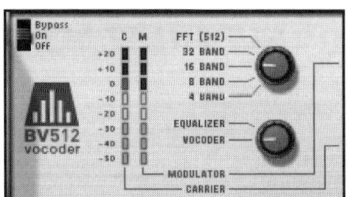

Fig. 11-8

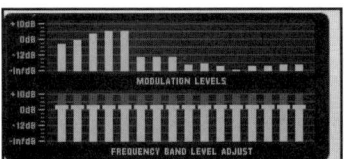

Fig. 11-9

Adjusting the level bands can increase the amplitude of the entire sound or just the chosen frequencies.

The top portion, which includes Hold, Attack, and Decay, affects the Envelope Follower parameters. Increasing the Attack softens the overall sound, whereas increasing the Release brings a more legato feel.

The Hold button freezes the envelope at a specific time. CV control is available from the rear of the unit, and using an LFO or Matrix sequencer can create really interesting rhythmic effects beyond just the parameters available on the BV512.

Fig. 11-10

The Shift parameter shifts the carrier signal up and down and can create phaser-style effects.

The HF Emphasis knob boosts the high frequencies in the Carrier signal, giving the tone of the overall sound a more cutting edge.

The Dry/Wet controls the balance between the modulator and vocoded sound. This should be left fully wet for classic vocoder applications.

In addition to sequencing with the BV512, it is possible to vocode in real time, using a microphone. This involves routing from the physical input to the Modulator input on the synth and connecting a microphone to the appropriate input.

This allows you to create the singing synthesizer sounds often heard in such bands as Trans Am.

THE SIDE-CHAIN BASS LINE

The use of side-chaining is often used in various style of music. Let's take a look at a side-chain bass line frequently heard in progressive and tech house tracks. It often sounds as if the bass sounds are in reverse and has a sucking quality to it.

The concept is simple. The bass synthesizer is run through a compressor, only the compressor is being triggered by another source via its Side-Chain input.

Create a Malstrom synthesizer and load the Killer Bass patch from the Bass folder.

With the Malstrom selected, create an M-Class compressor.

The M-Class Compressor will automatically cable itself between the Malstrom's outputs and the Mixer inputs.

Next, create a ReDrum. Cable the Stereo output of the ReDrum to the Side-Chain input of the compressor.

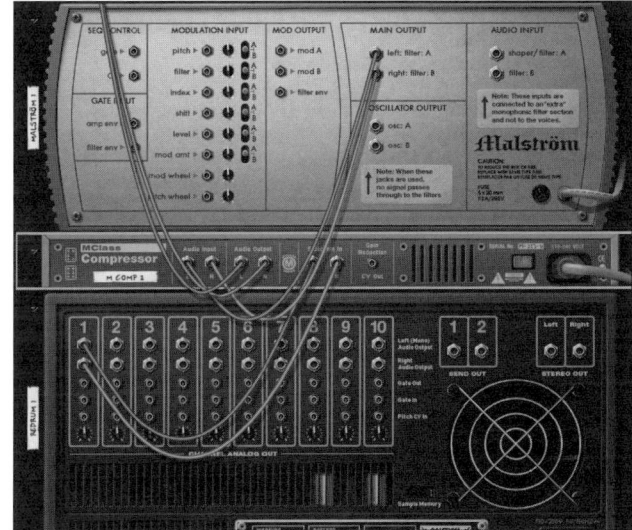

Fig. 11-11

On the M-Class Compressor, set the Ratio its highest setting (infinite:1).

Lower the Threshold to the left.

The Attack should be at its fastest setting, fully left, while the Release should be set fully right.

On the ReDrum, program a quarter-note kick drum pattern, using buttons 1, 5, 9, and 13.

Finally, record a bass line for the Malstrom track. You'll hear the classic side-chain bass line.

Fig. 11-12

ANALOG DRUM SEQUENCER

On the enclosed DVD or available from the Hal Leonard website, you will find a Combinator patch called Analog Drum Sequencer, which consists of a 14:2 mixer, ReDrum, and ten Subtractors. The ReDrum, which has no sounds loaded into it, is used to trigger ten Subtractors, each having an analog drum sound loaded into it. The Subtractors' outputs are connected to the 14:2, as a submixer, but it is possible to create ten Mix Channel devices and route each Subtractor to its own separate channel on the main mixer.

Fig. 11-13

To open, simply double-click on the Combi file located on the DVD, or create a Combinator and use the patch browser to navigate to the DVD containing the file.

Once the file is opened, click the Run button on the ReDrum transport and you'll hear a very basic pattern playing.

Select the Show Devices button, tab to the rear of the rack, and examine the wiring.

In Fig. 11.14, you'll find the Gate output of Channel 1 on the ReDrum is routed to the Gate input of the Subtractor's sequencer control. The Audio output of the Subtractor 1 is routed to the mixer.

This method of sequencing can be used with any of the instruments within

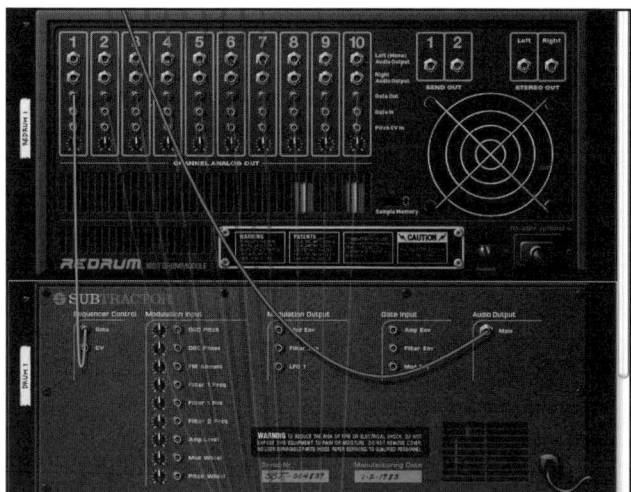

Fig. 11-14

Reason. Why not use the ReDrum with a Kong Drum Designer—an excellent combination!

THE REGROOVE MIXER

Up until now, you've been focusing on creative ways of routing signals within the rack. The ReGroove mixer gives you creative control over MIDI note data.

Imagine having a session drummer or bass player on hand to play on your tracks. Perhaps you're looking for cutting-edge grooves for hip-hop from top producers or an MPC-60. All of these options and more are readily available from the vast library of groove template presets.

Fig. 11-15

Reason's ReGroove mixer combines quantization, shuffle, and groove templates into a thirty-two-channel mixer. The mixer interface is shows eight channels at a time, but has four banks (A through D), giving a total of thirty-two channels to work with. Let's take a look at how to set up and use the ReGroove mixer.

SETTING UP THE REGROOVE MIXER

To begin, open the Chapter 11—ReGroove Mixer song file located on the DVD or available for download at the Hal Leonard website.

Once the file is open, you'll find a ReDrum drum machine with a eight-bar drum loop on the sequencer. The drum loop was first created with the ReDrum and then copied to the sequencer, using the Copy Pattern to Track function found in the Edit menu.

Hit Play and listen to the basic kick, snare, and high-hat sequence.

You could begin using the ReGroove mixer right away, but it would be better to separate each sound into a separate note lane.

Fig. 11-16

To do this, open the sequencer Tool window by selecting F8 on your computer keyboard.

At the bottom of available MIDI processing tabs, you'll find the Extract Notes to Lanes function.

With the MIDI clip selected, click Explode and then Move.

The MIDI clip will explode into separate lanes for the kick, snare, and high hat.

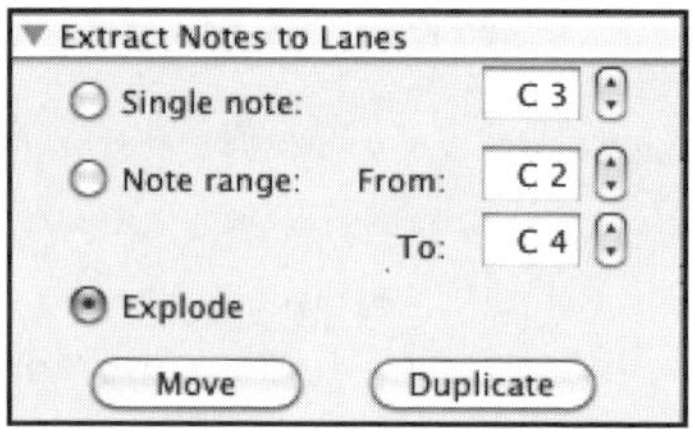

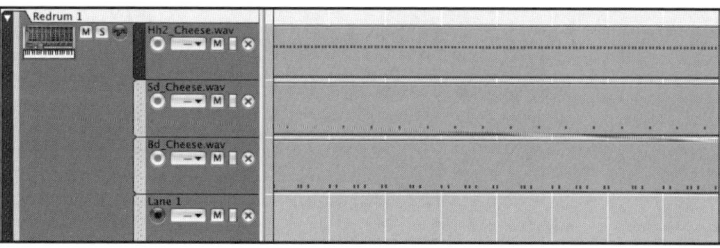

Fig. 11-17

Assign each of the new pattern lanes to a mixer channel on the ReGroove mixer via the drop-down menu. The drop-down menu is located next to the Record Ready button. It will open up to reveal four banks (A through D).

Fig. 11-18

Assign the kick to channel A1.

Assign the snare to channel A2.

Assign the high hat to channel A3.

Next, open the ReGroove mixer via the ReGroove Mixer button located on the Transport.

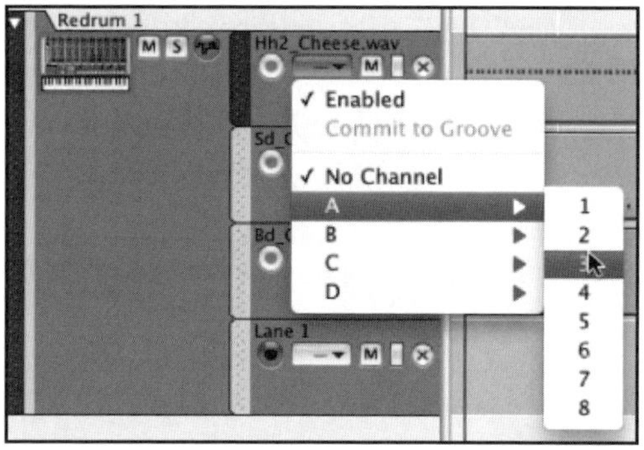

GLOBAL PARAMETERS

On the left side of the ReGroove mixer, you'll find the Global parameters.

Fig. 11-19

The Global parameters are Bank Selection, Anchor Point, and Global Shuffle.

Fig. 11-20

Bank Selection

At the top you will see letters A, B, C, and D. Selecting one of the four options will change the shown mixer to reveal eight additional channel strips, thirty-two channels in total.

Anchor Point

This parameter is used as an offset for the ReGroove mixer. In instances when you would not wish the ReGroove mixer to start at Measure 1, the anchor point offers an offset of up to seventeen bars. This feature is great for intros and pickups, where you would wish to delay the start of the ReGroove mixer processing.

Fig. 11-21

It's also worth mentioning that any time signature change will result in the groove's restarting. This can be used to great effect with long MIDI clips or clips of unusual lengths.

Global Shuffle

Shuffle is a rhythmic programming of moving every even-numbered division closer to the odd-numbered ones—like playing a triplet, but skipping the second note. It is a difficult function to describe, but quite easy to hear.

The global shuffle offers a program-wide setting for varying degrees of shuffle (or swing). It provides a cadence to straight programmed notes.

At 50 percent, the shuffle effect is essentially turned off, with no discernable difference to the programming. A setting of 66 percent yields a perfect triplet.

The global shuffle works with any device that's offers the shuffle function, such as the ReDrum, RPG-8, and Matrix Pattern Sequencer. There are also global shuffle options for any of the channels on the ReGroove mixer.

REGROOVE CHANNEL STRIP

The ReGroove channel strip is tied directly to the assignment on the sequencer page. In this tutorial, the first three channels of the ReGroove mixer have been assigned to the kick, snare, and high hat.

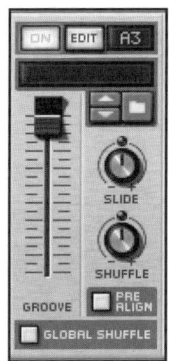

You'll be using channel A3 to explore the channel strip. This channel is assigned to the high hat, which is playing a straight sixteenth-note sequence.

You'll begin by investigating the Slide and Shuffle parameters.

Shuffle

As previously described, shuffle changes the rhythm of a straight sequence. Move the Shuffle knob to the right and you'll hear the shuffle in full effect.

The Shuffle knob offers a range of 25 to 75 percent. At a value of 66 percent, you'll   **Fig. 11-22**
be hearing a perfect triplet.

I typically use a shuffle setting of 55 to 60 percent.

Before continuing, return the Shuffle knob to 50 percent.

Slide

This feature could easily be labeled Rush and Drag. It moves note data earlier or later in time, which gives some dramatic effects. Musicians will sometimes play notes early to create a sense of urgency. By that same token, they may wish to add a laid-back feel by playing notes later.

The Slide knob shifts notes by up to 120 ticks (plus or minus) to generate this effect.

BROWSE GROOVE PATCH

Just above the Slide knob, you'll find the Browse Groove Patch button. Pressing this button opens the patch browser into the ReGroove Patches folder.

Here, you'll find six folders with multiple groove patches.

If you haven't done so already, hit Play on the Transport and audition the different groove patches in real time:

Bass-Comp

Bass grooves played by session musicians containing timing, velocity, and note length information.

DRUMMER

Drum grooves played by a session drummer containing timing and velocity.

MPC-60

Grooves taken from the Akai MPC-60, originally designed by Roger Linn. It has become a staple in hip-hop production.

PERCUSSION

Shaker and Tambourine grooves played by a session musician, with timing and velocity information.

PROGRAMMED

Grooves programmed by producers for hip-hop and pop-rock production.

VINYL

Grooves taken from samples of classic vinyl records, with timing and velocity information.

Groove Amount Fader

After you've explored the available grooves, select Sloppy Cruise.grov from the Programmed > Hiphop folder.

On the left side of the channel strip, you will find a fader. This is used to adjust the amount of the selected groove. By default, it's set at 100 percent; sliding the fader down will decrease the amount of the groove effect.

GROOVE SETTINGS

Selecting the Edit button at the top of the channel strip will open the Groove Settings tab of the floating Tool window.

This window gives you even more control over the selected groove, with parameter sliders for timing impact, velocity impact, and note length impact.

The range offered is 0 to 200 percent.

The random timing injects timing randomization up to 120 ticks.

These parameters work in conjunction with the groove amount fader on the ReGroove mixer and permit precise customization over the groove's impact on the MIDI clip. This way, you may adjust timing and velocity data independently of each other.

REGROOVE MIXER TIPS

Experimentation is key when using the ReGroove mixer, but here are some tips that may help you get the most out of this feature.

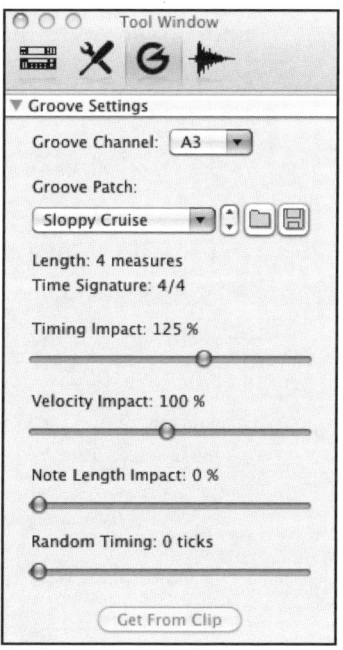

Fig. 11-23

- Use the same groove with different variations on timing and velocity impacts. You may find different grooves that work well with each other, but more often than not, the grooves may clash. By using the same groove algorithms with different settings will help your grooves to lock.
- Don't forget to use the Shuffle and Slide knobs with groove patches.
- Less is more. The ReGroove mixer offers a wide resolution, but you may find that the subtleties in randomization and timing can have a huge impact on the groove your programming.
- Use your ears. Try not to focus on what the data sliders and knobs are showing. Your ears are the best judge of how something sounds. Again, less is more.

COMMIT TO GROOVE

The ReGroove mixer applies its effect to the playback of the MIDI data, meaning it's done in real time as you play the track. However, there may be times when you wish to edit the grooves manually from the sequencer window. To do this, you will need to use the function Commit to Groove

There are two ways to engage this function.

All Grooves

All pattern lanes are tied to a specific track. If you wish to commit all the grooves for that track, simply select the track and click Commit to Groove from the Edit menu.

All the grooves will be printed to the MIDI clips on the sequencer page and the groove channel selection will be deselected.

Single Note Lanes

If you wish to only commit one note lane out of two or more, you'll need to disable the groove select on lanes you don't wish to commit. For instance, if you only wish to commit the high-hat track, you would need to disable the kick and snare tracks.

Once the grooves have been disabled, you may use the Commit to Groove on the note lane's Groove Select drop-down menu.

CREATING GROOVES

It is possible to extract groove information from any MIDI clip, whether it's played, programmed, imported, or copied from a device.

Let's look at how to extract a groove from a Dr. OctoRex patch.

- Start by creating a Dr. OctoRex Loop Player.
- Next, select Percussion > Tabla 75–2 from the patch browser.
- Now, select loop Slot 2 and open the programmer.
- Click the Copy Loop to Track button.
- You should now have four MIDI clips on the Dr. OctoRex track on the sequencer window.
- With the Groove Setting tab selected on the floating Tool window, select a blank groove channel (A4).
- Right-click or use Control + Click on one of the MIDI clips on the Dr. OctoRex note lane and select Get Groove from Clip. (You may also use the Edit menu.)
- A new groove will appear in the Groove Setting window named User 1.
- Finally, change the groove selection on the sequencer channels for the kick, snare, and high-hat lanes on the ReDrum track.

If you like the new groove and wish you use it again, you should save it via the Save Patch button on the Groove Settings window of the floating Tool window.

Tips for Creating Grooves

Try to use grooves with a sixteenth-note resolution. Also, keep in mind that grooves that are not constant will introduce gaps in the groove extraction. For example, if you have a sixteenth-note sequence that's missing some sixteenth notes, the groove, when applied, will not have groove information for the blank sections. Not that this is a bad thing, just something to keep in mind when creating grooves.

Grooves work best in even multiples of two (one, two, four, or eight measures).

Avoid broad ranges in velocities on your source clip, as this may cause unwanted dips in velocity information.

IN CONCLUSION

As you can see, the ReGroove mixer is a powerful tool for injecting a humanized feel to a static groove. With a little finesse, your tracks will take on a whole new level of expression and emotion.

Building an Arrangement

BEFORE YOU BEGIN

When beginning the task of writing a song, I personally find that it is important to be in the right mind-set. I always recommend being well rested and having eaten some food to ensure solid focus. It's also important to take a ten-minute break every forty-five minutes to an hour, to help maintain adequate performance while working. I also find that it's easier to block out at least three hours or more to work uninterrupted. There's nothing more frustrating than having the phone ring every five minutes, so you may wish to minimize such distractions. I'm also not a fan of working longer than eight hours in any one session, but if you're in the "zone," then by all means, run with it. However you choose to work long hours at a stretch, be sure to keep yourself well hydrated and, again, take regular breaks.

SONG STRUCTURE

Song writing can be a difficult task, especially for a first-time songwriter. Even seasoned professionals often suffer from writer's block or have a hard time with structure, especially if they are writing in an unfamiliar genre.

A variety of sources available from books and the Internet are dedicated to song writing and structure. Much of the structural issues you may encounter depend on the genre of music you are writing. Rock and pop music will differ greatly from jazz and classical. Even electronic dance music is comprised of several genres and subgenres.

Critical listening can be a great process, whereby the listener consciously notes the changes in structure of an already completed song. Using this song as a reference track to help guide you through the process of structuring your own song can really speed things up and prevent unwanted frustration.

In this chapter, you'll be creating a short electronic dance track in the genre of bass music; more specifically, dubstep.

Where most songs of this genre tend to be five to six minutes in length, the track you ill be creating is about three minutes.

This song features a simplified structure including an intro, main, middle eight (or breakdown) and coda (outro). You'll also be exploring how to use Reason's Block sequencer, a function that lends itself to working with loop based music.

Your first task will be to create the main part of the song. We'll then bring it into the block sequencer and finish building out the other parts of the song.

GETTING STARTED

Begin by opening the Reason song file "Building an Arrangement," found on the enclosed DVD or available for download from the Hal Leonard website.

Once the song is open, you'll find that I chose the template "Empty + FX" as the starting point. This template includes three time-based effects already connected to the main mixer via sends 1, 2, and 3, as well as the mastering effects via the Master Bus Insert section.

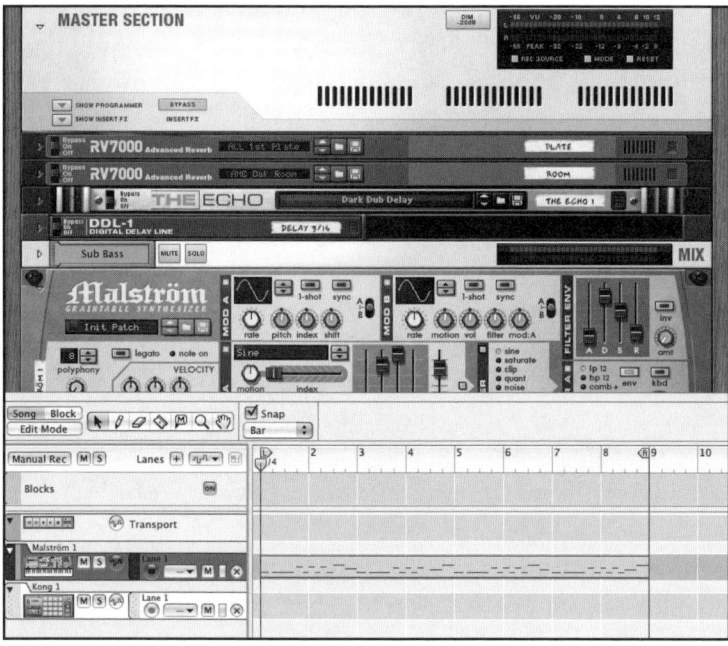

Fig. 12-1

By default, the master insert effects are bypassed, but go ahead and deselect the Bypass InsertFX to make them active. The M-Class Maximizer is the only effect currently set to process signals. Having this engaged will prevent the stereo bus from clipping and protect your monitors (and your ears).

On the sequencer, you'll find an eight-bar MIDI clip for a Malstrom synthesizer. The current patch is a sine wave sub bass, which is created when initializing the Malstrom.

You will also find a Kong, with a custom set of effects loaded into it. All these sounds are included in the Reason Factory sound bank and I've left a few slots open, in case you wished to load your own.

THE MAIN SECTION

You'll begin by building up the main section of the song, starting with the drums and bass.

Create a Dr. OctoRex

From the Create menu, select Instruments >Dr. OctoRex Loop Player.

Next, on the patch browser, select Dr. OctoRex Patches > Drums > Electronic Drums > Dubstep > Elec Drums / Dubstep Loops 140 –1.drex.

On the Dr. OctoRex, select Slot 2, DbStp02_Aggrostep.

Unfold the programmer and click the Copy Loop to Track button.

Finally, deselect the Enable Loop Playback on the main interface.

Press Play and listen to the drum loop and bass line together.

The drum loop has a heavy swing with a lot of triplet notes. The bass line is recorded straight and requires some tweaking to lock it into the drum loop.

Get Groove from Clip

Select the Dr. OctoRex MIDI clip and open the Tool window (F8) to the Groove tab. Select Get from Clip at the bottom of the window.

Before leaving this window, be sure to save the new user clip as AggroStep.

Assigning the Groove

On the Malstrom track, assign the Select Groove drop-down menu to A1, which will have the AggroStep groove loaded.

Press Play and listen to the results. Although the difference is subtle, the sub bass now locks to the Dr. OctoRex Loop Player perfectly.

Print the output of the groove assignment by clicking the Select Groove drop-down menu and selecting Commit to Groove.

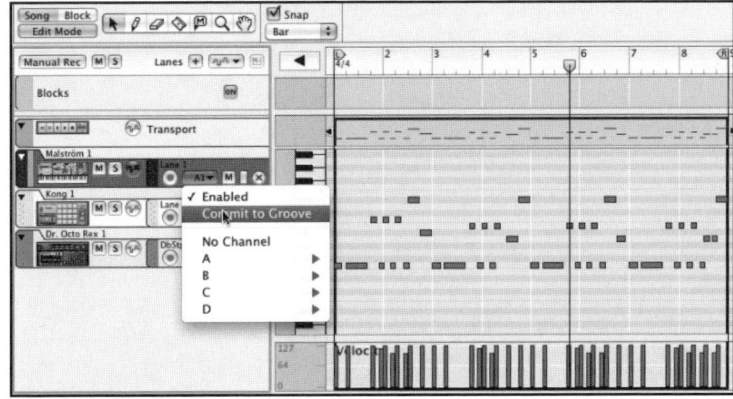

Fig. 12-2

Layering Drums

Next, you'll need to build up the drum track by recording the kick and snare pattern played from the Dr. OctoRex.

First, create a Kong Drum Designer and select the preset from Kong Patches > Kong Kits (mapped for keyboard) > Club Kits > UK Funky [k].kong.

You'll use the kick on C1 and the clap on D1.

To make things easier, I suggest turning on the Quantize During Recording function and set your quantization to 1/8 T (eighth-note triplet). I also suggest turning your Snap value to 1/8 T (eighth-note triplet).

Do your best to play the sequence as close to the Dr. OctoRex loop as possible. You may find it easier to pencil in the notes.

- Clap (D2) should be on the third beat of every bar.
- 1.3.1.0
- 2.3.1.0
- 3.3.1.0
- 4.3.1.0
- 5.3.1.0
- 6.3.1.0
- 7.3.1.0
- 8.3.1.0
- Kick (C1) should be on the following:
- 1.1.1.0
- 2.1.1.0
- 2.4.4.0
- 3.1.1.0
- 3.4.3.160
- 4.1.1.0
- 4.1.3.80
- 4.2.2.80
- 4.2.3.80
- 4.4.3.80
- 5.1.1.0
- 6.1.1.0
- 6.4.1.0
- 6.4.2.80

- 6.4.3.160
- 7.1.1.0
- 8.1.1.0
- 8.1.3.160
- 8.2.2.80
- 8.2.3.160
- 8.4.3.160

Once all the notes are in place, you may notice that some of the kicks may be a little off. Use the Select Groove drop-down menu containing the AggroStep preset you created earlier. Your new MIDI clip should mirror the Dr. OctoRex, adding depth and punch to the drum tracks.

Note that some of the kick velocities are still a bit high, where they should be lower. An easy fix for this is to open the Tool window to the Groove Settings tab and adjust the velocity impact to 200 percent.

Finally, print the groove by clicking the Select Groove drop-down menu and selecting Commit to Groove. If you go back and look at the MIDI data after they have been committed, you'll find some subtle timing variations to most of the MIDI notes, which really locks in the groove.

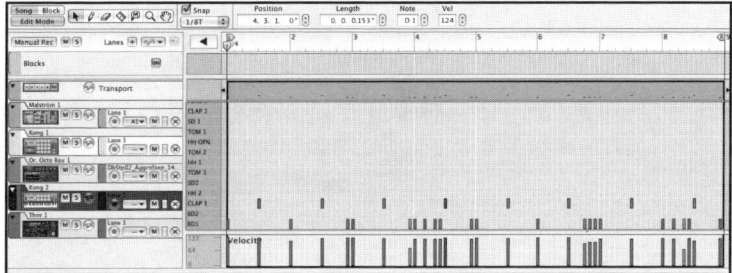

Fig. 12-3

Wobble Bass I

From the Create menu, select Instruments > Thor Polysonic Synthesizer. From the patch browser, select Thor Patches > Lead Synths > GammaPoisoning.

Listening to this sequence, you'll find that it's too low and needs to be transposed up one octave. Either select all the notes and move them up one octave manually, or use the Transpose tab from the Sequencer Tool tab of the Tool window by setting the transpose to 12 semitones and clicking Apply.

Now that you've got the sound in the right octave, let's make one tweak to the GammaPoisoning patch that will help provide definition to the sound.

Click the Show Programmer button and change LFO 1's waveform from a triangle to a sine wave.

Before moving on to the next section, you'll first need to tweak the current MIDI clip.

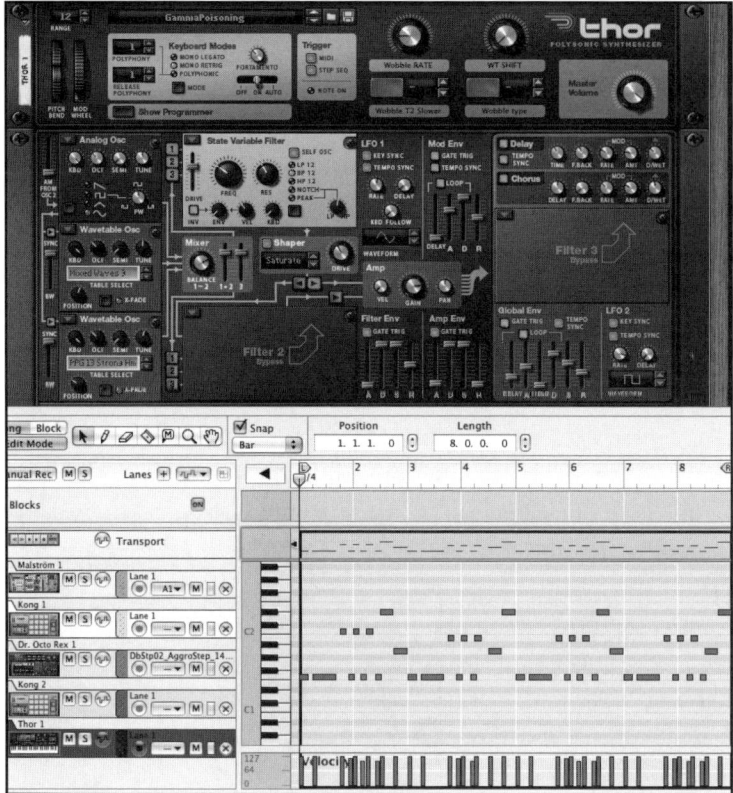

Fig. 12-4

In Fig. 12.5, note how the last two notes of Measures 2 and 4 are selected. You need to quantize these notes and fix the note length. This can be done manually, but try using the sequencer tools from the Tool window.

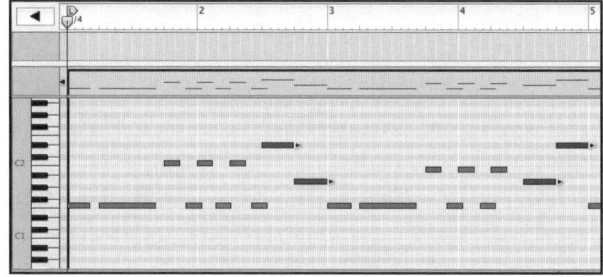

Fig. 12-5

First, select note D#2. Either right-click or from the Edit menu, click Select Notes of Same Pitch.

Next, from the sequencer Tool window, set the Quantize value to eighth notes and hit Apply.

On the Note Lengths tab, set the fix row to 0.1.0.0 and hit Apply.

Next, select note A2 and follow the same process.

Wobble Bass 2

From the Create menu, select Instruments > Thor Polysonic Synthesizer. From the patch browser, select Thor Patches > Lead Synths > VenusFlyTrap.

Click the Show Programmer button and change LFO 1's waveform from a triangle to a sine wave.

Click the Show Programmer button and set LFO 1's Kbd Follow knob to 0 (full left).

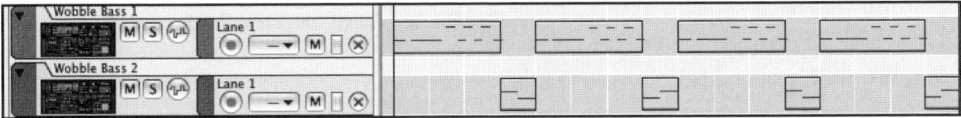

Fig. 12-6

Using the Razor tool, make slices on the Wobble Bass 1 MIDI clip at the following points:

- 2.3.1.0
- 3.1.1.0
- 4.3.1.0
- 5.1.1.0
- 6.3.1.0
- 7.1.1.0
- 8.3.1.0

Move the slices down onto the Wobble Bass 2 track.

Listen to the changes that have been made. You've just created a "call and response" with the two wobble bass sounds, which adds a subtle variation to the overall sound and creates a dynamic element.

Wobble Bass 3

With the Wobble Bass 2 track selected, click Duplicate Tracks and Devices from the Edit menu.

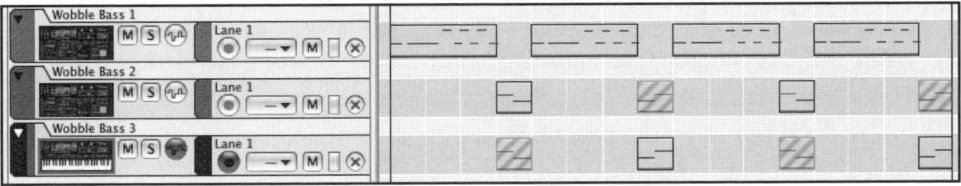

Fig. 12-7

On the newly created Thor, adjust the Kbd Follow knob to 32.

Using the Mute tool, mute the first and third clip on the Wobble Bass 3 track and the second and fourth clip on Wobble Bass 2.

An alternative method of muting (and unmuting) is to simply select the clips and then press the M key on your computer keyboard.

Renaming your tracks is a great practice to get into, so if you haven't done so already, take a minute now to rename each of the tracks with a suitable name.

Fig. 12-9

Kong FX

Now, let's add some sound effects to further enhance the rhythm of the groove. Using F1 and G1, alternate

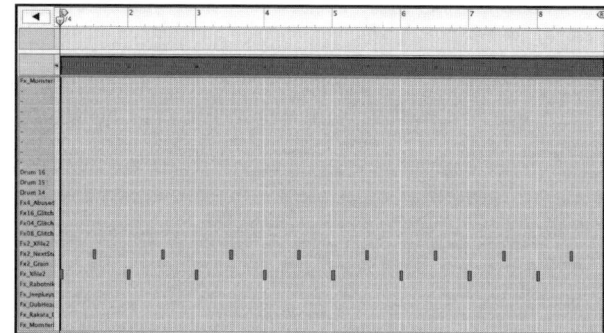

Fig. 12-10

on the first and third beat of each measure, starting with F1.

Remember to assign the Select Groove drop-down to A1 (AggroStep) and commit the groove.

BLOCKS

It is entirely possible to work with Reason without ever needing to use the Blocks function, but I would be remiss if I didn't mention this useful tool while building an arrangement.

Keep in mind, it's not necessary to work this way, but I find it invaluable and time saving when done properly.

Working with Blocks is very similar to working with patterns on a drum machine. You may have any number of tracks with recorded sequenced materials that can be easily and quickly replicated throughout your song. Any new MIDI clips recorded from Song mode will override the data contained in a block. This allows for variations to be easily created and applied on data throughout the entire song.

To utilize the Block function, you'll first need to either record or, in your case, copy and paste the MIDI clips into the Block mode of the sequencer.

Select all the MIDI clips by rubber-band selecting or using the key command Command + A if using a Mac or Control + A if using Windows. Once all the clips have been selected, use the copy key command Command + C if using a Mac or Control + C if using Windows.

Fig. 12-11

Next, engage the Block mode from the Transport (See Fig. 12.10).

The upper left corner of the sequencer window contains the Song, Block, and Edit buttons. These controls allow us to switch between the different modes.

Click the Block button or use the key command B to engage the Block mode.

Once Block mode is engaged, paste in the copied MIDI clips. You should now see the same sequence of MIDI clips you created earlier. Without the loop button engaged on the Transport, the sequence will automatically loop between the beginning and end markers. The L and R locators allow for looping a section within the block, for the purpose of editing and arranging.

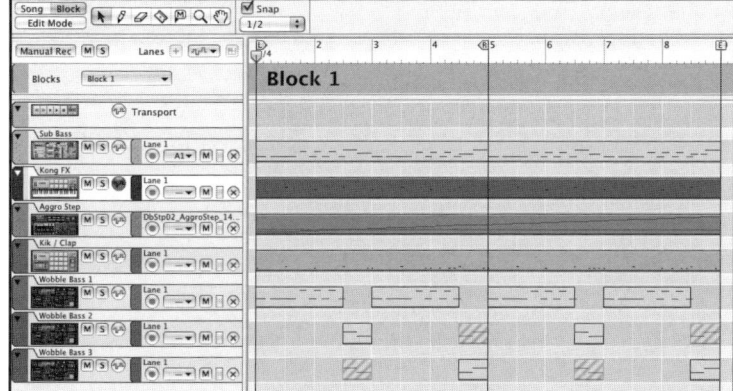

Fig. 12-12

Any MIDI clips outside the range of the block (denoted by the End marker) will be ignored from Song mode. This is useful if you have different ideas for MIDI clips, which can be held in Block mode without affecting the playback while in Song mode.

Fig. 12-13

To rename a block, simply double-click on the title located in the colored bar running across the top of the Block View window and input the title Main.

On the track list in the upper left corner, there is a box labeled Main. Clicking in this box reveals a drop-down list of thirty-two available blocks.

The recording and editing features function the same in Block mode as they do when working in Song mode. To edit a MIDI clip, simply double-click to open the Editor view.

A quick method for toggling between Edit mode and Block mode is to use the key command Shift + Tab. The MIDI editors are only available from within the mode from which they originated. For example, you can only edit MIDI data created in Block mode from the Block view. The same can be said for any data recorded in Song view.

Block Sequencing

Switch back to Song mode by clicking the Song button or use the key command B on your computer keyboard.

To sequence a block, click and drag with the Pencil tool from Measure 17 to Measure 49.

The first block is always designated as the default clip. Click on the name of the block to reveal the drop-down list, which will enable you to select a different block.

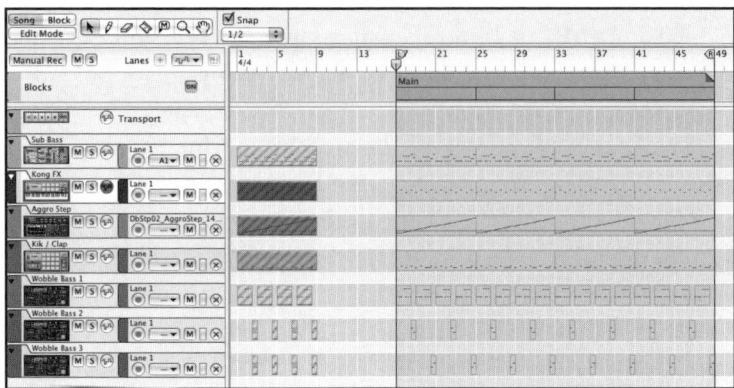

Fig. 12-14

It is also possible to use Option + Click if using a Mac or Alt + Click if using Windows and Drag to copy a block into a new destination. When copying, be sure to click on the bottom half of the block, below the block name.

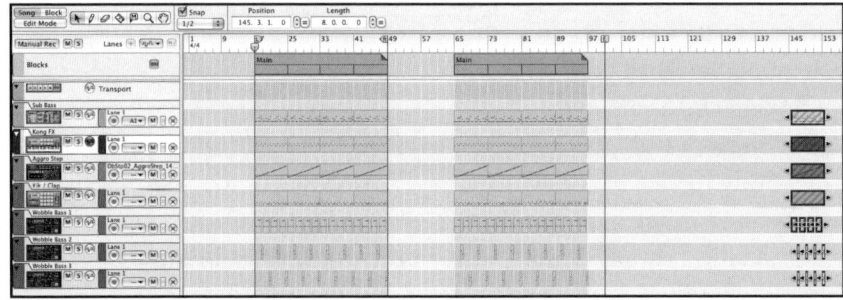

Fig. 12-15

Copy the main block from Measure 17 to Measure 65. Also, mute the MIDI clips originally recorded from Song mode and move them to Measure 145.

INTRO

The intro section of a song helps to set the tone of the entire piece. Also, tracks that are DJ friendly will typically include sixteen to thirty-two bars, allowing enough time for two tracks to be mixed together.

In the case of this track, you're already set to record a sixteen-bar intro. You'll be using elements from the main section with some additional effects, or what I like to call ear candy.

Drums

You'll start by creating a high-hat sequence, using the AggroStep loop from the Dr. OctoRex Loop Player.

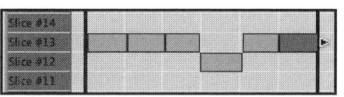

Copy the AggroStep drum loop from Measure 145 to Measure 1 and unmute it.

Fig. 12-16

Next, set the Left (L) locator to 2.1.1.0 and the Right (R) locator to 2.3.1.0.

With the Slice tool, cut the MIDI clip at the locator positions. You may have to change the Snap value to make some of the selections.

Once you've made the slices, delete the first and last part so that you are left with just the loop.

Double-click to enter Edit mode.

Rearrange the slices so they resemble the image shown in Fig. 12.15.

Exit out of Edit mode and move the clip to the beginning of Measure 1.

Copy the clip by using Command + C if using a Mac or Control + C if using Windows, and paste the clip by using Command + V if using Mac or Control + V if using Windows. Note that once you've copied the clip, the SPL moves to the end of the clip and with each successive paste, the SPL moves to the end of the clip. This is a fast and easy method for duplicating clips.

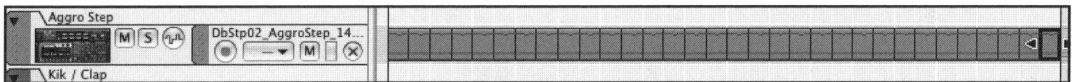

Fig. 12-17

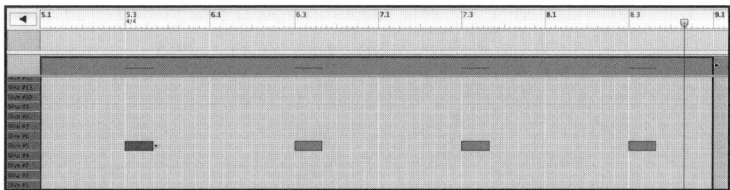

Duplicate the clip as described, to Measure 17.

Select the + button at the top of the track list to create a new note lane for the AggroStep track.

Next, using the Pencil tool, create

Fig. 12-18

a blank MIDI clip from Measure 5 to Measure 9 (four bars).

Double-click the newly created clip to enter Edit mode.

With the Pencil tool, draw in a MIDI notes on the Slice 5 row at every third beat. Make sure the note length is at least 0.0.2.160 long.

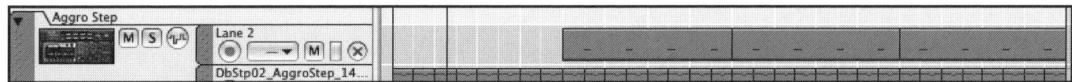

Fig. 12-19

Select Shift + Tab to exit out of Edit mode. Duplicate the snare clip two times, ending at Measure 17.

Next, let's add some kick drum from the Kick/Snare track, using the Kong Drum Designer.

Using the Pencil tool, create a one-measure clip at Measure 9.

Double-click the clip to enter Edit mode and draw in a single note on the BD1 row at 9.1.1.0.

Click Shift + Tab to exit out of Edit mode.

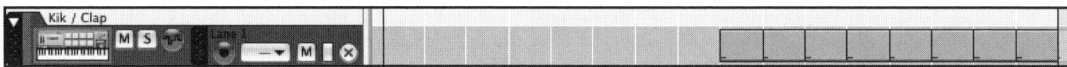

Fig. 12-19

Duplicate the kick drum clip to Measure 17.

Select the clips at Measures 15 and 16 and use the key command Command + J if using a Mac or Control + J if using Windows to join the two into one two-measure clip.

Double-click to enter edit mode.

Now, you'll create a kick drum roll leading up to the main section of the song.

In Measure 15, add a kick drum on every quarter note.

Fig. 12-20

Change the Snap value to eighth notes. At Measure 16, place a kick drum note on every eighth note. You may have to resize your MIDI note so that the notes don't overlap.

Change the Snap value to sixteenth notes and create eight sixteenth notes from 16.3.1.0 to Measure 17.

Kong FX

The Kong FX patch used here isn't a preset. Instead, it is one I created for this tutorial from scratch. However, all the samples used to create this patch are included in the Reason Factory Soundbank. If you wish to add more sounds to the patch, the process is quite easy.

ADDING CUSTOM SOUNDS
First, navigate to the Kong FX Instrument in the rack.

Next, select a blank slot, such as Drum 14.

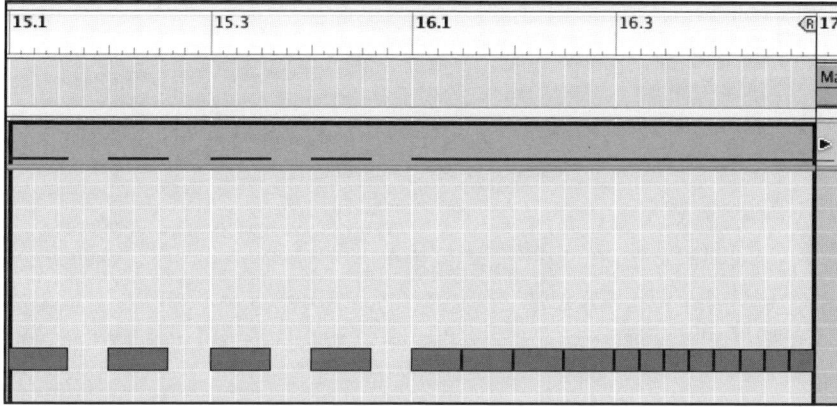

Fig. 12-21

Then, select the Browse Drum Patch button, located on the left side of the main interface. With the browser open, select the Reason Factory Soundbank and navigate to the Kong Patches folder. From the Kong Sound and Samples folder, select Noises and FX or Found Sounds.

Additional sounds can be found in the Redrum Drum Kits > xclusive drums-sorted.

You may also have a collection of samples to use or your own recorded samples, which may also be loaded into the Kong.

SEQUENCING THE KONG FX INSTRUMENT

Begin by creating a sixteen-measure clip with the Pencil tool from Measures 1 to 17, and double-click to enter the Edit mode.

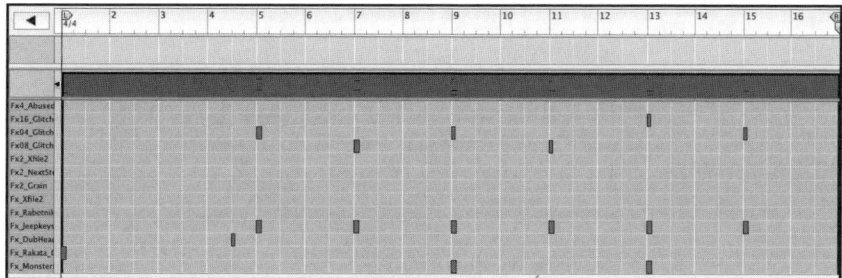

Fig. 12-22

Starting from the bottom, enter the following notes (Most notes are on the first beat of the measure except for FX_Dubhead):

- FX_Monster: 9, 13
- FX_Rakata_Gun: 1
- FX_Dubhead: 4.3.1.0

- FX_Jeepkeys: 5, 7, 9, 11, 13, 15
- FX08_Glitch: 7, 11
- FX04_Glitch: 5, 9, 15
- FX16_Glitch: 13

Wobble Bass I

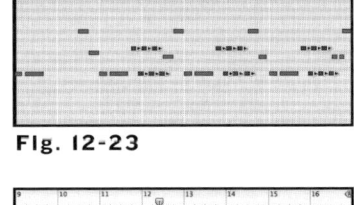

The final clip you will be adding to this arrangement is the Wobble Bass 1 track, including some additional edits.

First, copy the Sub Bass clip on Measure 145 to the Wobble Bass 1 track at Measure 9.

Fig. 12-23

Transpose the entire sequence up one octave (either manually or from the Pitch section of the sequencer Tool window).

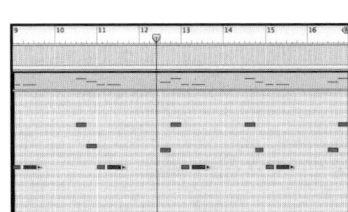

Next, double-click the clip to enter Edit mode.

Start by deleting the short sets of alternating notes in the middle of each phrase (as shown in Fig. 23).

Next, delete the second-to-last note (A1) in the clip at 16.3.3.160.

Fig. 12-24

Follow this by extending note A1 at 16.3.1.0 to 0.1.0.0 in length.

Finally, shorten all the second F1 notes to 0.1.1.0 (as shown in Fig. 12.24).

Listen to changes all your hard work has made.

ADDING ELEMENTS (MAIN SECTION)

As you move through the main section of the song, it becomes apparent that it sounds a little sparse. In this section, let's add some ethereal sounds in the background and a drum roll at the end of the sequence, to liven things up.

Cymbal FX

One of my absolute favorite sounds of the many offered by Reason is the bowed cymbal effect found in the Orkester Sound Library.

To employ this, first create an NN-XT Advanced sampler.

Press the patch browser and navigate to Orkester Sound Bank > Percussion > CYM FX.sxt.

Alternate between notes D3 and E3 on the keyboard every two bars or so. It doesn't need to be exact; rather, the sounds need to move in waves, dynamically getting louder and softer by turn.

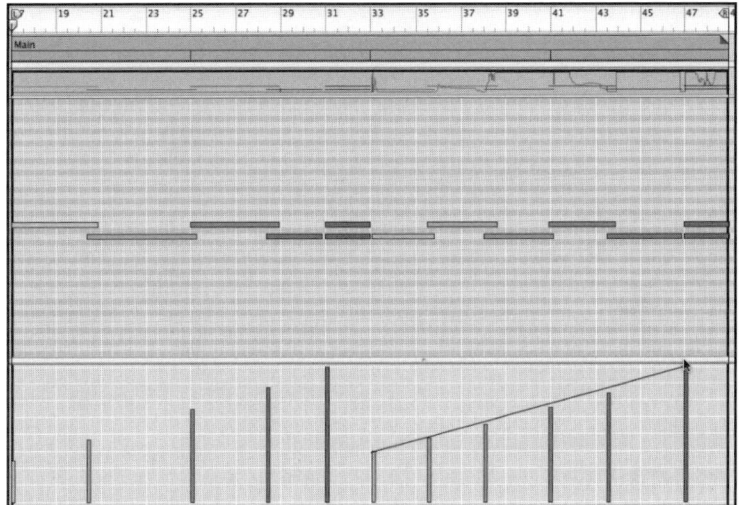

Fig. 12-25

However, at Measures 31 and 47, press both D3 and E3 together for two bars.

Also, adjusting the velocities can help with shaping the overall feeling.

Note how I have created a crescendo, each note getting progressively louder as it approaches Measures 31 and 47.

Creating a crescendo is a quick and easy task.

Start by selecting the Pencil tool.

Next, hold the Option key if using a Mac or the Alt key if using Windows until the pencil turns into a crosshair.

Click and drag your mouse until a horizontal line appears. For a crescendo, start the click at a lower level and drag the line so that it ends at the maximum when at Measure 31.

Repeat the same process for Measures 33 to 47.

Rise Effect

Another type of fun effect is referred to as Stingers. Radio producers use them quite often because they are great effects for adding tension and cueing the listener to an upcoming change. Different categories of stingers include rise, fall, swoops, sweeps, and so on.

In this case, you'll be using a rise effect, whereby the sound increases in pitch and amplitude over time.

First, set up a Combinator from the Create > Other menus.

From the patch browser, select Combinator Patches > Sound FX > Reach4theStars.cmb.

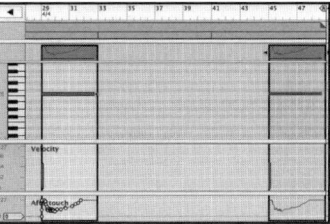

Fig. 12-26

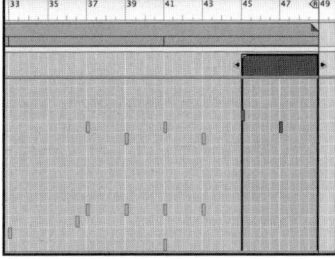

Fig. 12-27

In a lower octave, create a single four-measure note starting at Measure 29. Copy the clip to Measure 45.

Kong FX

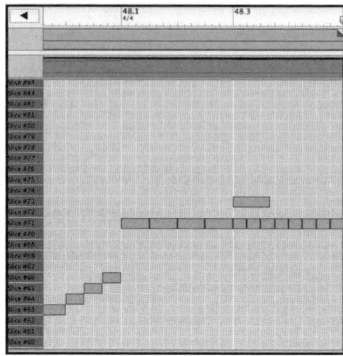

Select the Kong FX track and create a new note lane by clicking the + button at the top of the track list.

Copy the clip from Measure 1 onto the new note lane, starting at Measure 33.

Resize the clip so that it begins at Measure 45 and then double-click to enter Edit mode.

Delete the notes on the FX_Monster and FX_Dubhead **Fig. 12-28** lane.

You should now have a four-measure clip containing two notes.

Drum Roll

As the song progresses toward the end of the main section, let's add a drum roll to indicate the change into the breakdown, or middle eight.

Because you've already created the drum roll at the end of the intro section, simply copy this same drum roll to the end of the main section.

However, you'll need to fix the last two bars of the AggroStep loop, as it is on an eighth-note triplet, and if left as is, will create a sloppy mess.

To correct the timing, copy the AggroStep loop at Measure 145 to Measure 41.

Double-click to enter Edit mode.

Select all the notes at Measure 48 and quantize them to a sixteenth note.

INTRO AND MAIN

You should now have an entire sequence that includes an intro and main section with multiple effects and drum rolls.

In the next section, you'll rebuild the track from the breakdown back into the main section.

BREAK DOWN

The breakdown, or middle eight, offers a rest for your listener. For electronic dance music, it's imperative to allow the audience a chance to catch its breath while building back up to the main section of the song.

For this track, you'll use the intro with some additional effects and new elements.

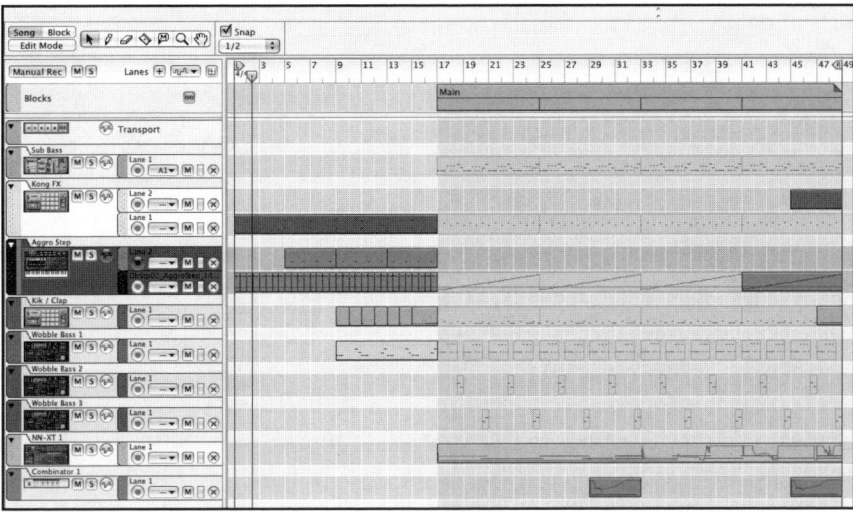

Fig. 12-29

Editing Clips

Start by copying all the clips in the intro section up to Measure 49.

Double-click the Kong FX clip to enter Edit mode.

At Measure 49, move the note from the FX_Rakata_Gun row to the FX_Monster row, just underneath it.

Press Shift + Tab to exit out of Edit mode.

Copy the Kick/Snare clip from Measure 57 to Measure 49.

Adding Effects

With the drum roll and additional effects leading into the main section, you need an equally dramatic explosion of sound to guide the arrangement into the breakdown.

Let's add some additional sound effects at the beginning of the breakdown.

EXPLOSION

Click Combinator from the Create > Other menus.

From the patch browser, select Combinator Patches > Synth FX > HyperSpace Explosion.cmb.

Starting at Measure 49, record a four-measure clip, using note C1.

IMPACT

Now, let's add an additional layer of an impact sample.

First, create an NN-XT Advanced sampler.

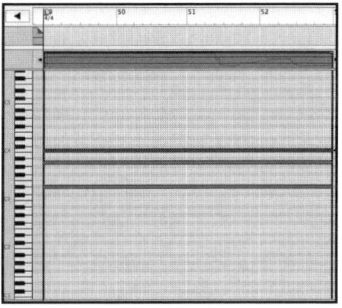

Fig. 12-30

Fig. 12-31

Press the patch browser and navigate to NN-XT Sampler Patches > Sound FX>Impacts.sxt.

Starting at Measure 49, record a four-measure clip, using notes A3 and C4.

Adding Percussion

Next, let's introduce a new percussion element that will play throughout the rest of the track.

First, create a Dr. OctoRex Loop Player.

Initialize the Dr. OctoRex from the Edit menu.

Click on Slot 1 to open the loop browser and then select Dr.Rex Percussion Loops > Tabla 075 bpm > Tabla_01_075.rx2.

Set the left locator (L) to Measure 53 and the right locator (R) to measure 55.

Open the Dr. OctoRex programmer and click the Copy Loop to Track button.

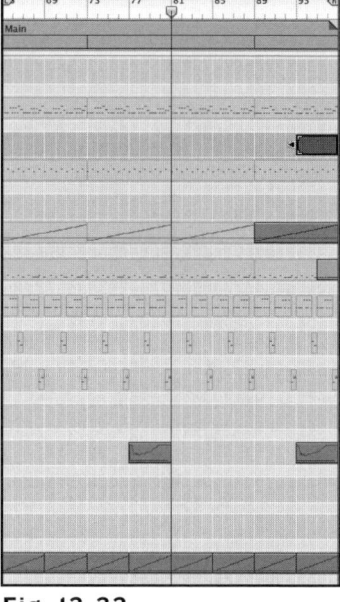

Fig. 12-32

The original tempo of the loop is 75 bpm, but your song is playing at 140 bmp, almost double time. You'll need to scale the tempo to get it to play closer to the original tempo.

To do this, select the MIDI clip and open the sequencer tools in the floating Tool window (F8).

Open the Scale Tempo tab and click the Half button.

The MIDI clip will now be twice as long, with the notes scaled to half time.

Duplicate the Tabla loop to the end of Measure 97.

Finally, set the Select Groove drop-down menu to A1—AggroStep and increase the Shuffle knob setting to 56 percent.

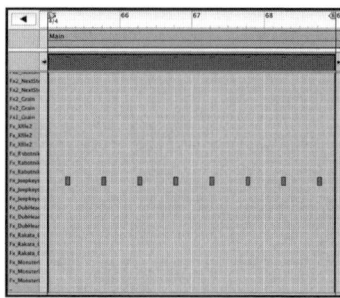

Fig. 12-33

Add the Sub Bass

Your last task for the breakdown will be to copy the Sub Bass MIDI clip from Measure 145 to Measure 57 and unmute it.

THE SECOND MAIN SECTION

The main section repeats again after the breakdown, starting at Measure 65. I'm a big fan of continuing to build and modify sections so they're not static. A great way of doing this is to add some additional parts and modify existing ones.

But before you start adding new parts, first copy all the additional parts added in the first main section. These include the Drum Roll on the Kick/Snare, Rise, modified AggroStep, Cym Fx, and modified Kong FX track.

The new destinations for the clips are as follows:

- Rise: 77, 93
- Kick/Snare: 95
- AggroStep: 89

You've already added the Tabla percussion loop to play along with the main section. Now, let's add another part from the Kong FX and modify Wobble Bass 1.

Kong FX

Select the Kong FX track and click the + button at the top of the track list.

Next, with the Pencil tool, create a four-measure clip, starting at Measure 65.

Double-click to enter Edit mode.

Place a note on every second and fourth quarter note in the MIDI clip on the FX_ Jeepkeys row.

Press Shift + Tab to switch to Song mode and then duplicate the MIDI clip to Measure 97.

Wobble Bass I

The Wobble Bass 1 patch, coupled with the Wobble Bass 2 and 3, make for a wicked wobbly bass line with a great rhythm and cadence. However, you can inject the sound with a glitch heavy vibe by automating the LFO 1's rate.

To begin, navigate to Wobble Bass 1 in the rack.

Right-click, or control click, on the LFO 1's rate knob and select Edit Automation.

A new lane will appear under the note lane of Wobble Bass 1.

With the Pencil tool, draw in a four-measure clip.

With the new clip selected, press Shift + Tab to enter Edit mode. (By double-clicking you can expand the clip from Song view; while it's possible to edit this way, it is far easier to work in Edit mode.)

In Fig. 12.34, you see the LFO 1 Rate parameter automation lane. Each of the horizontal lines represents a different rate.

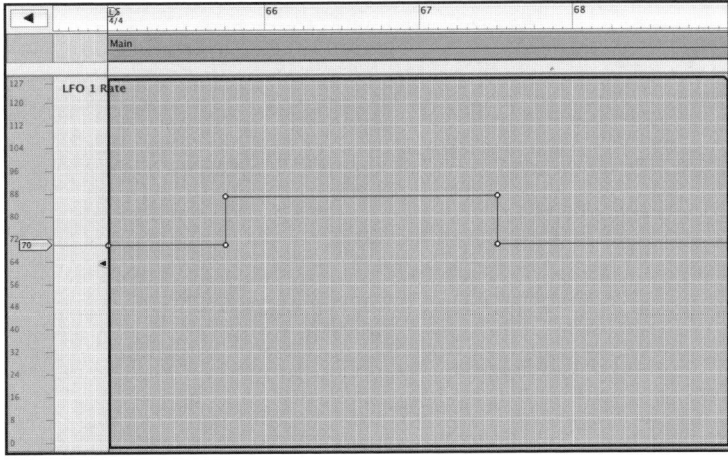

Fig. 12-34

Set your Snap value to 1/8 T (eighth-note triplet).

You can use the Pencil tool to draw in nodes, which are break points in the automation lane. Note that it is important to be accurate when editing these parameters.

To make a change, you'll need to select two nodes. The first will be where the automation starts and the second is the change you wish to make.

Working with nodes can be difficult because it can be a little fiddly and requires some patience, but it's well worth the effort in the end.

Once you have created some nodes, you may wish to edit their values and position. This can be done using the Selector tool.

Pressing and holding the Command key if using a Mac or the Control key if using Windows will switch the Selector tool to the Pencil tool. This enables you to toggle between the tools very quickly.

Also, any of the nodes can be selected by using the rubber-band selection technique. Once selected, it is possible to move nodes together.

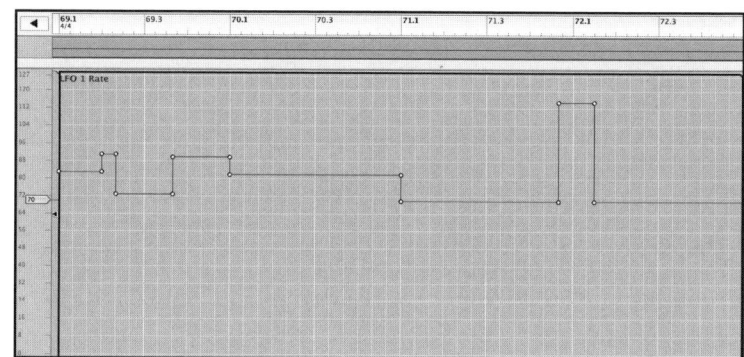

You can also copy automation by selecting nodes and holding down the Option key if using a Mac or the Alt key if using Windows while dragging (remember to release the Option or **Fig. 12-35** Alt key last, or you'll move the data instead of copying them).

MEASURE 65

For the first four-measure segment, re-create the following automation plot. Keep in mind; in most cases you'll need two nodes at each value, the start and the change.

- 65.1.1.0: 70
- 65.4.1.0: 70, 87
- 67.3.1.0: 87, 70

MEASURE 69

Copy the automation clip from Measure 65 to Measure 69.

Create the following automation plot:

- 69.1.1.0: 83
- 69.2.1.0: 83, 91

- 69.2.2.80: 91, 73
- 69.3.3.160: 73, 90
- 70.1.1.0: 90, 82
- 71.1.1.0: 82, 70
- 71.4.3.160: 70, 115
- 72.1.3.0: 115, 70

MEASURE 73

Copy the previous automation clip from Measure 69 to Measure 73.

Create the following automation plot:

- 73.1.1.0: 83
- 73.2.1.0: 83, 91
- 73.2.2.80: 91, 73
- 73.3.3.160: 73, 90
- 74.1.1.0: 90, 82
- 75.1.1.0: 82, 70
- 75.4.3.160: 70, 100
- 76.1.3.0: 100, 70

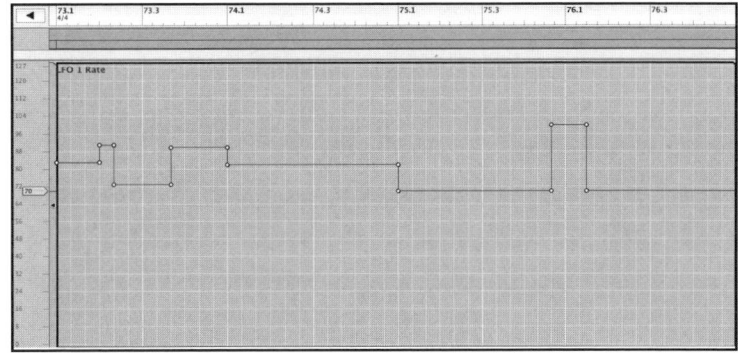

Fig. 12-36

MEASURE 77

Copy the automation clip at Measure 65 to Measure 77.

MEASURE 81

Copy the automation from Measure 73 to Measure 81.

Create the following automation plot:

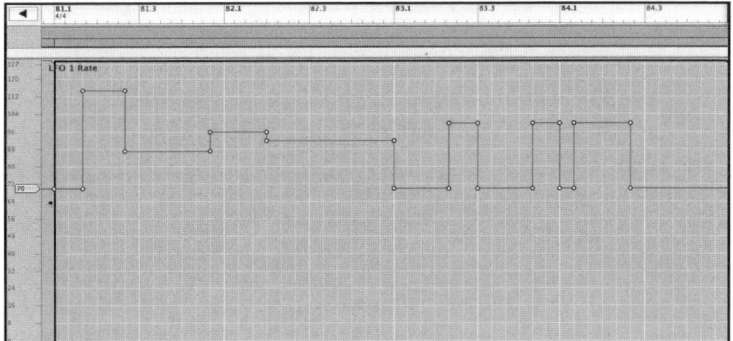

Fig. 12-37

- 81.1.1.0: 70
- 81.1.3.160: 70, 115
- 81.2.3.160: 115, 87
- 81.4.3.160: 87, 96
- 82.2.1.0: 96, 92
- 83.1.1.0: 92, 70
- 83.2.2.80: 70, 100

- 83.3.1.0: 100, 70
- 83.4.2.80: 70, 100
- 84.1.1.0: 100, 70
- 84.1.2.80: 70, 100
- 84.2.3.160: 100, 70

MEASURE 85

Copy the automation clip at Measure 81 to Measure 85.

Create the following automation plot:

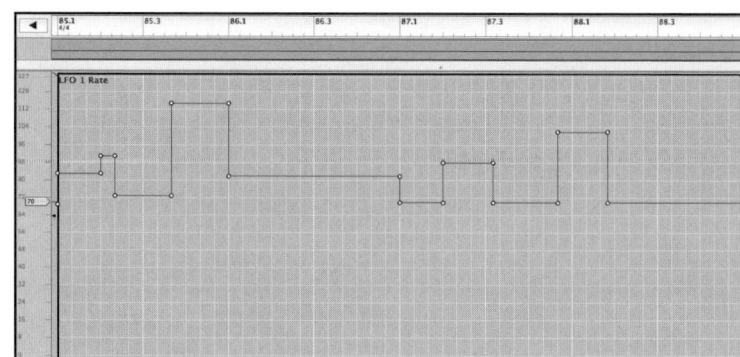

Fig. 12-38

- 85.1.1.0: 83
- 85.2.1.0: 83, 91
- 85.2.2.80: 91, 73
- 85.3.3.160: 73, 115
- 86.1.10: 115, 82
- 87.1.1.0: 82, 70
- 87.2.1.0: 70, 88
- 87.3.1.160: 88, 70
- 87.4.3.160: 70, 102
- 88.1.4.80: 102, 70

MEASURE 89

Copy the automation clip at Measure 73 to Measure 89.

MEASURE 93

Copy the automation clip at Measure 77 to Measure 93.

You should now have eight automation clips on the parameter automation lane for LFO 1's rate on the Wobble Bass 1 track.

If you haven't listened to it yet, sit back and bask in the glory of all the hard work undertaken to re-create this sound.

CODA (OUTRO)

The coda, or outro, of a song can take many forms. Depending on the genre, it may either slowly fade out over the chorus or stop abruptly.

In the case of electronic dance music, there's a need to have the song devolve over time by stripping away components. This idea lends itself to the concept of a DJ-friendly track, where the end becomes sparser as the DJ proceeds to mix in a new track.

For the ending of the track you are working on, you'll be re-creating the intro or breakdown in reverse.

Start by unmuting and moving the MIDI clips from Measure 145 to Measure 97.

Delete the Wobble Bass 1, 2, and 3 clips.

You should have four MIDI clips on the tracks Sub Bass, Kong FX, AggroStep, and Kick/Snare.

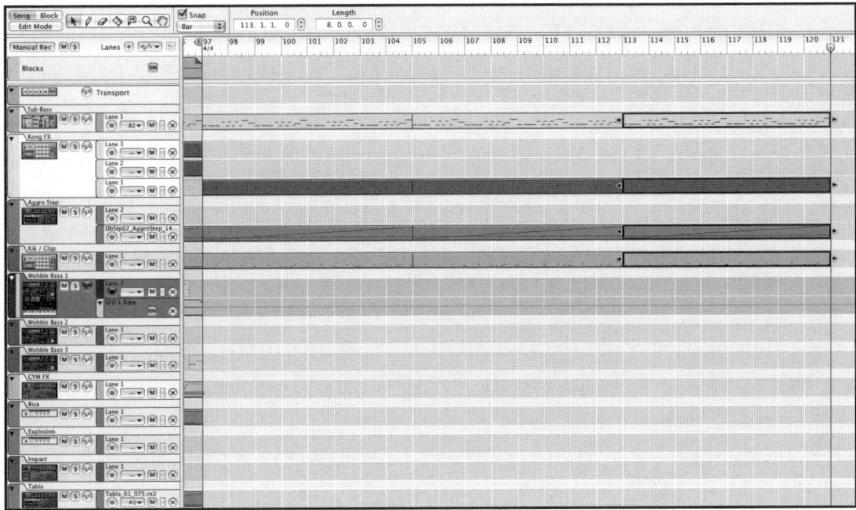

Fig. 12-39

Duplicate these clips two more times, which will end at Measure 121.

Copy the Wobble Bass 1 MIDI clip at Measure 57 to Measures 97 and 105.

Next, add the ending elements of the main sections to create a mini build that ends at Measure 113.

This includes the following steps:

- First, copy the Rise clip from Measure 93 to Measure 109.

- On the Kick/Snare track, shorten the clip starting at Measure 105 by two measures and copy the drum roll from Measure 95 to Measure 111. Delete the clip starting at Measure 113.

- Delete the AggroStep clip at Measure 105 and replace it with the clip at Measure 89.

- On the Kong FX track, duplicate the four-measure clip created for the second main section (lane three) to Measure 21. Also, copy the four-measure effects clip (lane two) at Measure 93 to Measure 109.

- Duplicate the Tabla clip to Measure 121.

- Copy the CYM FX clip Measure 65 to Measure 97. With the Razor tool, slice the clip at Measure 121 and delete the last half of the clip. You will also have to enter Edit mode to delete and shorten any clips that are outside the length of clip.

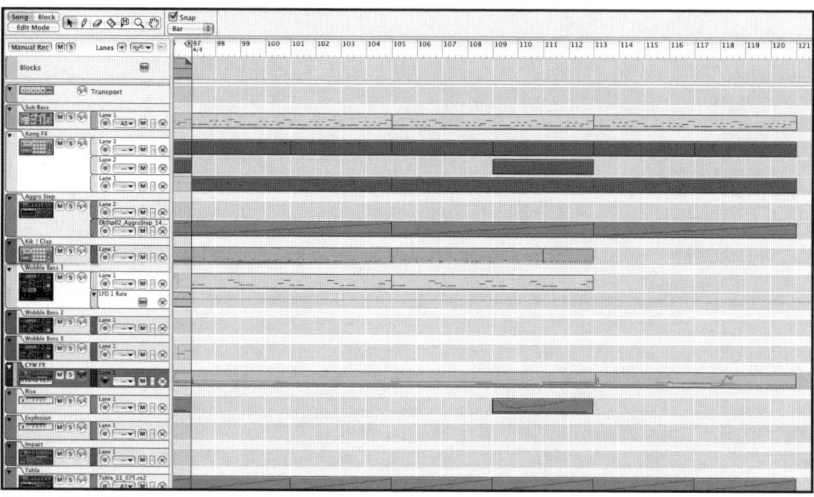

Fig. 12-40

Your coda should now resemble Fig. 12.40.

Finally, let's add a couple of hits to the Kong FX track at Measure 113 (lane one).

Enter Edit mode by double-clicking on the clip.

Pencil in a note on the FX_Monster row at Measures 113 and 117.

Extend the clip to Measure 122 and pencil in a note on the FX_Rakata_Gun row at Measure 121.

IN CONCLUSION

Congratulations! You've created a short but sweet dubstep tune. Truth be told, I'm pretty happy with the way this track has turned out, although at its present length it's a bit short for the genre, and so I'll definitely continue to work on it. If you take on

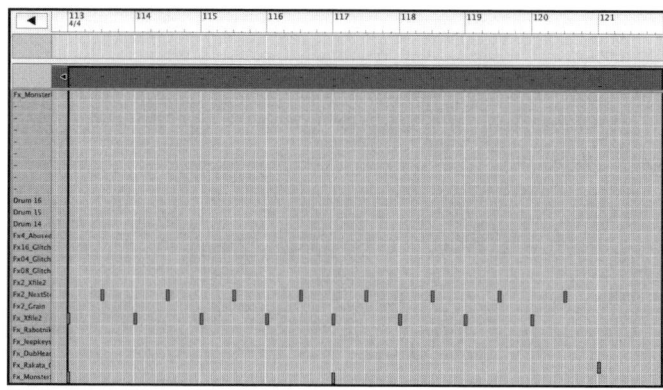

Fig. 12-41

the challenge to expand/remix this track, I'd love to hear your work. Send any copies to: morphous@tsunamibassexperience.com.

In the next chapter, you'll be diving into Reason's mixer to learn how to really bring out the best in this track via the mixing process.

The Art and Science of Mixing

BEFORE YOU BEGIN MIXING

When working in audio engineering, it is really necessary to use both sides of your brain. Using the clinical, analytical side enables you to focus on the science of sound, while the creative artistic side allows you to work as if you are painting on an aural canvas. Although it can take many years of hard work and dedication to train your ears properly, don't let that deter you. We all start from the same place and you'll be amazed at what you can accomplish with some steady effort, focused practice, and determination.

A few words of advice before you begin your mixing session work. I find it's really important to be well rested, but this especially holds true regarding your ears. Although you might feel inspired, the last thing you want to do is try to mix after you've come home from a noisy club or a concert. You should always try to start a mixing session with fresh ears, and a good night's sleep does wonders for this. Also it's a good idea to have eaten a little something, to enable you to focus properly during the session. I also like to block out a solid four to eight hours of working time. Again, it is advisable to turn off the phone and close the web browser, to minimize distractions. And remember to take a ten-minute break every forty-five minutes or so. Take proper care and give your ears a rest, while letting your brain focus on something else, to maintain stamina. This will also help you from overtaxing your ears and aids in keeping the mix fresh and in perspective.

I'm often asked, "What's the most important tool in your arsenal?" I never fail to respond strongly, "Your *ears*!" I cannot emphasize enough how important it is to protect your hearing. If you know you are going to a club or loud concert, then be sure to bring along some hearing protection. Every pharmacy carries sets or packs of small, disposable earplugs that you should have on hand. If you find you are not happy with the muffled sound these can produce, then I highly recommend making the investment in custom-molded in-ear attenuators. You've only got one pair of ears and once you've damaged or lost your hearing, there's little that can be done to get it back.

Mixing music can easily be compared to painting. Starting off with a blank sonic canvas, all the instruments and effects used in your song serve as the subjective components of your aural painting. Each sound can be equated to a different shape and color. Just as painters use different styles of brushes to create textures on their canvas, your main brush is the mixing board itself. It allows you to blend the sounds together. Making a particular sound louder pushes the sonic image closer to you. The Pan knobs control the perception of where that sound exists on your canvas with regard to left, right, and center.

As you move through this chapter, you'll learn about the mixing board and the basic tools it contains, so that you can use it effectively to shape your sound and bring your aural painting to vivid, stereo life.

REFERENCE MIX

Another tool I use quite often is called a reference mix. This is a professionally produced and mastered track that you can listen to, as a reference, as needed, to provide a guide finding the right balance of sounds within your own track (keeping in mind that your goal is not to reproduce someone else's track).

For instance, I personally find it easier for my brain to first identify the sound of correct balance between the kick drum and bass by listening to a properly mixed track before I begin working on my own mix. However, if I were to dive into my mixing work without hearing such a reference, it takes a lot more energy and time to achieve the correct balance in my sound.

That being said, to do this I usually look for a reference mix that is similar in style to the track I will be mixing, genre being most important; for example, it doesn't make sense to use a rock song as a reference for an electronic track.

Once you've selected a reference track to use, make sure to keep it on hand so you can refer to it throughout the mixing process. A good practice to adopt is to listen to the reference track for a couple of minutes after every break you take, before you resume working. This will allow you to retune your ears and brain. Remember that it is very important to take regular breaks every forty-five minutes to an hour while working, to prevent fatigue and ensure you are working in an optimal state.

A reference mix is also useful for setting the appropriate balance of your studio monitors and subwoofer.

Ideally, the listening levels should be set to around 85 dB.

UNDERSTANDING THE MIXER

The mixer, which is modeled after the SSL9000K, features an incredible amount of control, and for some, this may seem somewhat intimidating.

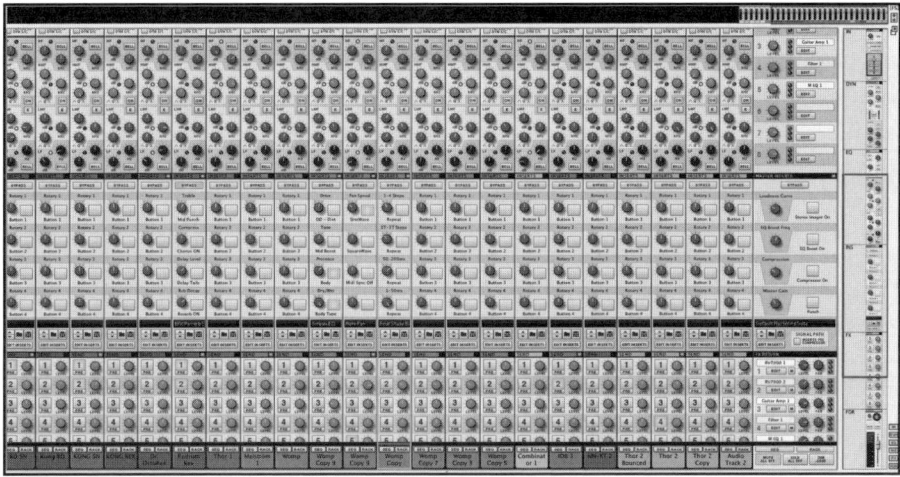

Fig. 13-1

Whatever you think at first glance, do not let the initial complexity of the mixer intimidate you. Its purpose is to function the same as the 14:2 mixer, albeit with many more bells and whistles, but essentially, it is the same. Let's take a closer look and break down what is displayed, to better understand how it functions.

Input

The Input section offers control over gain and the signal path of the dynamics, the EQ, and the Insert section.

INPUT GAIN
The Input Gain controls the input of the signal coming from either an audio input on the Hardware Interface or a designated instrument.

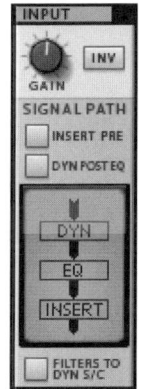

Fig. 13-2

SIGNAL PATH
The dedicated buttons of the Signal Path section allow you to modify the signal flow. The default has the signal running through the dynamics, EQ, and inserts. These buttons switch the order to offer various combinations.

Dynamics

The Dynamics section offer a dedicated compressor and gate with key input to enable side-chain effects.

COMPRESSOR
The compressor offers the standard controls with ratio, threshold, and release. The Peak button switches the compressor from an average setting to a peak setting, whereas the Fast button changes the attack of the compressor.

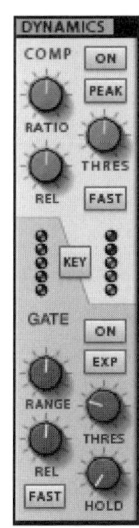

Fig. 13-3

GATE

The gate has controls over range, threshold, release, and hold. It may also be switched to Expander mode via the EXP button.

Expanders work the opposite of the gate, where as a signal crosses the threshold, it is made louder.

EQ

HIGH- AND LOW-SHELF FILTERS

The red HF and black LF sections of the EQ are shelf filters. The Bell button switches from shelf to bell curve.

HMF

The High-Mid-Frequency section is a fully parametric equalizer with frequency, gain, and Q controls.

LMF

The Low-Mid-Frequency section is also a fully functioning parametric equalizer that offers the same controls as the HMF, only it operates at a lower frequency range.

Fig. 13-4

Insert

The Insert section offers the same controls found on the programmer of the Mix and Audio devices found in the rack.

At the bottom of the section are the Browse and Save Effects buttons. Pressing the Browse Patch button allows you to peruse a multitude of great-sounding preset effects.

INSERT FX CONTROLS

Four programmable knobs and buttons are available for which multiple parameters may be gathered together and set to a single knob or button. This functions very similar to the Combinator controls. It is also duplicates the controls found on the Insert Programmer section of any mix or audio track device.

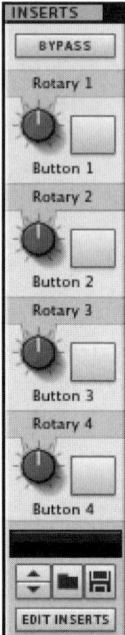

Fig. 13-5

FX Sends

The FX Sends section offers eight sends with level controls and dedicated pre buttons to switch any send to Prefader mode.

Fig. 13-6

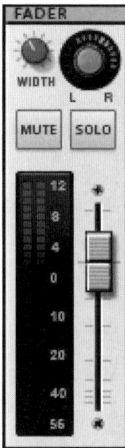

Fig. 13-7

Fader

The Fader section offers the usual controls, with a level fader and Solo and Mute buttons.

PAN

The Pan control offers a width control that goes way beyond simple left and right. The width allows you to dial in and place your sound within the stereo field with precision and control.

With the width set to hard left, it essentially turns any stereo signal into mono.

Master Section

The master section is the heart and soul of any console. It offers extensive control over the FX send and return, master inserts, the master fader level control, monitor control, and the famous SSL Stereo Bus compressor.

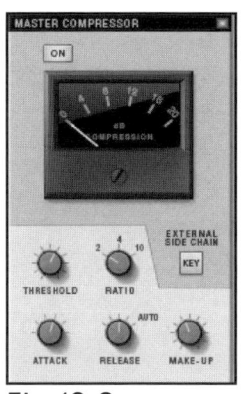

Fig. 13-8

MASTER COMPRESSOR

The master compressor is faithfully modeled on the much-sought-after SSL Stereo Bus compressor.

This device provides the sonic glue that helps gel your tracks together and gives your sound a professional and polished sheen. It features the standard compression controls, with a key input and VU meter settings.

FX SEND

Dedicated FX Send controls allow you to control the levels going to a designated effects device.

This is incredibly helpful when sending multiple sends to an effect, because it gives you the ability to lower the gain stage before the effects without changing the overall balance of the sends.

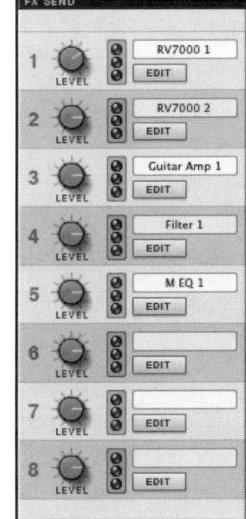

Fig. 13-9

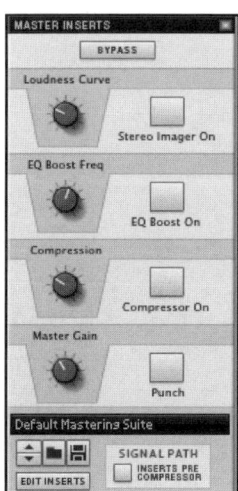

Fig. 13-10

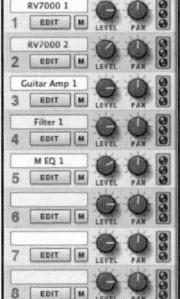

Fig. 13-11

MASTER INSERT

The master insert section offers the same control as the channel insert section, with similar dedicated control knobs and buttons. A wide variety of master effects patches are also included.

FX RETURN

The FX Return section offers level and pan control over sound coming from any effect.

MASTER FADER

The master fader offers level control over the entire mix. In addition, it adds a Level knob for the control room output and enables independent monitoring of each FX send and return.

THE BIG METER

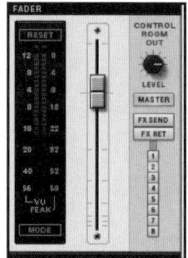

Another useful tool in Reason is the Big Meter, found on the Hardware Interface. It allows you to accurately view levels via different modes.

Begin by selecting the button located under Audio Output 1 and 2. This button will glow red to indicate when it is engaged and sets the channel that will be displayed by the Big Meter.

Located on the left side of the Big Meter are a number of different parameters, including the Meter modes, Peak Hold settings, VU offset, and Channel Selection.

Fig. 13-12

VU Meter

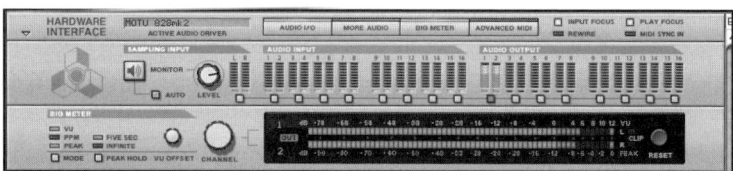

Fig. 13-13

The VU meter, or volume unit meter, is a visual meter based on the design of an average loudness setting. This meter represents the slowest of the three settings, averaging around 300 milliseconds. It's the closest meter available to ascertain how humans perceive loudness as sound. The original VU meters were designed with a needle and offered a typical range of –20 dB to +3 dB.

PPM

The PPM, or peak performance meter, is a quasi-peak meter that's faster than the VU meter at 10 milliseconds, but not as fast as the peak meter. While the VU meter displays an average level between the highest peak and lowest trough, the PPM provides a more accurate reading of the peak values. The 10-millisecond response time allows for a different detail of the displayed value, but note that it is still not as accurate as the true peak meter.

Peak Meter

The peak meter accurately depicts peak levels with a 0-millisecond response time. Its ultrafast response time instantly displays the highest peaks within the audio signal.

Using the Mode button allows you to cycle through the different types of meters. Continue to cycle through and it will split the meter, permitting two modes to be displayed at once. The different combinations include VU and Peak as well as PPM and Peak.

You will need to switch between the different settings, depending on what element you are working on within the mix.

Peak Hold

This offers two settings, known as Five Seconds and Infinite, respectively.

FIVE SECONDS

This setting will hold the highest Peak setting for five seconds before resetting itself to catch the next-highest peak. This is a useful setting for monitoring the peak levels throughout the entire duration of the track.

INFINITE

This setting holds the highest registered peak indefinitely. This setting is useful if you are looking for any excess clipping that might have occurred either during a recording session or during the mix down. The Reset button is used to clear the peaks or clipping from the mix.

VU Offset

The VU Offset knob enables the scaling of the VU meter from 0 to +20. You will maintain the default setting of +12 during this mixing session.

Channel Selector

The channel selector allows you to select the channel for the Big Meter. This has already been set by the Selection button, and does not need to be changed.

Clip Indicator

This indicator shows when the output has been exceeded, which may occur during the digital clipping process. Use the Reset button to clear the clip indicator.

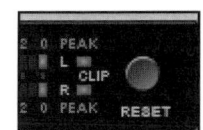

Reason 6 uses a floating-point processor for the computation of audio signals, which results in an almost infinite headroom and the inability to clip internally. The clip LEDs indicate when there is a danger of clipping the physical audio hardware and should always be observed.

Fig. 13-14

MIXER METERS

The mixer also features multimeter modes, including Peak, VU, and PPM. Although this meter isn't as advanced (or big) as the Big Meter, it provides useful information while working with the mixer, without your having to toggle to the rack view.

I typically keep an eye on the mixer meter and reference the Big Meter when necessary.

GAIN STAGE

One thing to always consider when mixing is the gain stage. There are several places in which to control the gain or loudness of your instruments. In addition to the faders on

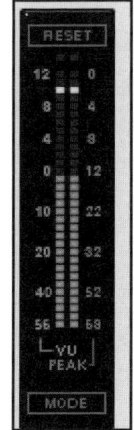

Fig. 13-15

the mixer, all the instruments in Reason have their own main volume control built into their respective control panels. The most important thing to keep in mind is to make sure you do not overdrive the master fader, also referred to as a stereo bus, on the mixer. Your goal is to leave enough headroom on each individual track to enable gain and adjustment by other means during the mixing process. If you make each track too loud, then you're actually making the task of mixing harder on yourself than it needs to be, akin to painting yourself into a corner. Personally, I like to keep my mixing channels set more toward the middle, thereby leaving lots of room to boost the softer-sounding instruments. This will prevent overdriving of the master fader and will further facilitate your mixing session.

Another thing to consider is that mixing is always subjective. There are no hard-and-fast rules when it comes to mixing; however, I'll demonstrate some guidelines that you can follow. It's important to understand how these guidelines operate, before attempting to deviate from them (much like knowing the rules before you break them!). As you move through this chapter, in which I'll be showing you insight into my approach to mixing, you'll start to develop your own style and approach to serve your sense of style and subjectivity.

THE STATIC MIX

A static mix is the starting point where you set your basic levels and Pan control. It's called static because it's similar to a snapshot. Later in this chapter, you'll explore more about automation to help make your mix more dynamic.

During the Building an Arrangement chapter, all of your levels were pretty rough. This is because the M-Class Maximizer was engaged during your production, and as a result, a considerable amount of limiting may have occurred.

A common problem I find when teaching mixing to students is the levels they try to use are often too high at the start, thereby leaving very little headroom in which to mix properly.

When playing a single track with an output of 0 db, having the mixer level set to 0 db is appropriate.

In this mix session, we will be working with several tracks. If all the levels were set at 0 db, then the output would be too loud and you incur the risk of the dreaded digital clipping, which often results in an overly harsh distortion.

Although using a compressor or limiter may prevent digital clipping, in trade you would be compromising the sound quality, so it is not recommended.

I find it best to adjust all the levels to a combined output of –6 dB. Later you'll be utilizing the Mastering Suite to polish the mix and ensure your track is loud enough to compete with commercially released tracks. However, it's important to get your static mix in place with an adequate buffer of headroom, to enable the inclusion of additional effects such as reverb and compression.

Your goal is to achieve an overall balance within the track, so that every instrument can be heard appropriately and adequately.

MIXING SESSION

If you completed the Building an Arrangement chapter, you may use this session to start mixing. However, if you had any issues or wish to check your work, the Reason song file Chapter 13—The Art and Science of Mixing may also be utilized.

This Reason song file is located on the enclosed DVD or is available for download via the Hal Leonard website.

Once the song is open, you'll begin by creating a static mix, but first, let's bypass the Master FX.

DRUMS

When starting the static mix, typically I will start with the busiest section of the song and focus on just the drums.

First, select the second Main block and hit P on your computer keyboard. This will set the locators around the selected section and start playback with the Loop mode engaged.

The main source of the drums is generated from the Dr. OctoRex AggroStep and the Kong Kick/Snare.

You could start adjusting levels, EQ, and compression, but the effects would be global over the instrument and not the individual sounds. It's always best to have as much separation as possible when mixing.

To that end, let's route the kick and snare from the Dr. OctoRex to separate the mix channels.

Dr. OctoRex Outputs

Stop the song from playing and select the AggroStep track on the sequencer page. **Fig. 13-16** Then, set your MIDI controller's octave to C1.

In the rack, open the Dr. OctoRex programmer and press the Select Slice by MIDI button, located just above the Select Loop and Load Slot interface. This allows you to select slices via your MIDI keyboard controller.

Next, create two new mix channels by selecting Create > Other > Mix Channel.

Tab to switch to the rear of the rack and route Outputs 1 and 2 to the first mix channel and Outputs 3 and 4 to the second.

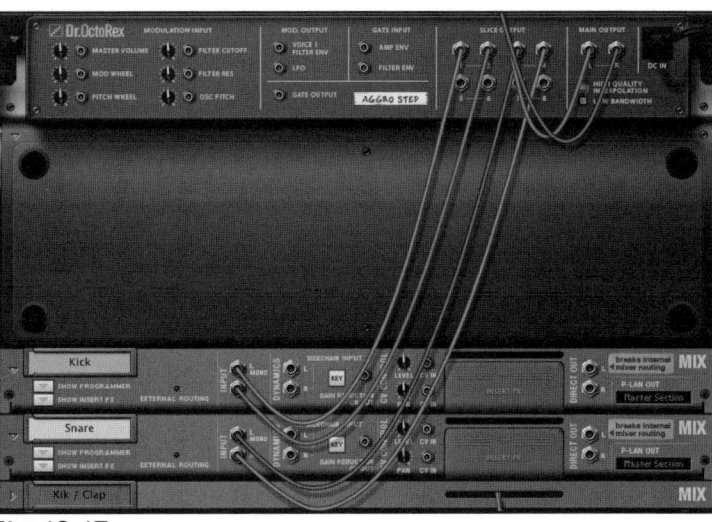

Fig. 13-17

Rename the mix channels Kick and Snare.

Tab back to the front of the rack.

Play the keyboard, starting at C1. Route each kick drum to Output 1 and 2 and each snare to output 3 and 4 via the Slice Output knob of the programmer.

Here's a list of routings.

- C1: Kick
- C#1: Kick
- E1: Snare
- G#1: Kick
- A1: Kick
- C#2: Snare
- D2: Snare
- F2: Kick
- F#2: Kick
- G2: Kick
- C3: Snare
- D#3: Kick
- E3: Kick
- F3: Kick
- F#3: Kick
- G#3: Kick
- A3: Kick
- A#3: Snare
- B3: Kick
- C4: Kick
- F#4: Snare
- A#4: Kick
- B4: Kick
- D#5: Snare
- E5: Snare
- F5: Kick
- F#5: Kick
- G5: Kick
- G#5: Kick
- A5: Kick

- D6: Snare
- F#6: Kick
- G6: Kick
- G#6: Kick
- A#6: Kick
- B6: Kick
- C7: Snare
- E7: Kick

Once you've completed the task of routing the drums, solo the three mix channels in the rack and press Play. The sound should play back as originally heard and you can listen to each drum separately to check for any misplaced routings.

Kong—Kick/Clap

Next, you're going to do the same process with the Kick and Clap sound of the Kong.

Start by creating a new mix channel and naming it Clap.

Tab to the rear of the rack and route Outputs 3 and 4 to the inputs of the new mix channel.

Tab back to the front and select Pad 3.

Select the Show Drums and FX button on the left side of the interface.

Set the drum output to 3 and 4.

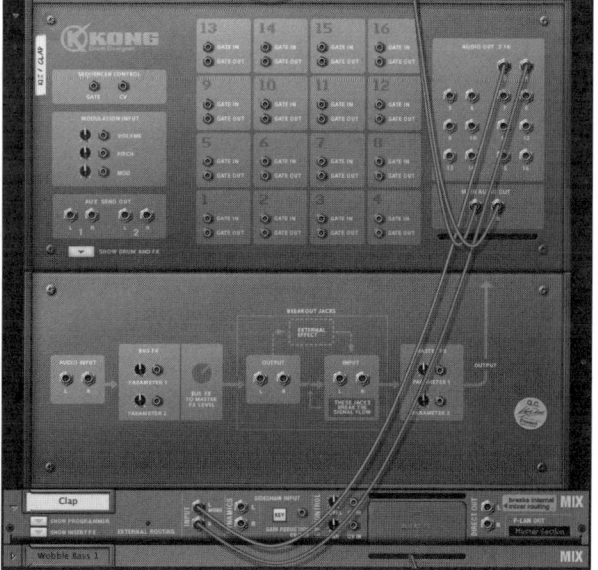

Fig. 13-18

Fig. 13-19

Mixing Drum Tracks

On the mixer, bring all the faders down to their lowest settings. Nothing should be heard.

After carefully comparing the Dr. OctoRex (AggroStep) loop with the other sounds in the arrangement, I've determined that the entire loop could be louder. Luckily, the Volume knob on the Dr. OctoRex boosts all outputs and not just the main.

Bring the Dr. OctoRex Loop player (AggroStep) up to full right (127).

Start by bringing up the AggroStep Kick to –6.27 dB.

Next, bring the Kong Kick/Clap up to –6.64 dB. You want the initial crack of the AggoStep, blended with the girth of the Kong Kick.

Next, bring up the AggroStep Snare to –6.37.

Now, bring up the Clap fader to –7.0.

Finally, increase the AggroStep fader (high hat patter) to –6.37.

The drums should now have a good balance. One thing to remember about the Dr. OctoRex—Aggrostep: Even though you've separated the Kick and Snare into separate channels, their volume levels should remain relative to each other, as their all working together creates the loop. If you were to boost or cut any of the elements too much, the loop will become unbalanced.

DRUM SUB MIX

Now that the drum levels are set, you may find that you'd like to boost or cut the levels of all the tracks, which can ruin the delicate balance of the drum mix. Unfortunately, Reason 6 doesn't offer fader groups, which would normally allow you to adjust levels while keeping the mix intact.

However, there is a way to create a submix of the drums.

First, create a mix channel and name it Drum Sub Mix.

With the new mix channel selected, create a 14:2 mixer, which should automatically cable itself to the inputs.

Every mix channel has direct outputs located on the rear of the

Fig. 13-20

device. This allows you to use the channel strip but send the output somewhere other than the stereo bus.

For each drum sound, route the direct outputs of the mix channel to an input on the 14:2 mixer.

Now as you add instruments and find the need to change the overall volume of the drums, you can adjust the fader of the Drum Sub Mix track. As a bonus, you can add compression to the drum mix by either the onboard compressor of the channel strip or by inserting an M-Class Compressor onto the track.

Sub Bass

One of the hardest tasks in mixing is to get the sub bass and kick drum to work together. The difficulty lies in the fact they both occupy much of the same frequency spectrum.

A great trick is to employ the side-chain circuit on the sub bass compressor triggered from the kick drum. You've already learned how to do this with the M-Class Compressor in the chapter on advanced routing, but here instead, you'll set up the side-chain bass by using the channel strip compressor.

Tab to the rear of the rack and navigate to the Kick/Clap mix channel.

Click the Show Insert FX button to reveal the Insert FX section.

As shown in Fig. 13.21, route the output of the insert labeled "To Device" to the side-chain input's Dynamics input on the Sub Bass mix channel.

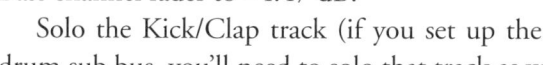

This will send a copy of the kick drum to the side-chain input, causing the compressor to react to the kick drum.

Navigate back to the mixer and set the Sub Bass channel fader to –4.47 dB.

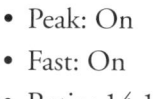

Fig. 13-21

Solo the Kick/Clap track (if you set up the drum sub bus, you'll need to solo that track as well) and the Sub Bass track.

Next, engage the compressor and make the following settings:

- Peak: On
- Fast: On
- Ratio: 14.1:1
- Threshold: 31.35 dB
- Release: 709 ms

Now, every kick drum will cause the compressor to react, which forces the level of the Sub Bass down. You're not looking for an extreme setting like the one used in the advanced routing section; rather, a subtle effect that allows the kick to cut through momentarily. This is a great way to control the bass of both tracks without the use of equalization.

Now both the Kick and Sub Bass are loud and punchy, without a buildup of excessive low-end frequencies.

Wobble Bass

Bring the volume level fader of Wobble Bass 1 up to –7.05 dB.

Bring the volume level fader of Wobble Bass 2 up to –6.64 dB.

Bring the volume level fader of Wobble Bass 3 up to –6.82 dB.

Solo the Sub Bass and the three Wobble Bass tracks and have a listen. The Sub Bass should sit just underneath the Wobble Bass sounds. By muting the Sub Bass, you should hear a definite drop in low-end frequencies.

Kong FX

The Kong FX instrument contains a lot of different effects and so it is better to separate these sounds onto different tracks.

First, select the Kong FX instrument, and from the Create menu click Other > Mix Channel. You'll need six of these in total, so duplicate the process five more times, or use Option if using a Mac or Alt if using Windows + Drag upon the mix channel five times.

On the Kong FX instrument, unfold the Show Drums and FX tab.

Click on each pad and route the Drum Outputs accordingly, as follows:

Fig. 13-22

- Pad 1: Outputs 3 and 4
- Pad 2: Outputs 5 and 6
- Pad 3: Outputs 7 and 8
- Pad 4: Outputs 9 and 10
- Pad 6: Outputs 11 and 12
- Pad 8: Outputs 13 and 14

The last three glitch effects on Pads 10, 11, and 12 will remain routed to the main outputs (1 and 2).

Tab to the rear of the rack and physically wire the outputs to the mix channel inputs on their respective channels.

On the mixer, set the levels for each channel to the following:

- Kong FX 1–2: 6.05 dB
- Kong FX 3–4: 3.73 dB
- Kong FX 5–6: 3.33 dB
- Kong FX 7–8: 4.27 dB
- Kong FX 9–10: 7.10 dB
- Kong FX 11–12: 4.15 dB

- Kong FX 13–14: 1.80 dB

Having a separation of these sound effects will allow you to add time-based effects and equalization independently.

Cymbal FX

Bring the volume fader for the Cymbal FX up to –7.66 dB.

Rise

Bring the volume fader for the Rise sound effect up to –7.61 dB.

Tabla

Finally, bring the volume fader for the Tabla track up to –5.30 dB.

Explosion and Impact

At this point, you've now set the basic levels for nearly all the tracks.

Turn off the Loop function and start the song from the beginning.

Set the volume fade levels for the following tracks:

- Explosion: 4.95 dB
- Impact: 4.57 dB

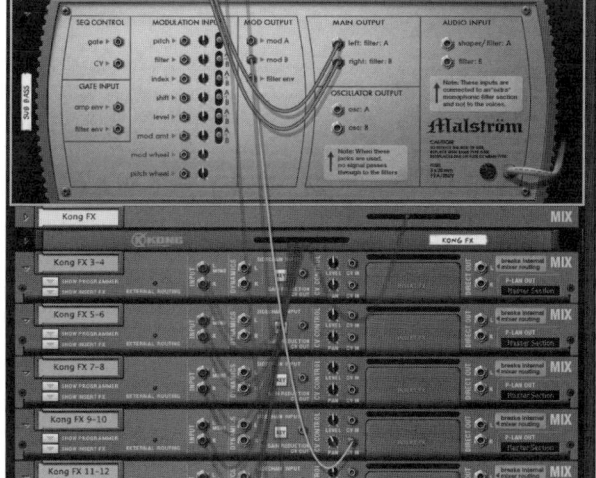

Fig. 13-23

PAN SETTINGS

Most of the tracks in this song are stereo, but adjusting the pan levels even in small amounts will help the overall mix.

To begin with, tracks with low-frequency information are subject to phasing issues. To guard against this, adjust the width of the Sub Bass and the Kick/Clap track (Kick).

The Sub Bass is a simple sine wave, which contains no stereo information. Turn the wide knob all the way to the left, which effectively turns the signal mono.

The same can be said for the kick coming from the Kick/Clap track. By changing the width to the left, the sound becomes more focused, thereby providing more impact.

Usually all individual drum sounds should be in mono, but the AggroStep loop is stereo and changing the width on any of its tracks will compromise the sound and integrity of the loop.

Depending on the genre of music, you might try panning the tracks out slightly. This provides a little breathing room for the mix and instruments, without seeming cluttered.

For instance, the Sub Bass and the Kick occupy much of the same frequency range, so shifting the Sub Bass by –1 and the Kick by +1 will give a bit of separation. I doubt you'd notice, but in the end, it will help the mix.

In fact, I'm a big fan of shifting each track slightly, by 1 or 2. Try alternating every track + or –1.

Kong FX

The Kong FX track has three glitch effects on Pads 10, 11, and 12.

Leave the Pan set to 0 or center.

On the Kong, select Pad 10 and set its pan value to –13.

Select Pad 11 and set its pan value to 12.

Finally, select Pad 12 and set its pan value to –1.

Kong FX 9–10

This sample is repeated every bar during the second main section. Let's set up an auto-pan by using the LFO from the Sub Bass's Mod B.

First, navigate to the Malstrom synthesizer in the rack.

Set Mod B to sync with a rate of 4/4.

Tab to the rear, grab a cable from the Mod B output section, and cable it to the Pan CV input of Kong FX 9–10.

Adjust the CV Scale knob to 55.

The Mix Channel pan value should be set to 0.

Kong FX 11–12 and 13–14

Adjust the width of both tracks to 100 and set the pan values to –12 and +12, respectively.

ADDING EFFECTS

Now that you've gotten the levels and pan set for the static mix, let's use some of the onboard effects to shape the sound of some of your instruments.

I learned a valuable lesson once when assisting with a veteran engineer. He was very particular about the selection of microphone preamps, microphones, and microphone placement. It was a little nerve-racking as we spent what I considered an inordinate amount of time fussing with setting and placement.

After we recorded all the instruments, I was stunned to see (and hear) that he didn't need to use any equalization or compression and that every sound was near perfect.

At the end of the day, his knowledge and expertise taught me a lot about effects and when *not* to use them.

Not everybody has an extensive mic locker or rack of outboard gear at his or her disposal, so we do our best. Luckily, a vast collection of these tools is available within the software, which can help resolve most issues.

Let it be said that just because you have the ability to use multiple effects on every track, doesn't necessarily mean you should use multiple effects on every track. Think of these effects as tools to help fix problems. In this particular song, you're using mostly samples, all of which were recorded with an attention to detail. It's safe to say you won't need the use a ton of effects processors, as most of these sounds were already processed when they were created.

And once again I'll repeat my mantra, "Less is more!"

EQ and Filters

As has been discussed throughout this book, equalization can be used creatively, but more often than not, it's used to correct issues. Most issues arise not from the sound by itself, but while combining sounds in the same frequency spectrum.

SUB BASS
For example, take the Sub Bass and Kick Drum sounds.

We solved a lot of issues concerning the battle of these two for sonic space, with the creative use of compression and the side-chain input.

However, if you solo the Sub Bass track and listen carefully, you'll hear some clicky high-end frequencies created with each transient. I prefer the bass to be smoother, so we'll use the parametric equalizer, combined with the filters, to remove some of this unwanted clutter.

Fig. 13.24 shows an image of the filter and EQ section.

Start by setting up a loop around the main section and solo the Sub Bass.

Turn the EQ on and engage the E button.

Set the HMF knob to 2.84 kHz, the gain to –18 dB, and the Q to 1.40

Set the LMF to 200 Hz, the gain to –5.08, and the Q to 1.33.

Set the LF to 40.7 and the gain to –5.08dB

Next, engage the HPF and set its frequency to 40.7 Hz.

Finally, engage the LPF and set its frequency to 553.6 Hz.

With these settings, you have effectively gotten rid of the clickiness of the sound and tamed the woofy low frequency.

Fig. 13-24

USING HIGH-PASS FILTERS
One of the biggest problems when mixing is the buildup of low frequencies. When teaching, I always tell my students to define the low end, meaning what instruments are responsible

for the low-end frequencies of the song. In the case of your current song, it would be the Sub Bass and Kick Drum.

A good rule to follow is that anything that isn't responsible for generating low frequencies should have a high-pass filter enabled and set to 120 Hz.

This may sound extreme, but think about this: Any number of tracks could be generating frequencies at 60 Hz. Most of this 60 Hz is probably –20 dB or lower, and not really noticeable.

Now imagine having twenty-four tracks all generating 60 Hz at –20 dB. Bear in mind that with each instance of the sixty-cycle wave, the perceived loudness will increase by 3 dB. Twenty-four tracks playing together would create an excessive buildup of low frequencies and would more than likely render the Sub Bass and Kick drum muddy and unfocused.

By removing frequencies of 120 Hz and down, you're clearing the way for your Sub Bass and Kick Drum, both of which you want to sound huge for this track.

First, go ahead and set up a 120 Hz HPF on every track. A quick and easy way of doing this is to use the Copy Channel Effects from the Edit menu.

Start by initiating a HPF on the Kong FX track and set the frequency knob to 120 Hz. With the track selected click Edit > Copy Channel Settings > Filters and EQ

Once it's copied, simply right-click (Control + Click) on the background of a channel strip and select Paste Channel Settings: EQ.

Do this for all tracks except the following:

- Kong FX 3–4: 41.8 Hz
- Drum Sub-Mix: 40.7 Hz
- Aggro Kick: 45.2 Hz
- Aggro Snare: 35.6
- Kick/Clap: 50.3
- Clap: 35.6
- Wobble Bass 1, 2, and 3: 72 Hz
- Explosion: 56.5 Hz
- Impact: 57.7 Hz
- Tabla: 52 Hz

Also, engage the HF filter on the Drum Sub-Mix track and set the frequency to 16 kHz. This will roll off on the sharpness of the high hats.

Compression

Compression is another tool I try to use sparingly. You'll be using the stereo bus compressor and the M-Class Mastering Suite on the master inserts, so you don't want to overcompress the sounds too much.

Fig. 13-25

I've determined that the Drum Sub-Mix could use a little compression to tighten up its sound.

On the Drum Sub-Mix track, engage the compressor.

Do not use the Fast or Peak settings.

Set Threshold to –25.08 dB.

Set Ratio to 4.06:1.

Set Release to 554 ms.

Send FX

Send effects offer a lot with regard to sound design. They can be used to create a sense of space by sending multiple tracks to a reverb, giving the illusion that all the tracks were recorded in the same space. They are also a great way to save on processing. You could put an RV7000 advanced reverb on every track with similar settings, or send a copy of the signal from every track to one RV7000.

SCREAM

Let's set up a Scream Destruction Unit for the Wobble Bass tracks.

On the mixer, right-click (Control + Click) on the background and select Create Send FX > Scream 4 Distortion.

In the FX Return box of the master section, you'll find that Slot 5 now has a Scream effects unit listed.

Click Edit button just underneath the label.

The rack opens to the newly created Scream effect.

Make the following settings on the Scream:

Fig. 13-26

- Damage Control: 47
- Damage Type: Digital
- Parameter 1: 45
- Parameter 2: 86
- Low Cut: 10
- Mid Cut: 0
- High Cut: 9
- Body Resonance: 47
- Scale: 68
- Auto: 0
- Body Type: B
- Master Level: 80

On the mixer, engage the FX5 button for all three of the Wobble Bass tracks.

On the FX return, set the level to –5.17 dB.

Solo the three Wobble Bass tracks and have a listen to the nasty digital distortion that's been created.

REVERBS

Next, let's send some tracks to the reverbs on Sends 1 and 2.

- Kong FX: FX2—14.65 dB
- Kong FX 7–8: FX1 and FX2—12 dB
- Drum Sub-Mix: FX2—21.99 dB
- CYM FX: FX1—1.34 dB, FX2—3.33 dB
- Rise: FX1 and FX2—8.20 dB
- Explosion: FX1—4.86, FX2—3.93
- Impact: FX1 and FX2—4.23
- Tabla: FX2—12 dB

AUTOMATION

Now you will use some automation to make your static mix a bit more dynamic.

Sub Bass

The Sub Bass track comes in heavy during the first main section of the track. During the breakdown section, there's a lot less sound and the Sub Bass appears to sound a little heavy.

Let's set up some automation to lower the Sub Bass during this section.

Right-click (Control + Click) on the channel fader and select Edit automation.

A new parameter automation lane is created in the sequencer.

Set the SPL just before the breakdown section and hit Play.

Once the song moves into the breakdown section, press Record.

A new MIDI clip will be recorded on the Sub Bass track.

Grab the Level Fader and move it down to –5.54.

Hit Stop just before the start of the second main section.

If the recording isn't precise, edit the automation by selecting the clip and enter Edit mode.

The volume change should occur at Measure 57 or before and then end at Measure 65.

Bring the bass down only 1 dB may not seem like it's affecting much, but remember a change in 3 dB is perceived as twice as loud. It's just enough so that when the Sub Bass comes in again, there is an additional element of drama.

Next, copy the automation clip to Measure 113.

Delay

Delays are an excellent effect for adding a polyrhythmic element to your track.

Already created in the effects section are two delays, the DDL-1 and The Echo.

DDL-1

Start by selecting the Edit button on FX4 return. The current setting is 3/16 notes. Set the step length to 1/8T.

Move the SPL to just before the second main section.

On the Kong FX 9–10, right-click (Control + Click) the FX4 Send on and select Edit Automation. A new automation parameter track is created in the sequencer window.

Now, press Record. Once the SPL reaches Mmeasure 65, click the FX4 Send on. Once the SPL reaches Measure 113, click the FX4 Send button to turn it off.

THE ECHO

Select the Edit button under FX3 Return. On The Echo, select patch Pschodelrium from the General Delay folder.

Turn the Diffusion button off and set the mode to Triggered.

On the mixer, turn the FX3 Send button on for the AggroStep Snare. Set the Send level to −12.06 dB

Next, turn the FX3 Send button on for the Explosion track and set the Send level to −12.07 dB.

Move the SPL a few measures before the breakdown.

On The Echo, right-click (Control + Click) the Trigger button and a new parameter automation lane will be created on the Sequencer window.

Now, press Record. Wait until the SPL passes the initial transient of the hit and then press and hold the Trigger button. Release the trigger around Measure 52.4.1.0.

Press the trigger at Measure 57 and hold for one measure.

Press the trigger at Measure 61 and hold for one measure.

Fig. 13-27

Press the trigger one last time at Measure 63 and hold for one measure.

As you can see, adding automation is an easy task that allows for dynamic control over parameters, which will certainly bring your mix to life.

At this point, I'm pretty happy with the current state of the song. It's sometimes difficult to determine when you are finished with a song, as there are an infinite number of possibilities with effects and instruments, but in your case, let's move on the master bus and finalizing stage of your mix.

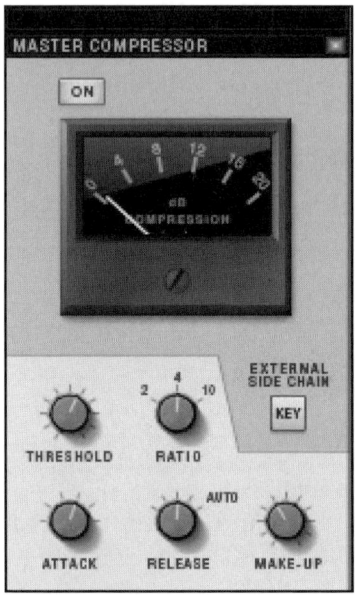

Fig. 13-28

FINALIZING THE MIX AND MASTERING FX

The last process of creating a track is using the built-in stereo bus compressor and the suite of M-Class master effects of the mixer.

Let's begin by engaging the master compressor.

Master Compressor

The master compressor is based on the SSL9000K's master bus compressor. If you don't have access to a real SSL, then there are hardware rack units and software emulations available. Reason 6 offers its own version of the compressor, and although I haven't tested it against the authenticity of a real SSL compressor, I think it sounds fantastic.

Using the master compressor is like adding a sonic glue that smoothes everything over and helps the mix gel. Think of it like adding a coat of varnish or polyurethane to your mix. It adds sheen and gloss, yet is transparent.

As always, I prefer to leave things on the subtle side.

Let's use the method described previously in this book to set up and use the compressor.

First, set Ratio to its highest setting, 10.

Set Threshold to its lowest setting, –30 dB.

Set Attack and Release to their fastest setting.

On the sequencer, set a loop of the entire song and press Play.

As the song is playing, make the following adjustments:

• Attack: 3 ms
• Release: 0.6 s
• Threshold: –12.76 dB
• Ratio: 4

- Makeup Gain: 3.0 dB

Now, let's investigate the M-Class mastering effects.

What Is Mastering?

Mastering is the final step in audio production, done before your project is sent for mass reproduction. This process entails critical listening within an acoustically designed room and employs the use of high-end audio equipment to fix any anomalies that may be present in the mix. A mastering engineer will also balance out the loudness of each track so that the overall collection of songs or album will flow properly. Mastering engineers have also been known to help with determining the order of tracks on an album. They lend an objective, experienced take on your music, with an end result that is polished and professional. Luckily, Reason 6 ships with the M-Class Mastering Suite, a collection of excellent-sounding plug-ins that will give your track that same kind of professional polish.

Using the M-Class Mastering Suite

The last process you engage for your song before mixing down is to use the Default Mastering Suite, which consists of a M-Class EQ, stereo imager, compressor, and maximizer. This final element of your track will ultimately give it a finished polish. Bear in mind, if you plan to send your track to a mastering engineer, something I highly recommend, then you'll want to go easy on these effects, as the mastering engineer will be adding his or her own magic. When sending tracks out to a mastering engineer, make sure you are delivering a premaster version of the data.

A premaster is a finished track, but one that contains little compression or EQ on the stereo bus and has at least 5 dB of headroom, which will allow the engineer to make the track sound its best.

Let's assume for now that you are going to be mastering the track yourself.

There are several different mastering presets. Many are useful for different genres of music, so feel free to explore them. For the purposes of this tutorial, we'll be using the Default Mastering Suite.

Although the Default Mastering Suite has dedicated controls mapped to the programmer, I tend to ignore these and work with the processors directly.

M-CLASS EQ

You've spent some time ensuring the frequencies of the track were balanced during the mixing stage, so you will only require minimal use of the EQ to sweeten the mix.

Make sure the EQ is set to On and set the parameters as follows:

Fig. 13-29

- Lo Cut: On
- Low Shelf: Freq 48.2 Hz, Gain 0.6, Q 1.15
- Param 1: Freq 44.8 Hz, Gain 0.6 Hz, Q 11.0
- Param 2: Freq 473.7 Hz, Gain –0.9, Q 5.0
- Hi Shelf: Freq 12 kHz, Gain –0.6, Q 1.49

M-CLASS STEREO IMAGER

The stereo imager splits the signal into two frequency bands and allows for the widening of higher frequencies, while narrowing low frequencies.

Fig. 13-30

Make sure the stereo image is turned on and set the parameters as follows:
- Solo Lo Band
- Adjust X-Over frequency to 400 Hz
- Lo Band: Adjust Low Width to –20
- Solo Hi Band
- Hi Band: Adjust High Width to 15

This is a fantastic processor that helps make your track sound bigger than life. Keep in mind that widening the low-frequency band will result in a weaker-sounding low end. Also take care that too much widening might create phasing issues when summing to mono.

M-CLASS COMPRESSOR

The compressor will help gel the track together, giving it a denser feel. Without compression, your song might have the image of several tracks layered together, as opposed to one solid track.

Be careful of overcompression, as this will suck the life out of the track by effectively eliminating the dynamic range. The goal is to *not* hear the compression, but to thicken up the sound while keeping it transparent.

You've already added a layer of compression with the master bus compressor, so you'll want to go easy with this effect. Compression does not add, it multiplies. For example, running a signal through three compressors set at 3:1 ratio will yield a 27:1 outcome (3 x 3 x 3 = 27).

Make sure the compressor is turned on and set the parameters to the following:
- Input Gain: 3.1 dB
- Threshold: –13.6 dB

Fig. 13-31

- Soft Knee: Off
- Ratio: 1.75:1
- Attack: 78 ms
- Release: 223 ms
- Output Gain: 2.0 dB

M-CLASS MAXIMIZER

The maximizer is your secret weapon for making your tracks as loud as any commercially released track. It features a brick wall limiter that prevents the output from clipping your audio interface's digital-to-analog converters.

Make sure the maximizer is on and set the parameters to the following:

Fig. 13-32

- Input Gain: 3.0 dB
- Limiter: Enabled
- Look Ahead: Enabled
- Attack: Fast
- Release: Auto
- Output Gain: –0.2 dB

Mastering: Final Thoughts

With these tools, you'll be able to accomplish most mastering tasks. I do wish there was a RMS meter included in the Big Meter display. To work around this, I typically will export the track and review it in another application to check the RMS levels. If you have this capability, try to aim for an RMS level of –10 to –12.

If you own a CD that was made in the mid-1980s and compare it to a CD that was manufactured today, you'll notice the level of the older CD seems to be much lower. Most of those CDs tracks were mastered with an RMS level of –14.

Those levels are perfectly acceptable, even when compared to today's levels, but the loudness wars have forced most commercially produced music to be overcompressed. Producers want tracks so loud that people have to turn their stereo down, which is absurd and detrimental to sound quality.

Again, a good compromise between sound levels and compression is about –10.

If you don't have access to an RMS meter, don't worry about it. Use your reference track and trust your ears and you'll be fine.

EXPORTING YOUR SONG

Now let's learn how to export your song so you can share it with the world.

End of Song Marker

The first thing you need to do is set the End of Song marker. Make sure to listen to your track once with the Loop function off. You want to make sure that any reverb tails or delays play out to silence. If not, the reverb will be cut short and the sound will end too abruptly. Note how I have set the E marker to just past Bar 125.

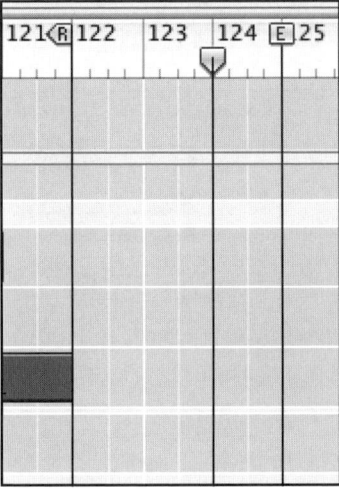

Fig. 13-33

Export Song

Next, select Export Song as Audio File from the File menu.

NAME THE SONG

A dialog box will open for you to name the song. I chose the title Reason 6 Demo. You can also choose what format with which to export the data. The choices available are .aiff or .wav files. Either one is fine, as they have essentially the same quality. The default file for Mac is in AIFF format; whereas WAVE is used for Windows-based PCs.

Once you've selected the correct format, click the Save button.

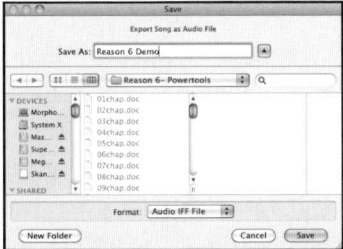

Fig. 13-34

EXPORT SETTINGS

The next window displayed is the Audio Export Settings. You can select your sample rate and bit depth, and determine whether you want to use Dither.

SAMPLE RATE

To burn this song on to a CD, you first need to confirm that the sample rate is set correctly. The settings range from 11,025 Hz to 192,000 Hz. The standard sample rate for an audio CDs is 44,100 Hz, which is also happens to be the default setting.

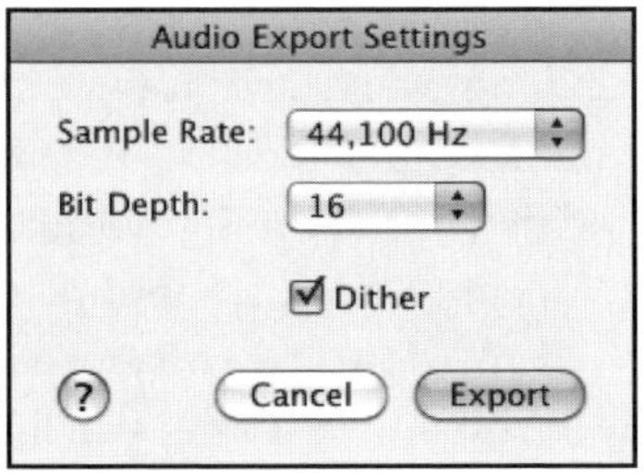

BIT DEPTH

The bit depth gives you the option of either 24- or 16-bit settings. The 24-bit setting provides higher quality and would be ideal if you were sending this to a mastering

Fig. 13-35

engineer or if you wanted to import the song into another program. However, 16-bit is the standard for audio CDs—and is also the default setting.

DITHER

Dithering is a process you use to get from a 24-bit file to a 16-bit file without any loss in quality. Imagine for a moment that your session is 24 bits. If you choose to export the audio at 16 bit without using Dither, the program will chop off the top 8 bits, thereby affecting the quality of the export.

This is when dithering can come in handy. The process of dithering involves adding super-high-frequency noise into your file. The high frequency is well above human hearing, so you won't actually hear it. Now, when the program needs to remove 8 bits, it removes the high-frequency noise and the result is a 16-bit file that sounds like your 24-bit file.

Fig. 13-36

Because you're burning this song to a CD, keep Dither on and hit Export.

Export

Next, you'll see the Export Audio progress gauge.

Finally, your song appears as a file on the desktop. Congratulate yourself on a mix well done.

Reason 6 Demo.aif

Fig. 13-37

Performing Live with Reason

The ability to perform live using Reason became a reality with the advent of the Combinator. Reason has always had the capability of enabling the use of multiple controllers to play a variety of instruments in real time, simultaneously.

With the Combinator and the new Dr. OctoRex, it is now possible to load up several sections of a song and have them trigger via MIDI notes in unison.

Fig. 14.1 shows a basic setup that I have created to be used for the live playback of backing tracks.

In the rack you will find six Dr. OctoRexes loaded with loops. Each Dr. OctoRex has the same loop loaded into various slots. This to enable you to create a basic song structure that can then be triggered by selecting keys E0 to B0 as designated to a MIDI controller.

Selecting E0 will cause Loop Slot 1 to trigger in each of the six Dr. OctoRexes. Notice how some slots are left blank intentionally to create

Fig. 14-1

a build, which is accomplished by adding new elements as you play higher notes on the scale.

In the arrangement window you will find the Combinator track, which controls all six Dr. OctoRexes, as well as each individual Dr. Octorex. This permits greater flexibility in triggering individual loops on the fly.

Another benefit that Reason offers is the ability to lock a controller to a specific device. The master keyboard will always follow the selection displayed in the Arrangement window, so it's possible to set up multiple controllers to control several different facets of a live setup.

Let's take a look at how to build a live rack and lock a controller to a designated device.

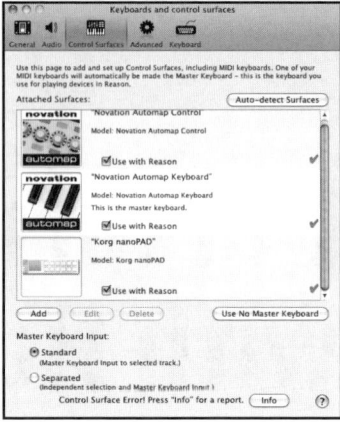

Fig. 14-2

BUILDING A LIVE SET RACK

- With a new session open, create a Combinator.
- Within the Show Device window, a red bar across the top of the section indicates the selection.
- Create a 14:2 mixer.
- Select the mixer inside the Combinator and create three Dr. OctoRex Loop Players.
- For the first Dr. OctoRex, load Beyer Lekebusch/ Bottom Loops from the Dr. OctoRex Patches > Drums > Electronic Drums > Beyer Lekebusch folder.
- Then, for the second Dr. OctoRex, load Beyer Lekebusch/Top Loops −1 from the Dr. OctoRex Patches > Drums > Electronic Drums > Beyer Lekebusch folder.

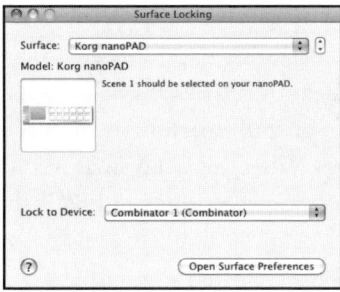

Fig. 14-3

- And then, for the third Dr. OctoRex, load Percussion/Tabla 75 −2 from the Dr. OctoRex Patches > Percussion folder.
- Next, navigate to the C0 octave of your keyboard controller, which is three octaves down from middle C.
- Press E0 on your controller.
- All three Dr. OctoRex Loop Players will start playing Slot 1 in unison.
- Press F0 and all three of the Dr. OctoRex Loop Players will play Slot 2 in unison. The same procedure can be repeated for any key from E0 to B0.

Locking a Controller to a Device

If you have more than one controller available, with Reason it's possible to lock a device to a specific instrument or another device.

First, confirm that Reason recognizes your controller via Preferences > Control Surfaces.

If your controller isn't displayed, try activating the Auto-detect Surfaces button. You also have the option to add a controller manually or to use one of the generic model settings listed in the Other menu option.

In my case, I've added a Korg nanoPAD. Note that I also have a Novation Remote controller that's been assigned

Once Reason recognizes your controller, you can lock a device to it.

OPTIONS > SURFACE LOCKING
Select Surface Locking from the Options menu.

Under Surface, select the controller to be locked. In this case, you will be selecting the Korg nanoPAD.

Under Lock to Device, select the Combinator.

Now, when you navigate to a different device, the nanoPAD will always be available to trigger the Combinator, including all three Dr. OctoRexes, in unison.

EDIT MENU >SURFACE LOCK DEVICE
The Edit menu can be used to choose a controller and select the device to which to lock it. In this case, selecting Edit > Lock Korg nanoPAD to this device would be the correct setting. An even easier way to make this selection is to right-click on the device and select the Lock nanoPAD setting.

Another great way to introduce additional variation into a mix is by creating tracks for each device within your Combinator. Fig. 14.4 displays three Dr. OctoRex Loop Players and the mixer. As the Novation controller is set up to be your master controller, you are able select any of these tracks and have control over the device, independent of the nanoPAD control over the combinator.

Fig. 14-4

REMOTE OVERRIDE

Many controllers come complete with ready-made templates for user-friendly, plug-and-play control over Reason. These templates usually consist of a logical layout of controls for each available device, while also affording a full breadth of control of every parameter.

However, you may find that when working on a set for live performance, these logically designed templates won't provide you an easy way to control parameters. If you find yourself constantly juggling between tracks, its useful to know that there is an easier way.

Edit Remote Override

Selecting Edit Remote Override from the Options menu enables you to remap any parameter of any device to any available physical controller.

When you first engage Edit Remote Override, you see that all of the devices in the rack are grayed out. When you select a device, you'll see either blue arrows or yellow circles, depending on

Fig. 14-5

which track has been selected by our Master Keyboard input.

The blue arrows (see Fig. 14.5) denote all the available parameters that can be remapped.

In Fig. 14.6, you see the same mixer with the Master Keyboard input selected on the designated track. Notice how, now, the previously displayed blue arrows have been replaced with yellow circles. This is to distinguish the parameters that have already been routed to the controller.

Fig. 14-6

It's important to bear in mind, when approaching the Remote Override, that any parameter assigned will take precedent over preexisting or previously routed parameters.

For instance, if I were to override Channel 1's fader assignment by remote, then any device that would normally use the fader designated to your controller would lose its control.

It's definitely a trade-off because once you commit to overriding some parameters, you will lose a bit of functionality. However, for use in a live set, this is a positive attribute because such ability gives you total customization over your set.

Having multiple controllers provides some excellent benefits, especially when you can lock controllers, override parameters, and command full control using your master keyboard input. It is even possible to have multiple controllers mapped to the same parameter.

Programming Remote Overrides

To create an assignment, enable Edit Remote Override from the Options menu.

Next, select the device you wish to override.

Then double-click on the parameter you wish to override.

A yellow spinning lighting bolt will appear on the screen. Move the controller fader, knob, or button to assign this to a location. Once assigned, the parameter will maintain a static lightning bolt hovering above it.

Fig. 14-7

Another way to assign a controller is to right-click on a parameter and select Edit Remote Override Mapping.

Next, a text box will open and you can either manually assign the Control Surface and Control or use the Learn from Control Surface Input.

Incidentally, you do not have to be in Remote Edit Override Mode to remap a control. You can also do so from the standard view, by right-clicking on a parameter and selecting Edit Remote Override Mapping.

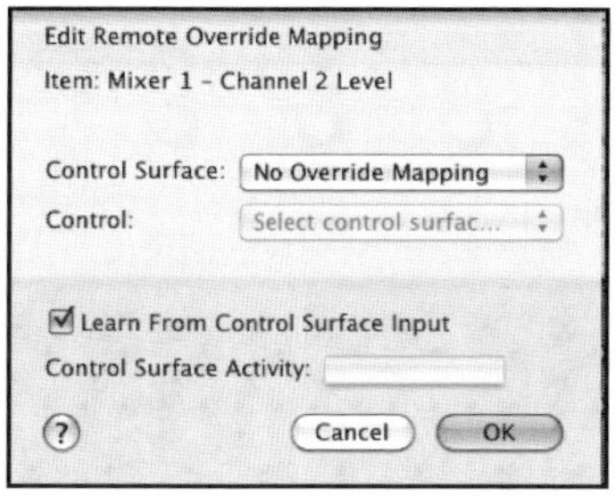

In Fig. 14.9, note how I've routed Filter Freq and Filter Res to Rotary 1 and then mapped this to Fader 4 on my controller. The ability to control multiple parameters via the programmer on the Combinator, and then to map these controls to a tactile knob or slider, really adds a new dimension to the live setup.

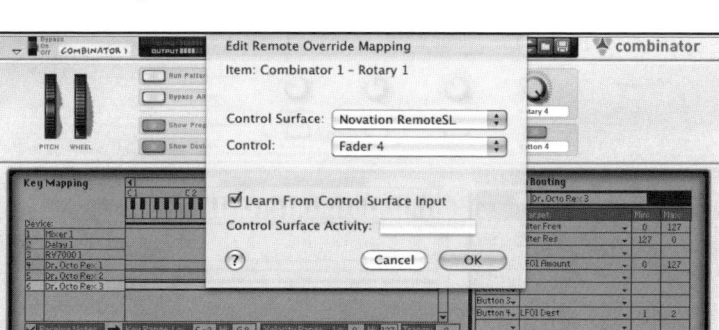

Fig. 14-8

Fig. 14-9

KEYBOARD CONTROL

Another useful function for assigning control is the Enable Keyboard Remote, also found under the Options menu.

This function permits the assignment of control to the computer keyboard.

Certain keys are blocked because they are already hardwired as key commands; for example, Q through U for Tool selection, or the numeric pad for Transport controls.

Most keys can be accessed with the use of Shift as a modifier.

Keyboard Control Edit Mode

Turn the Enable Keyboard Remote function on, to enter this mode to make assignments.

When selecting a device, note how all the assignable controls are denoted with a gold arrow. Double-clicking on an arrow causes a gold spinning square to appear.

Once a selection is made, a static gold box appears with the newly labeled keystroke.

Note that the value for the control is the minimum and maximum.

For instance, assigning a keystroke to a channel fader will cause the value to switch between 0 and 127.

While this can limit the functionality, it is especially useful for switches and buttons. If assigned to a button with multiple options, such as LFO waveform, the control will cycle through the available options.

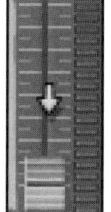

Fig. 14-10

ADDITIONAL OVERRIDES

Another useful option for controlling different aspects of Reason is Additional Overrides. These offer some great options for controlling Reason from your MIDI controller, many of which would not be possible from standard key commands.

In Fig. 14.11, you will see how to assign Move Loop One Loop Length Left to a pad on the Korg nanoKONTROL.

By pressing G#1 and A#1, you are able to move the L and R locators by a predefined value. This is a fantastic

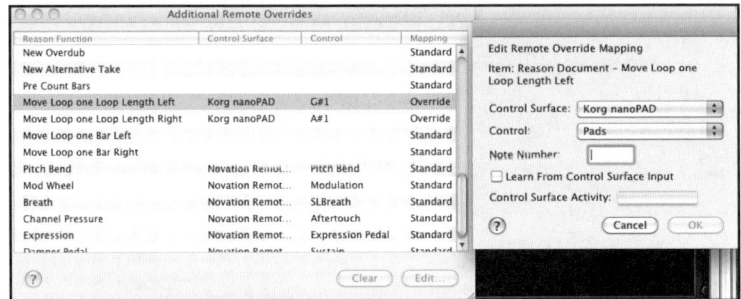

Fig. 14-11

way to loop sections of the Reason sequencer on the fly by using your controller.

DJING WITH REASON

You can perform a DJ style set using Reason, as it is easy to have multiple songs open and running simultaneously. While there is no method to sync two songs together without utilizing two separate computers, if you are a solo performer using one computer, you can use the number 1 on the numeric pad to repeatedly restart from the left locator. This function is very similar to the Tap Tempo button found on the Transport. It takes a little practice, but once you get the hang of it, you can manually synchronize two songs as long as the tempos match appropriately. To do this effectively, you will want to have a proper sound card with at least two stereo outputs, to provide the cue necessary to achieving successful transitions.

In the next chapter, you will explore ReWire and how to use Reason as a sound module within other programs.

ReWire

ReWire is a technology that allows for the usage of Reason as a sound module from within a third-party digital audio workstation.

Some of the benefits afforded by using ReWire include the ability to utilize third-party plug-ins and effects and hardware synthesizers, and to record audio.

Before ReWire, if you had wanted to synchronize two applications, you would be forced to use the IAC (inter-application connection), which offered only MIDI functionality in a tedious and clunky process.

With ReWire 2, you are now able to stream up to 256 audio tracks from Reason and over 4,000 MIDI tracks into Reason. Plus, you have the additional benefit of having the name of every Reason device show up in your host program. This makes it an especially elegant method for combining the power of Reason with other programs such as ProTools, Logic Pro, Cubase, Digital Performer, and Ableton Live to both record audio parts and use outboard synthesizers.

SETTING UP REWIRE

There are two data streams when working with ReWire. The audio stream is routed from Reason to the host application. The MIDI stream routes MIDI from the host to Reason. At the very least, the audio stream must be set up.

Audio ReWire

The setup process is pretty painless, as most functions are handled automatically.

I'll be using Logic Pro to demonstrate the process. Resources are available online from Propellerhead to show other applications.

You must first launch Logic before Reason. Launching Reason first will cause the two applications to be open without ReWire, but not to worry if you forget the correct order, as this will not damage anything on your system.

With Logic open, launch Reason.

The first thing to notice when Reason is launched is that the Hardware Interface unusually displays your audio driver, which now registers ReWire Slave Mode. This is to indicate that ReWire has been activated.

If you are planning on rewiring a completed Reason project, you will need to decide whether you'll be using the mixer in Reason and outputting a stereo mix, or whether to have each instrument set to its own channel within the host application. Either way, the process to be undertaken is essentially the same.

Fig. 15-1

Fig. 15-2

As you will be building a session from scratch to observe how to effectively use Reason as a sound module, you will first need to add some instruments.

Start by creating a Thor, Subtractor, and then a ReDrum.

Press Tab to display the rear of the rack and cable the instruments to the Audio Output section of the Hardware Interface. The Thor is connected to channels 1 and 2, the Subtractor is connected to channel 3, and the ReDrum is connected to Channels 5 and 6.

If you hit Play on either Transport, both programs will start to play in sync. Note that the L and R locators are both locked as well.

In Logic, you'll need to create

Fig. 15-3

three Aux tracks for the instruments connected to the Hardware Interface and to assign the input to the used Hardware Interface channels.

In Figure 15.4, you'll see three Aux tracks, each with its input set to the proper and respective channels. Notice that I've programmed a simple kick pattern to the ReDrum, as indicated by the resulting audio displayed on Aux 3 in Logic's mixer.

Fig. 15-4

If you were using Reason's sequencer to trigger the instruments from a song created in Reason, then you are now ready to add additional instruments and effects to your production.

MIDI ReWire

- If you are planning on triggering the Reason Instruments from within Logic, you will first need to set up the ReWire MIDI tracks.
- With most audio applications, simply creating a MIDI track and assigning its output to the proper Reason instrument is pretty straightforward.
- Logic is an object-based program and therefore needs to have the proper objects created within its environment to be able to access this functionality.

Fig. 15-5

- To execute this, first open Logic's environment from the Windows menu.
- By default, Logic opens to the Mixer layer in the environment. It doesn't matter where you place the ReWire objects, just as long as they exist within the environment.
- Then, from the New menu, select Internal > ReWire.

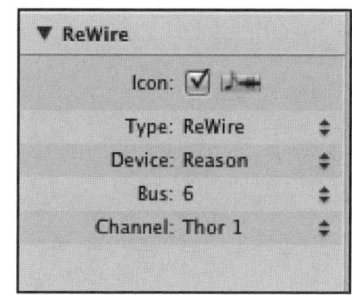

Fig. 15-6

The newly created object will appear in the Environment window.

With the ReWire object selected, turn your attention to the Parameter box in the upper left corner of the Environment window.

Now, confirm the following settings have been made.

TYPE
The type should be set to ReWire.

DEVICE

Any ReWire-capable devices will appear in this drop-down window. Ensure that this is set to Reason.

BUS

The default setting of 6 is the correct setting for Reason instruments.

CHANNEL

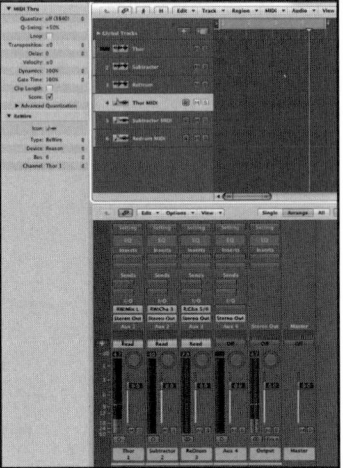

- Click on the Channel drop-down menu and select the Thor from the available list.
- Next, use the Option + Click method if using a Mac or Alt + Click if using Windows to create two more copies of the ReWire object.
- Change the channel settings for these ReWire objects to reflect the remaining instruments in your Reason rack.

Fig. 15-7

- Last, close the Environment window.
- Now, from Logic's Arrangement page, create a new track by double-clicking in the blank area just below the track listed as Aux 3.
- A new track entitled Aux 4 will be created.
- Right-click on the track name and navigate to Reassign Track > Mixer > ReWire.
- Now, assign the newly created ReWire track a more descriptive name by doubling-clicking on it and typing "Thor."

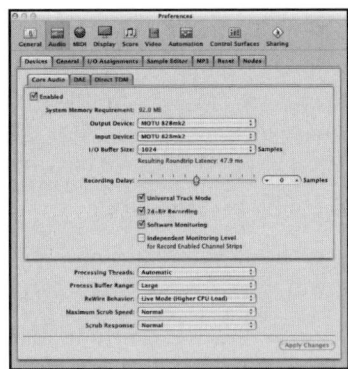

Fig. 15-8

- With the ReWire track Thor selected, double-click again to create a new track. Because the current track is also a ReWire track, Logic will create a new track of the same type of track listed in an ascending order.
- Follow this process to create one more track and rename it to reflect the channel assignment.

You now have a total of six tracks in the Arrangement window: three for the ReWire MIDI and three for the ReWire audio.

Now, selecting a ReWire MIDI track and playing a MIDI controller will send the MIDI signal to the instrument in the Reason rack. The output of the Reason instrument is routed to its respective designated audio track.

The last thing you'll need to do is set is the ReWire behavior found in the Logic audio preferences. To do this, change from playback to record.

Appendix:
The DVD ROM

On the enclosed DVD-ROM, I have included eighteen instructional videos to help you get acquainted with Reason. In addition, I've also included seven folders containing Reason song files to help with:

- Getting Started—Chapter 3
- Recording and Editing MIDI—Chapter 4
- Recording and Editing Audio—Chapter 5
- Reason FX—Chapter 9
- Advanced Routing—Chapter 11
- Building an Arrangement—Chapter 12
- The Art and Science of Mixing—Chapter 13

VIDEO TUTORIALS

The following tutorials are designed to accompany the Reason 6 Power Tools to help clarify and cement certain topics throughout the book.

1. Reason Overview Part 1

This video provides a quick overview of the software including menu structures, mixer, and rack.

2. Reason Overview Part 2

The second part of the Reason 6 overview shows the Transport.

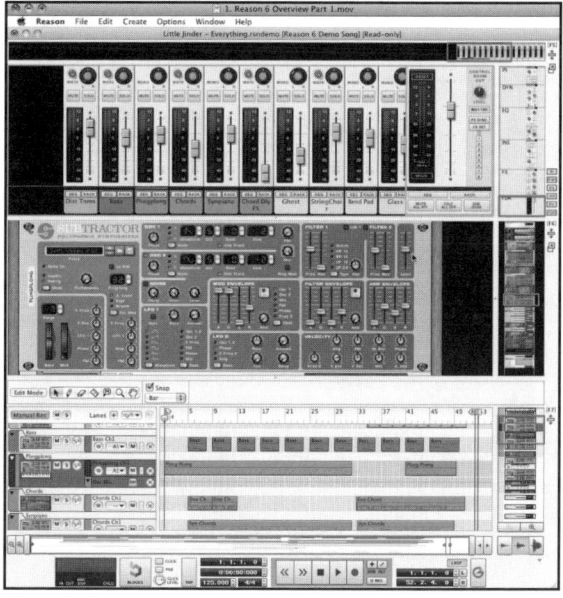

Fig. A-1

Fig. A-2

3. Recording and Editing MIDI

This video covers the signal flow, recording, and editing of MIDI.

Fig. A-3

4. Recording and Editing Audio

This video covers audio signal flow and how to record and edit audio on the sequencer page.

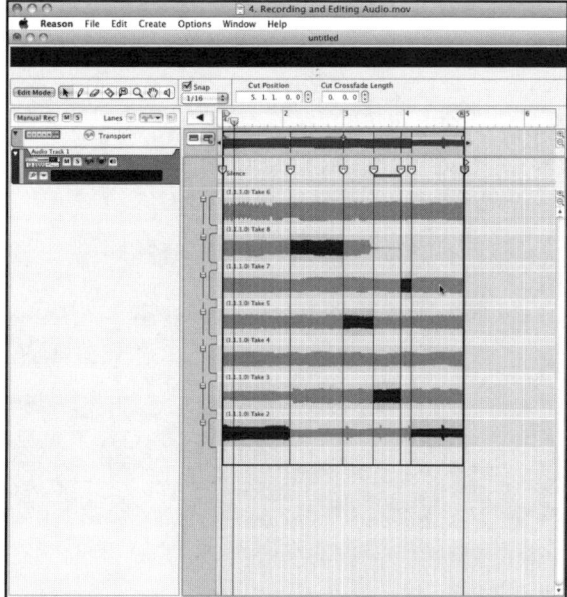

Fig. A-4

5. Synthesis

This video covers the basic operation of an analog subtractive synthesizer using the Subtractor synthesizer.

Fig. A-5

6. Subtractor

Using the concepts discussed in the Synthesis video, you'll further examine the Subtractor synthesizer.

Fig. A-6

7. Thor

This video tutorial covers the Thor Polysonic Synthesizer's synth controls, routing matrix, and Step Sequencer.

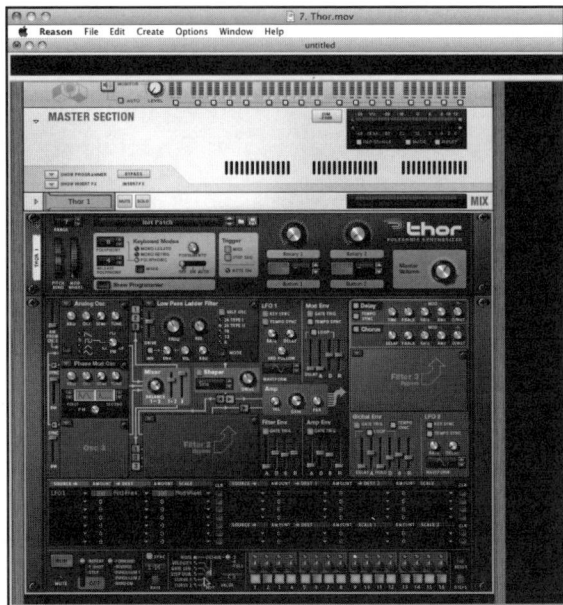

Fig. A-7

8. Malstrom

This video explains the operation and use of the Malstrom Graintable Synthesizer.

Fig. A-8

9. NN-19

This video tutorial covers the concept of sampling with examples from the NN-19 Digital Sampler.

Fig. A-9

IO. NN-XT

The NN-XT video tutorial explains advanced sampling techniques.

Fig. A-10

II. Dr. OctoRex

This video covers the use and operation of the Dr. OctoRex Loop Player.

Fig. A-II

12. ReDrum

This video covers the operation of the ReDrum drum machine.

Fig. A-12

13. Kong Drum Designer

This video tutorial explores the operation of the Kong Drum Designer.

Fig. A-13

14. ID8

This video covers the basic operation of the ID8 instrument device.

Fig. A-14

15. Reason FX

This video covers several of the Reason FX including the Line 6 amp simulator, Pulveriser, The Echo, Alligator, and more.

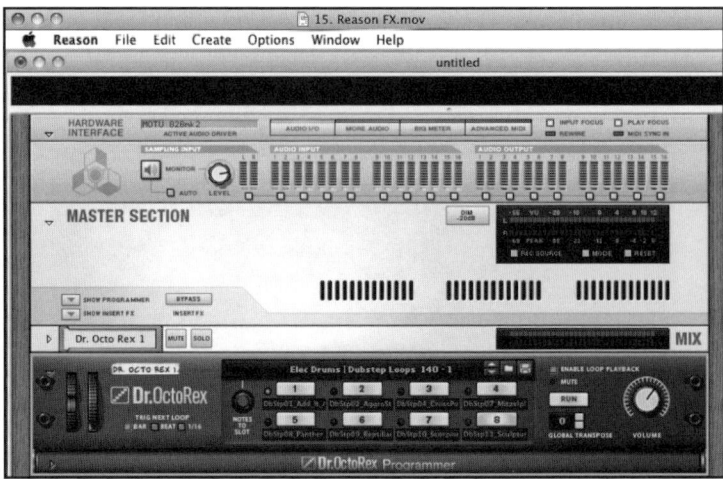

Fig. A-15

16. Arrangement Overview

This video provides an overview to the chapter on arranging.

Fig. A-16

17. Mixing

This video provides and overview to the chapter on mixing. Topics include separating elements of the track, sub mixing, and compression.

Fig. A-17

18. Mastering FX and Exporting

The final video covers Reason's mastering effects and how to mix down your song.

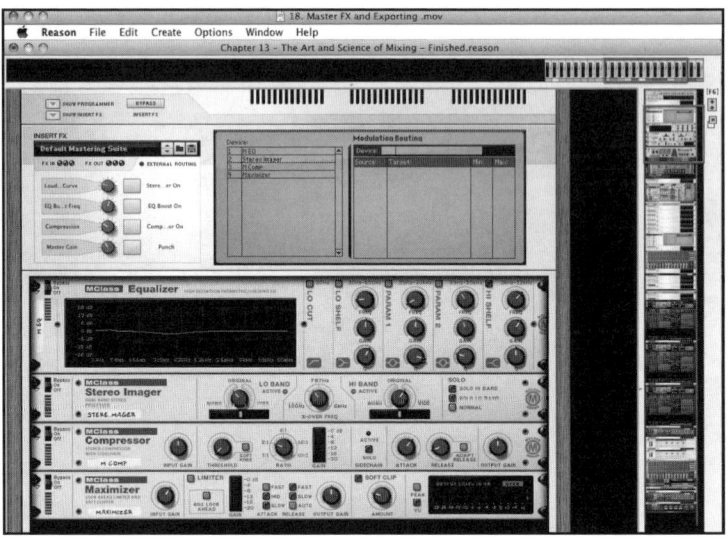

Fig. A-18

REASON SONG FILES AND MATERIALS

The following folders contain files that are to be used in conjunction with their respective chapters. Some folders offer start and finished versions of the song and additional materials.

Chapter 3—Getting Started.reason

This folder contains a song file starts with a blank template.

Chapter 4—Recording and Editing MIDI

This folder contains a song file with a Subtractor and ReDrum to be used for recording and editing MIDI. It also contains a finished file with which to check your work.

Chapter 5—Recording and Editing Audio

This folder contains two song files. The Recording Audio song file is set up with an audio track for recording. The Editing Audio song file contains four tracks with audio, for you to perform edits.

Chapter 9—Reason Effects

This folder contains a song file with one instance of the Dr. OctoRex Loop Player, for you to experiment with effects.

Chapter 11—Advanced Routing

This folder contains a song file with a ReDrum drum machine used to demonstrate the ReGroove Mixer. It also contains the "bad_bwoyy.wave" sample to be used with the NN-XT and a file containing an analog drum sequencer.

Chapter 12—Building an Arrangement

This folder contains a song file with a single MIDI clip and two instruments. This is the starting point for building an arrangement. The Chapter 13—The Art and Science of Mixing song file may be used to check your work at the end of chapter 12.

Chapter 13—The Art and Science of Mixing

This folder contains two song files. The first is the finished chapter 12 file. The "Finished" version contains the final mixed version of the chapter 13 and may be used to check your work.

REASON 6 DEMO.AFF

This is an .aiff file bounced down from the The Art and Science of Mixing song file.

Index